KISS YOUR
RESUME
GOODBYE

6 RULES THAT RULE
THE JOB MARKET
FOR LEADERS, EXECUTIVES
AND THOSE WHO LOVE THEM

KISS YOUR
RESUME
GOODBYE

6 RULES THAT RULE
THE JOB MARKET
FOR LEADERS, EXECUTIVES
AND THOSE WHO LOVE THEM

Ronald R. Evans

HUDSON
HOUSE

Cataloging in Publication Data

Evans, Ronald R., Kiss Your Resume Goodbye

ISBN: 1-58776-807-0

1. (Business)

Library of Congress Control Number: 2003105181

Manufactured in the United States of America

HUDSON HOUSE

675 Dutchess Turnpike, Poughkeepsie, NY 12603
www.hudsonhousepub.com
(800) 724-1100

TABLE OF CONTENTS

DIAGRAMS AND ILLUSTRATIONS

DEDICATION

This book is dedicated to the millions of professionals who change jobs each year hoping to better their lives. You are the heroes and heroines of the free market system and embody the resilience and strength of the free market. May the *Six Rules That Rule the Job Market* guide your job hunting to fulfillment and prosperity.

ACKNOWLEDGEMENTS

I am deeply grateful to many faithful colleagues, business leaders, friends and family who generously shared their time, energy and expertise in order to give this book life. Veteran CEOs, managers, engineers, Ivy League MBAs and diligent attorneys have provided insightful and constructive feedback that enriched this book and made it so much more meaningful. Thank you all.

My heartfelt thanks to Roberta J. Buland for her editorial assistance and to Aaron Bieber for his artistic skill and thoughtful involvement in the graphic elements of this work.

WHY READ THIS BOOK?

What you might not know about changing jobs could fill an entire book: this book. Many people are impressed by the high profile job changes of well-known business moguls and CEOs as chronicled in the national media. We are entertained and amused by tales from the polo club and mahogany-paneled boardroom. But have you ever wondered how most professionals change jobs? How do the millions of managers, business leaders, sales and marketing aces and technical geniuses who constitute the majority of the professional labor market actually go about changing jobs? What can be done to help those who may never warrant a column in the *Wall Street Journal*? How can anyone hope to rapidly change jobs or careers in the highly fragmented, confusing job market? What do you do with all that wonderful advice about self-actualization and following your passions? All these questions and many others I have been asked over the past 20 years can be summed up in the general question: Is it possible for job hunters and career changers to increase their effectiveness, improve their odds for success and speed up a positive outcome?

The answer is a resounding "Yes!"

You are unique and your circumstances are unique, but you share much in common with other professionals who are changing jobs or contemplating doing so. After two decades of interviewing and evaluating thousands of executives on behalf of some of the world's most prestigious organizations, I have become convinced that *the majority of professionals lack a strategic approach to one of the most important activities in their working lives: changing jobs.* Less than 5 percent of the smart, educated, wonderfully experienced people I have interviewed have a firm grip on themselves or the job market they are plunging into. Still fewer have a systematic approach for dealing with both. Bear in mind I'm counting the brightest engineers, the best marketing and sales professionals, brainy CFOs and even a few CEOs. Despite making brilliant contributions to current and former employers, many job hunters leave their brains and common sense at the door when they begin to look for a new job. The average talented professional appears to operate under the belief that if he/she can simply connect with the right recruiter (outplacement firm, career counselor, fill in the blank) things will eventually work out. Amazingly, such people abdicate personal responsibility for their own job search and overlook their personal value proposition (PVP), which is the most marketable asset each one of us possesses, as is discussed in chapter 5.

Fortunately there is a simple alternative, but it is only available for those who are willing to take charge of their job changing process. And now we are face-to-face with the premise of this book: *You are the only one qualified to plan and execute your own job search.* In the past you may have wanted to do so, but perhaps you felt you lacked the knowledge and resources to develop a game plan. Those days are history because what you lacked is now in your hands.

Before you venture further into this book I should let you in on a little secret: I hate to read. I also hate to waste time - mine or anyone else's. So you might understand my reluctance to write about the topic of careers and changing jobs when there is already so much written on these subjects. Frankly, the only way I could justify writing this book was to offer a uniquely strategic approach to this subject that is so concise you will be able to read it in one easy sitting. But the real magic of this book is that if you diligently work through the exercises and apply the concepts you will be able to:

1) Save yourself, your family and prospective employers precious time, frustration and money;

2) Transform the quality of your personal life by taking control of your job hunt or career change; and

3) Significantly increase the likelihood of landing a job that leverages your proven skills and abilities.

At its core, **Kiss Your Resume Goodbye** is an elegant reversal of the process that top notch executive recruiters use to find great candidates for the companies they represent. There is no reason that you, as a candidate, cannot use this methodical approach starting from your end, to find employers that fit you like a glove.

If these are the results you are after, then this is your field manual. You might find it helpful to read through the entire book to see the whole picture, then reread it with a pad of paper in hand, working through the various questions, exercises and suggestions on how to apply the concepts to your particular situation.

SECTION I

YOUR PREDICAMENT

Chapter 1
THE THREE PILLARS
Establishing Your Foundation

If you are looking for a new job or a better one, you are not
alone. In fact almost everyone in the workforce knows people
who have been laid off, fired or voluntarily changed jobs during
the past few years. Simply reading the newspaper tells you this
phenomenon is much larger than your personal circle of contacts.
So you may not be surprised that in December 2001 the Center on
Budget and Policy Priorities, a non-partisan research organization
based in Washington D.C., released this statement:

> *The increase over the past 12 months in the number of
> unemployed workers was the largest such increase in any 12-
> month period in nearly 20 years. Labor Department data
> …show that between November 2000 and November 2001,
> the number of unemployed workers rose by 2.5 million —
> from 5.7 million to 8.2 million. Unemployment has not risen
> that much in a 12-month period since the period from
> December 1981 to December 1982.*

But you might be surprised to learn that our present economic troubles are not the main culprit. Huge cultural, economic and demographic trends are combining to create a very different employment world than previous generations have known. These forces are not the subject of this book, but suffice it to say that if your parents worked 30-40 years for one company before moving into a condo on a golf course, you will not. Consider the following job tenure data from the Web site of the Bureau of Labor Statistics (BLS). For the period 1983-2002 the median tenure with current employer averaged:

◆ 5.3 years for executive, administrative and managerial employees

◆ 5.8 years for engineers

◆ 4.4 years for mathematical and computer scientists

◆ 3.2 years for technical, sales and administrative support

Topping it all off, the BLS speculates that *the average college graduate will have no fewer than five careers and 15 jobs during his or her lifetime.* The bottom line is that changing jobs is not an exercise reserved for the unlucky few, but a survival skill that the majority of professionals in the twenty-first century must master. Regardless of economic cycles and regardless of whether you are looking for another job voluntarily or involuntarily, you are among several million people doing so. This means you are part of a large group likely to spend significant time, money and emotional energy on job hunting approaches that are proven failures. Whether you are a highly paid senior executive with 25 years of experience and a country club network, or a young professional just starting out, you are equally prone to doing it wrong. *The inability of experienced professionals to efficiently secure new jobs stands in frightening contrast to the growing frequency with which they are required to do so.*

During the past 20 years working with three global executive search consultancies as well as establishing my own executive recruiting firm, I have had a panoramic view of the best and brightest talent in America. Sadly, most of the professionals I have interviewed and evaluated were ill-prepared for the job market into which they were plunging. In addition to this, the 500-1000 unsolicited resumes I receive each month reveal a broad cross section of professionals who appear to be unfocused and floundering in their job transitions. It is my hope that the frustration and loss suffered by many of those I have interviewed and evaluated can be translated into practical guidance for the millions of professionals I have never met, including you.

If you are currently relying on a recruiter, job counselor, family member or spouse to tell you what to do and where to go, you are headed for disappointment. If you are broadcasting resumes to the entire world hoping someone else will figure out where you should fit in, you are wasting time and money, while alienating potential employers. If you are going to every networking event, social occasion and industry forum to distribute your resume, you are probably straining important relationships and expecting too much from people who cannot help you.

THE FOUNDATION

The foundation of successful job hunting and career changing has three pillars:

1) A clear knowledge of what you have to sell

2) A clearly defined market of buyers

3) A clear game plan linking you, the seller, with buyers

These approaches usually don't produce results for most people because they lack *the proper foundation.* This foundation is the same for all of us, regardless of age, experience, education, industry or functional expertise, and is made up of *three pillars.* Your ability to identify and establish all three pillars will determine the speed and effectiveness with which you change jobs. *The foundation of successful job hunting and career changing has three pillars:*

1. *A clear knowledge of what you have to sell*

2. *A clearly defined market of buyers*

3. *A clear game plan linking you, the seller, with buyers*

In my experience successful job hunters and career changers have a firm grasp on the three pillars while those who languish between jobs do not. In the chapters that follow I will share with you *Six Rules That Rule the Job Market* that will help you discover and establish your three pillars. It won't take you long to read **Kiss Your Resume Goodbye,** but if you diligently apply the concepts your entire game plan will be transformed. There is one and only one objective for this book: to give you an effective job hunting approach that will get you where you want to go smarter and faster.

But before we move on to the next chapter there is one more point to discuss: honesty. Are you willing to be brutally honest with yourself as you read further? Are you deeply motivated to do things differently? Will you do whatever it takes to jump-start your job hunting? Or do you simply want to complain about how difficult and unfair the entire process is? These are important questions to address because it is easier to complain than it is to take the radical steps required to change. Nothing in the book will make sense to you unless you are committed to developing a radically different perspective. If your current job hunting method is flawed, trying a radical alternative could be a smart move. Unless, of course, Yogi Berra is your career coach.

Phil Rizzuto - "Hey Yogi I think we're lost."

Yogi Berra - "Yeah, but we're making great time!"

If your current method of job hunting is not getting you the results you want, then it may be time to consider changing your approach to the entire process. Once you are ready to do things differently, truly committed to pursuing a radical, market driven alternative to the standard job searching activities, then your next move is to turn the page.

Chapter 2
HOW THE
JOB MARKET WORKS
Buyers, Sellers and Agents

Why do even the most brilliant, successful people have a tendency to become less rational when it comes to changing jobs? Perhaps it is for the same reason that surgeons do not operate on themselves or lawyers do not attempt to represent themselves in court. For most of us, applying logic and discipline to something as intensely personal as your career and income is quite difficult. But it is exactly what needs to be done. So let's begin by discussing the mechanics of the job market that will be critical to guiding your efforts. If you are a professional with several years of experience dealing with products or services, then **The Market Rule** will be very familiar to you and should give you great confidence. **The Market Rule** states that *the job market is like any other marketplace, driven by buyers, sellers and their agents. Understand the marketplace and you will avoid five classic misconceptions.*

To understand **The Market Rule**, let's begin with some descriptions of the supply and demand forces that shape this mar-

THE MARKET RULE

The job market is like any other marketplace, driven by buyers, sellers and their agents. Understand the marketplace and you will avoid five classic misconceptions.

ket. Although the job market is highly fragmented and inefficient, it still consists of buyers, sellers and agents. As with all other markets, it is important that you know which one you are, as well as correctly categorize others *and* understand how each is rewarded and by whom. The breakdown below should prove helpful to most job hunters:

Buyers: Companies and organizations that acquire talent

Sellers: Candidates, job hunters, career changers (that's you)

Agents: Intermediaries that represent either buyers or sellers. This group warrants discussion:

✦ *Buyer agents* represent employers, and include retained recruiters and *some* contingency recruiters.

◇ *Retained recruiters* or *executive search consultants* generally work the upper end of the market, as defined by an arbitrary compensation line, handle assignments exclusively and are usually paid regardless of outcome.

◇ *Contingency recruiters* usually work the middle and lower market portions. These recruiters often compete with each other on the same placement and are paid by the buyer only if the seller (you) is hired.

◇ *Headhunter* is a vague label applied to both retained and contingency recruiters. But regardless of labels, both are paid by the buyer (employer) not the seller.

15

✦ *Seller agents* include a variety of businesses such as career consultants, resume writers, resume distribution services, some executive coaches, some contingency firms, *and any other party who provides services to candidates.* They are usually paid by the seller with the notable exception of outplacement firms which are usually paid for by the seller's last employer.

Recruiting is a business with few agreed upon standards, so there are many exceptions to the generalizations above. But these descriptions cover the majority of agents. Most contingency recruiting firms do not represent the buyer exclusively; therefore, they compete with other contingency firms to fill positions. This often results in shopping candidates to several buyers simultaneously to increase the likelihood of receiving a fee, which creates the impression they are working for you. They are not. Finally, some firms have been known to work buyers and sellers simultaneously, charging candidates for assistance *and* companies for recruiting.

Myths and Misconceptions

Once you can differentiate among buyers, sellers and their agents, you will be able to avoid several classic job hunter misconceptions:

1) *A fantastic looking resume (on the most expensive paper) will catch someone's eye and I'll be saved!* Not true. Buyers are usually driven by specific needs and pretty resumes don't change what they need.

2) *My network will save me.* Only if your network is full of buyers or direct leads to buyers who understand your mar-

16

ketplace value (see chapter 5) will it save you. Networks and networking must be used carefully because they consume huge amounts of time and energy and have built-in deficiencies, as we shall see in Chapter 7.

3) *All I need to do is get in front of a buyer (company, recruiter, etc.), and once they see how great I am I'll be home free.* Unless the buyer needs someone exactly like you, this is rarely true. Pursuing face-to-face meetings without diligent research and targeting is a time waster.

4) *Recruiters help people like me find work.* Sorry, but the recruiter's customer is the buyer, not the seller (you). Like any prudent businessperson, recruiters focus on their customers first, which explains why many successful recruiters will often not return your phone call or email unless they believe you fit an assignment on which they are working. If this happens to you, don't take it personally.

5) *Outplacement firms, career counselors, etc., will find my next job for me.* Probably not in this lifetime, because agents working for sellers usually lack significant connections with buyers, a.k.a. your next employer. Outplacement firms are generally paid by companies to ease the pain of departing employees, and are not paid based upon results achieved for the seller (you, the candidate). Typical services include resume development and distribution, secretarial support, networking with other job hunters and coaching.

Keeping these five widely held misconceptions in mind will allow you to conserve your precious time, money and emotional energy. They are based upon faulty assumptions or are inherently inefficient, and as you study the economic relationships involved you will see why they don't work.

Now I suggest that you swallow hard and brace yourself for the next Rule which attacks the raw currency of the job market: your resume.

Chapter 3
KISS YOUR RESUME GOODBYE
Why Your Resume Won't Save You

Equipped with an understanding of the basic players in the job market, you may feel emboldened to attack the job market with renewed confidence and vigor. But how should you proceed? Should you follow the well-worn trail of the nameless, faceless millions who are writing, rewriting or sprucing up their resumes?

No. Save the ink and the hard drive space for more productive purposes. A resume is not what you need right now. As stated in **The Resume Rule**, *resumes are overused and ineffective tools for both buyer and seller.*

As you blink and reread **The Resume Rule**, some questions might begin forming in your mind, such as "How can a person conduct a legitimate job search without a resume?" "If resumes are the basic currency of the job market, aren't you a penniless job hunter without one?" "How am I going to tell the whole world how great I am without a resume?" While all these reactions are

THE RESUME RULE

> *Resumes are overused and ineffective tools for both buyer and seller.*

understandable, you have probably experienced the truth of **The Resume Rule** unbeknownst to you. If you have ever been in the position of hiring other professionals, you are probably aware that the ultimate selection for most jobs rarely hinges upon the quality and content of the resume. Most of us seem to sense this intuitively, yet we spend huge amounts of time crafting the perfect resume on the theory that it will "get us in the door." It could be argued that never in the history of capitalism have so many people pinned their economic futures on something as ineffective and undeserving as the resume. This idea even applies to those proud owners of really impressive resumes written with professional help and printed on expensive paper.

Shocking news like this can be tough to digest and old ways of thinking can be hard to change, so here are two simple reasons that support **The Resume Rule**:

1) *Resumes burden the buyer with the task of discerning your value.* As a buyer's agent who receives hundreds of resumes each week, let me assure you that every unsolicited resume arrives with this unspoken plea: "Help me figure out where I fit in!" Since you now know that buyers and agents working on their behalf are not in the business of helping job hunters, it makes sense that this is the wrong message for this audience. If you are not an immediate match for a buyer's need your resume usually disappears into a trash can or a database. Unfortunately, future contact with buyers who have already dispensed with your resume can be complicated *if they feel compelled to defend their initial reaction to your paperwork.* Imagine how this

problem can snowball for sellers relying on mass resume distribution!

2) *Buyers are drowning in resumes.* With millions mailed each week, millions more sent via email each week, and still more millions available via hundreds of Web sites, buyers are overwhelmed with resumes. To illustrate this let me share with you two email solicitations I recently received. One offers Internet access to over *"30 million resumes for only $695"* promising that I can *"find the perfect candidate for every position without having to deal with a wave of unqualified job seekers."* The second proclaims, *"Boy do we have resumes! Want some, they're free? Just click here, sign up and we'll email you great resumes."* It should come as no surprise that buyers have responded to this deluge with sophisticated scanning, filtering, storage and retrieval systems. Bottom line: Your resume has less chance of being seen today than ever before.

From these comments you might reasonably conclude that mass resume distribution may not advance the seller's cause to the extent most people hope. The dramatic increase in resume volume over the past decade has effectively diminished the time and attention paid to each individual resume. Furthermore, mass resume distribution assumes that job hunting is simply a matter of probability where your chances for success can be increased by more attempts, but ignores the very real risk of turning off certain buyers unnecessarily or prematurely. It happens all too often and there is no way that you, as the seller, will ever know.

So should you eliminate your resume entirely? No. But it should not be your primary job hunting tool. Think of your resume the way a football player thinks about his cleats: every football player realizes he must wear cleats to have the same traction as everyone else on the field, but the cleats themselves do not determine who wins the game. In the same manner, *resumes are necessary to play the job changing game, but they have little to do with winning.* Therefore, make your resume brief and factual and be certain to include dates for every job and degree. Also, include comprehensive contact information including email addresses, office, cell and home phone numbers. Limit offering your resume to when it is requested. The truth is that a resume is only supporting information for hiring organizations that already understand *who you are and what you can do for them.* And helping them understand this, which we call your *personal value proposition* (PVP), is the subject of the next several chapters.

Before we move on, however, it is helpful to define several key terms that will be used in upcoming chapters. Although the words *job, function, industry* and *career* are commonly used, they seem to carry different meanings depending upon who is using them. In order to minimize confusion, let me share with you some fairly standard definitions used in this book for each of these important terms.

Job - a specific set of duties, at a specific level, within a designated function within an organization

Function - a category of jobs performing a unique and specific role within an organization. Some of the most commonly recognized functions in the job market include engineering, finance and accounting, operations, marketing and sales.

Industry - a grouping of companies defined by the goods and services produced or by the raw materials utilized. SIC codes (Standard Industrial Classification) are a form of industry grouping. A few basic examples of broad industry groupings include: financial services, consumer products, manufacturing and professional services (law, accounting, consulting). The proliferation of technologies during the past two decades makes designations such as high technology too broad to be meaningful. It is better to classify by technology type, such as biotechnology, software or hardware.

Career - a series of jobs that a professional has held that collectively describes his/her work experience. Interestingly, there is a growing population of multiple career professionals -people with two or more distinctly different sets of jobs in different industries, functional roles, or both.

PVP (Personal Value Proposition) - your proven problem-solving expertise that addresses specific problems of an organization or industry.

Diagram #1

ANATOMY OF A JOB:
THREE REALMS OF KNOWLEDGE

FUNCTIONAL EXPERTISE

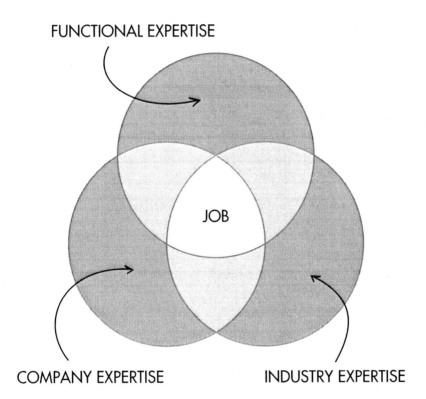

COMPANY EXPERTISE   INDUSTRY EXPERTISE

As Diagram #1 reveals, most jobs consist of three realms of knowledge or expertise: functional, industry and company. When it comes to finding another job, logic suggests that you direct your search within the area where two or three of these realms overlap.

Diagram #2

ANATOMY OF A CAREER

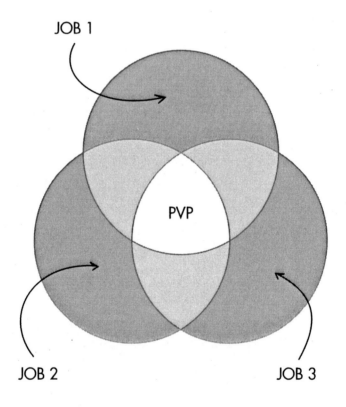

JOB 1

PVP

JOB 2   JOB 3

Diagram #2 shows the relationship between individual jobs and your personal value proposition (PVP), which is discussed in chapter 5. Your career is made up of a series of jobs and the central element of success at these jobs is your PVP.

Understanding yourself and your career is helpful, but it is not an end in itself; it only has value in the context of what the marketplace needs. With this in mind, it's time to unveil our next paradigm shifting concept in the following chapter.

Chapter 4
IT'S NOT ABOUT YOU
Focusing on the Buyer

In his best-selling book, *The 7 Habits of Highly Effective People,* management guru and author Steven Covey challenges his readers to "Begin with the end in mind..." Job hunters and career changers would do well to keep this concept foremost in their thoughts. It is particularly important to realize that the end result for the seller (you) looks quite different from the end result for the buyer, and the key to successful job hunting is to understand what the endgame is for the buyer. Let me explain.

As a job hunter you must begin by asking a more profound question than "How do I get my next job?" Sit back and reflect on what the buyer might be trying to accomplish by hiring someone. Ask yourself, "Why does a company or organization choose to hire someone in the first place? Is it because they have an empty box on the organizational chart? Are they simply smitten by people who make favorable impressions, or perhaps attended certain schools, or have an inside connection at the hiring organization?"

Certainly all of these factors may be influential, but they are not the primary force that drives the hiring of professionals. This is a big concept, and if you haven't guessed it by now then **The Hiring Rule** needs to be carved into your front door: *people get hired to solve the problems of the hiring organization.*

Simple idea, right? Wrong. Actually, it's not so simple (or trivial) at all! *It's not about you (the seller) and it never was; it's about the buyer.*

Correctly understood, **The Hiring Rule** will turn your world upside down. This concept represents a major paradigm shift for the vast majority of sellers. In fact, it never even occurs to most. For the sake of emphasis, don't jump to the next sentence, the next paragraph or the next chapter until you spend 60 seconds meditating on **The Hiring Rule**. It may sound like keen insight into the obvious, but once you thoroughly digest this concept, your job hunting paradigm will be forever changed.

Understanding the buyer's perspective involves being able to explain who you are and what you do in terms of the buyer's problems. We all have a strong tendency to lose our identity to functional titles, company names and industry classifications. "I'm the top hedgehog at XYZ company," we reply to anyone asking what we do. But if you think about it, that's not a very informative answer unless the inquirer happens to know your current employer well. Therefore, before you launch out into the job market you must rid yourself of that kind of thinking and the language that goes with it. It is imperative that you distinguish between the organization you work for and what you do. You must be able to differentiate between what you do and your

THE HIRING RULE

People get hired to solve the problems of the hiring organization.

department or function, and you must know the difference between you and your job title.

Why is this so important? First, because *the job market handles clearly defined sellers more efficiently than vaguely defined sellers.* If you cannot accurately describe what you do and how it adds value, how will the marketplace know what to do with you? Second, *different companies may refer to similar functions with different terms, a problem that becomes even more pronounced if you move between industries.* Therefore, the burden is on you to describe who you are and the value you add apart from company-specific or industry-specific labels and designations. To do so will require serious thought, time and energy on your part. Therefore, let me encourage you to reflect on the three *brutal* questions below, questions that will help you develop the three pillars of your job changing foundation. I call them *brutal* because they force you to confront the bottom line for both buyer and seller. Over the past two decades I have observed that few sellers seriously consider these questions, and fewer still attempt to answer them. Only the most purposeful, focused job seekers and career changers can answer the brutal questions.

1) What kinds of problems do you solve?

2) What kinds of organizations have these problems?

3) What would compel an organization to hire you to solve its problems?

These are not academic or philosophical questions and the answers are not vague ones. Rather, the answers to these questions are what the job market needs to understand about you. *If you*

know the answers to the three brutal questions and can clearly artic-
ulate them, you are miles ahead of those who do not. The answers
to these questions will form the foundation of your job hunting or
career changing process.

Now let's review. At the end of the day, sellers (job hunters)
must realize that it's all about buyers (employers) and solving their
problems, not about finding a new or better job. That is your
problem. Whether you have degrees from elite undergraduate or
graduate schools or carry a humble sheepskin from Wachamacallit
State University, buyers want to know if you can solve their problems. Sure, some companies will hire only graduates of prestigious schools, and some job seekers may have the inside track
because of special relationships. But these distinctions usually
become meaningful *after* it is determined whether or not you can
solve their problem. This is particularly true in difficult economic
times. *If you, as a seller, can give the buyer what he/she wants then*
you will end up with what you want: a job that draws upon your
proven problem-solving skills.

"That's all well and good," you might be thinking, "but all
I've got is my crummy old resume and it doesn't address these
questions." Don't panic. Just turn the page.

WHAT TO DO ABOUT YOUR PREDICAMENT

Chapter 5
TAKING INVENTORY
Discovering What You Have to Sell

No veteran executive would launch a new product or service without doing market research, or dare to make a strategic acquisition without performing due diligence. Yet these same executives and managers, turned loose in the job market, often fail to apply these very disciplines to themselves. For reasons I do not understand, when it comes to the most valuable asset you have (yourself), many people forget to rigorously apply the processes and disciplines that have brought them success throughout their career. This brings us to **The PVP Rule**: *you are responsible for clearly defining what you bring to the marketplace. This is your Personal Value Proposition (PVP).*

So before you launch out into the job market, perform some due diligence on yourself. Take inventory of what you have to sell. Begin the process by tackling the first question raised in chapter 4: "What kinds of problems do you solve?" Take a blank 8 1/2 by 11 inch writing pad and your favorite pen or pencil, find a quiet spot,

THE PVP RULE

You are responsible for clearly defining what you bring to the marketplace. This is your Personal Value Proposition (PVP).

brew a good cup of coffee or tea, and dedicate at least an hour to answer this question. Total time required may vary depending upon years of experience. (Those inclined to settle down in front of the computer keyboard might be challenged by additional distractions.) If you don't want or need much guidance, brainstorm answers to the question as stated: "What kinds of problems do you solve?" Those who would like more specific direction might find these steps helpful:

1) Gather your work papers, portfolio, recent projects, awards and other tangible reminders of successful projects, challenges or meaningful accomplishments. Read through the material, think through each project and reflect on each award or other reminder.

2) Select your three most fulfilling jobs or assignments from the past and write down what you did and how you did it. Then summarize each situation concisely for each job or project you identify.

3) Develop an exhaustive list of all work-related problems you have solved, going back to the beginning of your career and working your way to the present. Make it chronological if possible and be sure to provide details.

4) Create a problem-solving summary sheet highlighting key problems you have solved. *Carefully note any apparent patterns or themes.*

5) Create a summary statement of your problem-solving abilities in 100 words or less. Underneath, list supporting evidence.

These five steps should yield a concise summary of what you have to offer to the job market. Although it is best to start this exercise alone, you may need a reality check. *Enlist the help of a trusted advisor* who could be a colleague, spouse or friend to honestly critique your results. Remember, you are embarking on a radical path to find a new and better job; therefore accurate, honest feedback is essential to the process. It is imperative that you enlist the support of a person who has your permission to be objective and tough. If the person laughs, rolls his/her eyes or seriously challenges your results, you need to begin the exercise anew. Remember, *it is better to be laughed at by a friend who knows you than a buyer who doesn't.* Once your problem-solving observations and summary statement pass the reality test with your trusted advisor, you are ready to move on.

Forming Your PVP (Personal Value Proposition)

The traditional way to view your career is as a series of interdependent relationships among your job, function, company and industry. This is graphically displayed in Diagram #3 as a pyramid. Starting at the bottom, each level of the pyramid supports the section above it and as you go up, each section is more specific than the section beneath it. Thus, an industry consists of many companies, and each company consists of many different functions (such as operations, finance and marketing) and each function consists of many jobs. For the experienced professional, this is a logical representation of the fact that your specific job exists within a larger context. It is built upon your functional expertise, the company for which you work and the particular industry in which your company competes.

Diagram #3

OLD CAREER PARADIGM

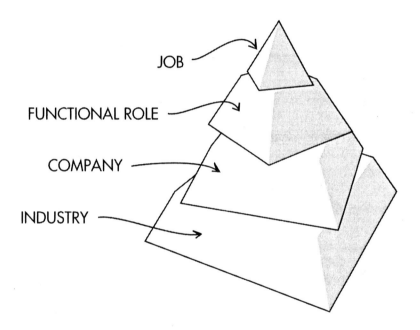

JOB

FUNCTIONAL ROLE

COMPANY

INDUSTRY

The shortcoming of Diagram #3 is that your job and career success depend upon something not shown here, something more fundamental and important than all these other elements. It is called your *Personal Value Proposition* or *PVP*. And this is what can be discovered from the self-inventory and discovery process you have begun. This is not the job objective printed at the top of your resume, nor is it a feel good or wannabe statement. Rather, it is a statement that clearly defines your problem-solving ability in the context of specific organizational or industry challenges. It answers the most important question of all: "Why would any organization hire a person like me?" Your PVP must be specific enough to steer you away from all organizations except those that require someone like you. Thus your PVP becomes the foundation for the bridge you are building that will lead to your next job.

In contrast to the pyramid depicting the old career paradigm, your PVP might be better illustrated by a flagpole as seen in Diagram #4. Imagine the very top of the flagpole represents your specific job, the sections below are your functional and industry expertise, and the foundation of the flagpole represents your PVP. Now consider the amount of movement these various portions of the pole experience when the wind blows. The top of the flagpole would experience the most change, representing the frequency with which most of us experience changes in job title, budget responsibility and reporting relationships. But as you progress down the pole, each section moves a bit less than the section above it. When you finally reach the foundation that secures the entire pole you are at the place where no discernable movement occurs. In a similar fashion, your PVP remains relatively constant in contrast to changes in your job status, the company for which you

Diagram #4

NEW CAREER PARADIGM

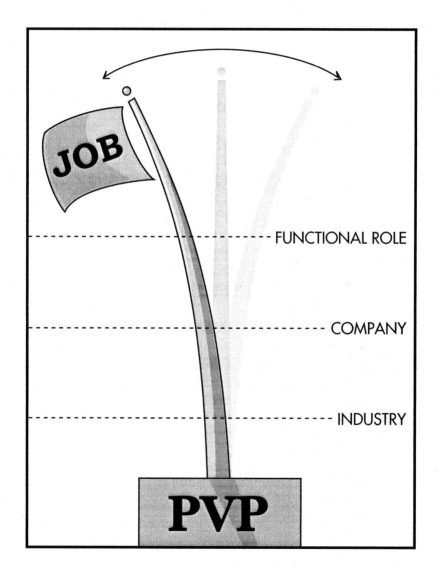

work or even the industry in which you have the most experience. If it changes at all, it does so very slowly. This is the essence of your work life and defines your contributions to any organization.

Developing your PVP is both intellectually challenging and creative work. Return to your summary of *what* types of problems you have solved and develop a succinct description of *how* you solved them. Reflect upon the intellectual and interpersonal skills used to solve these problems, as well as the business tools and processes you employed. There are many ways to go about this, but in order to stimulate your thinking I will share with you one simple method I often use to get at the *how* issue.

Over the years interviewing and evaluating sellers, I have observed that most executives can be classified as a **C** or an **O** based upon how they go about solving problems. The **C**'s are *Creators* and the **O**'s are *Optimizers.* Creators and optimizers are capable of functioning at any level within the organization, from the boardroom to the mailroom, but they approach problem-solving very differently.

C's are professionals who solve problems by creativity or initiation. They visualize solutions to problems quickly and are usually leading the charge during the early stages of problem-solving. Not surprisingly, *C*'s believe that most of the value in any solution lies in conceiving and initiating action. Everything else is simply implementation and maintenance. *C*'s can usually be found building new organizations or shaking up existing organizations, and frequently become entrepreneurs and business owners. Although they may be quite capable at execution and completion, they are inclined to leave them to others because they believe the primary value is in the creative act.

O's are professionals who solve problems and create value by optimizing any process, department or organization they touch. O's exhibit analytical, methodical and disciplined approaches to problem-solving. They are often found cleaning up, fixing or finishing what C's start. They pick up the broken pieces, figure out why things are not working and develop business value in situations where C's cannot. Where nothing is broken, optimizers are deft at fine-tuning systems to generate higher output. In the midst of great, complex disasters, the superstar O's can be found orchestrating high profile turnarounds. Although optimizers can be very creative and often initiate action, the real value they add is in mastering and perfecting the details of operations or execution.

Clearly C's and O's are both valuable and, in fact, often exist as complementary relationships within more progressive organizations. Although many people possess both C and O characteristics, one trait is generally dominant when problem-solving. The point here is that such distinctions are important when developing your own PVP. Therefore, two professionals in similar jobs can achieve excellent results using very different problem-solving approaches.

Hopefully this will stimulate you to think about yourself from a different point of view, and speed your development of the *how* portion of your PVP. Take some time right now and make a first draft of your PVP incorporating both *what* and *how*. You want to be able to identify several detailed examples of achievements so that you can clearly determine if your dominant problem-solving tendencies are as an Optimizer or a Creator.

The power of a well-written PVP was made painfully clear to me while working with venture capital funds and early stage technology companies. Young, promising companies routinely have spirited discussions about value propositions. Every one of these companies has unique capabilities, dazzling technology and brilliant people, yet just like you, each company must clearly define itself by a simply stated value proposition. Why is this so important? Because without a powerful value proposition a start-up company will not be able to attract capital, and without capital the business will die. This is the hard reality of capital markets and it is precisely the same for you, the job hunter or career changer. You are trying to attract capital in the form of a job and you must go through the same disciplined process so that you emerge with your PVP, which is your statement of marketplace value.

Clearly defining your PVP can be quite a struggle for many experienced professionals because you must think beyond the traditional clichés and words that you frequently use to describe your work and experience. Because some examples might help speed you along the way, four PVPs developed by talented executives from different industries and backgrounds follow. In the first example, a CEO demonstrates a well-written PVP that emerged from several hours of analyzing his past successes.

PERSONAL VALUE PROPOSITION #1
CEO

I lead, guide or structure complex, multifaceted business transitions. My creative successes include start-up businesses, restarts, reorganizations, acquisitions and divestitures where shaping the value equation is critical. I thrive under intense pressure in technology-driven industries, providing sound leadership during uncertainty and rapidly changing conditions. My tools are:

- *quick grasp of the "big picture"*

- *experience with complex financial structures*

- *deep grounding in all aspects of corporate law*

- *well-honed business planning and organizational skills*

- *strong interpersonal skills*

- *first-rate communications abilities*

- *management expertise with all facets of business operations*

- *good negotiating skills*

Using this PVP, the CEO in example #1 secured two complex consulting projects and identified a group of specialty businesses he had not previously known about, all before leaving his current job.

In the second example, a COO/CFO describes more of the process by revealing his PVP and his answers to the three brutal questions.

PERSONAL VALUE PROPOSITION #2

COO/CFO

I am a business leader who solves execution and implementation problems. I am an optimizer who identifies the people, culture and process problems hindering the fulfillment of business goals. My tools are leadership, analysis, business processes and systems. My proven successes are with start-ups, turnarounds and Fortune 500 business-es, heavily concentrated in software, services and private equity. I solve problems by:

a) disciplined analysis

b) strategic blueprinting

c) adjusting talent requirements to fix problems

d) clarifying customer wants/needs

e) identifying market opportunities

f) institutionalizing metrics to perpetuate success

My leadership is thoughtful, ethical, but intensely focused.

1. *What kinds of problems do I solve?*
   Execution-oriented problems. Specifically, cross-functional problems requiring confluent management of people, processes, profits driven by intense cost and timeline pressures.

2. *What kinds of organizations have these problems?*
   Lots. But the types I know best are dynamic, high growth or turnaround companies that have the potential for industry dominance but need strong operational leadership.

3. *What would compel an organization to hire me to solve its problems?*
   The organization must need a leader who can inspire a team, build strong customer relationships and drive enduring and superb financial results.

Some professionals may find it helpful to extend the PVP exercise all the way back to the formative years preceding professional life. In the third example, the Corporate Trainer is looking for problem-solving themes that might have surfaced during his formative years. Please note that this is not an exercise in self-indulgent reflection, but rather an effort to clearly identify or confirm problem-solving skills that may be easier to detect in the earlier stages of life. Obviously this assessment will not reveal much about industry or functional problem-solving because it is based on his youth. But you might be able to see entrepreneurial drive, *optimizer* versus *creator* tendencies or interpersonal problem-solving skills that later become critical to success in selling, negotiating or leading.

PERSONAL VALUE PROPOSITION #3

CORPORATE TRAINER

Childhood: Happy kid. Youngest in family. Loved playing outdoors, very active and adventuresome. Lots of friends, a natural leader, mischievous. Passionate about whatever I pursued. Successful on swim team.

K – 12: School was boring, but realized my potential midway through high school. Math and science were weaknesses, history and English were strengths. Captain of high school swim team, enjoyed team dynamics. Senior year city champs, but knocked off in state championship. I changed strokes to fill in for injured teammate; I was the "go to" guy in a pinch –thrived on adversity. Clueless about future, vocation. Guidance department not real helpful. Received kudos from teacher and classmates in public speaking class. Very independent. Leader in church youth group.

In between: Took off for a year between HS and college. Worked odd jobs, traveled to California for fun, Europe with church mission trip. Enjoyed diverse experiences. Manual labor was fun, but looks tough for older people ...maybe college is not such a bad idea.

College: Attacked college with vigor. Loved the intellectual environment, loved the new ideas, new information and passionate professors. Struggled to balance studies with leadership in campus ministry. Lots of public speaking, training and development work. A knack for practical solutions. Work well with diverse types of people. Friends describe me as practical, common sense type, very direct.

Developing a concise, accurate summary of your formative years of life may require several hours of reflection, discussions with siblings, parents and old friends. For many, it might yield insight into problem-solving themes and tendencies. Some sellers may not see much correlation between the formative years of life and current professional endeavors, but thousands of interviews have convinced me that for many people there definitely is such a correlation. In example #3 above, the Corporate Trainer identifies the early roots of a career that included public speaking and training activities. Themes of independence and exploration manifest C (creative problem solver) tendencies often found in entrepreneurs and change agents. Not surprisingly, years later this person achieved a string of successes as a speaker and corporate trainer, and also reconfigured technology services for an employer thus creating new revenue opportunities.

Even if you do not consider your developmental years, forming your PVP involves an exhaustive review of your career. In the fourth example, the General Manager gives us an in-depth look at what the PVP analysis process looks like before you draw your summary statement. He diagrams his expertise, chronicles successes through his entire career and concludes with lists of strengths, areas for development and the types of organizations and cultures he prefers.

PERSONAL VALUE PROPOSITION #4
GENERAL MANAGER

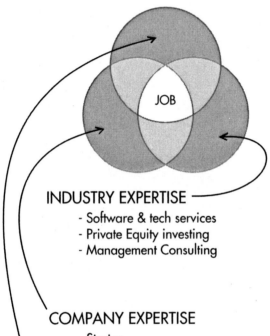

INDUSTRY EXPERTISE
- Software & tech services
- Private Equity investing
- Management Consulting

COMPANY EXPERTISE
- Startup
- Fortune 500
- Turnarounds
- High growth

FUNCTIONAL EXPERTISE
- CEO/President/COO
- P&L Management
- Strong in Finance, Sales, Marketing & Operations

SIGNIFICANT PROFESSIONAL ACCOMPLISHMENTS
AND PROBLEMS SOLVED

Company: XYZ Capital Management

Job Title: General Partner

Dates Held: Month, year - Present

Problem: Turnaround languishing wireless portfolio company

Actions: Determine viability of company/create strategic blueprint. Based on review of market, competition, opportunity sizing, positioning and company's management team, I/we:

1) Fired CEO/CTO

2) Hired new leadership team and key personnel

3) Created culture/inspired morale

4) Worked with new CEO to create "ecosystem" of advisors

5) Defined product offering

6) Refined business model value proposition

7) Identified market segments/partners/global geographic focus

8) Addressed intellectual property issues

Result: Portfolio company now poised to succeed

Company: XYZ Capital Management

Job Title: General Partner

Dates Held: Month, year – Month, Year

Problem: Rejuvenate the startup of a portfolio manufacturing company

Actions: Create strategic blueprint. Based on review of market, competition, opportunity sizing, positioning and company's management team, I/we:

1) Hired new President, CFO, COO, & VP Sales. COO & CFO were sourced personally

2) Worked with President/CFO to create financial models

3) Worked with President & VP Sales to devise marketing and sales plan

4) Introduced strategic advisors, recruited Board Director

Result: **Portfolio company is generating revenues and scaling down production**

Company: XYZ Capital Management

Job Title: General Partner

Dates Held: Month, Year – Month, Year

Problem: Floundering strategic alliance between AAA consulting and portfolio company

Actions: Built executive level relationships and touchstones *with multiple contacts.*

1. *Helped choreograph negotiations -involved directly and behind scenes.*

2. *Met with multiple partners within AAA consulting.*

3. *Introduced joint customer opportunity.*

4. *Addressed initial relationship and execution issues.*

5. *Transitioned new CEO to be lead on relationship.*

Result: **Maintain strong personal relationship with major international consulting partner**

Company: *XYZ Capital Management*

Job Title: *General Partner*

Dates Held: *Month, Year – Month, Year*

Problem: *Weak Limited Partner investor relations given difficult story and difficult venture environment*

Actions: *Create "best practice" caliber inaugural Limited Partner meeting. Orchestrated agenda, presenters, company features, logistics, deliverables, rehearsed presenters*

Result: **On a scale of 1 - 5 with 5 being best, Limited Partners rated overall meeting 4.63**

Company: CCC Inc.

Job Title: President/CEO

Dates Held: Month, Year – Month, Year

Problem: Closing window of opportunity for first mover product advantage

Actions: Create industry "statement" with a successful marketing launch in 120 days. Unlike other software companies at the time, I wanted to formally announce product launch with substance, i.e., signed partners, customers, industry analyst validation.

Results: 1) Announced 3 major strategic partners (Indira, AQ, BP); 2) Signed 4 customer beta installations; 3) Approximately 150 attended press conference, carried in periodicals/papers/radio stations and several industry analysts wrote about the company/product

Company: CCC Inc.

Job Title: President/CEO

Dates Held: Month, year – Month, Year

Problem: Built software company from ground up with no outside venture capital and limited funding from sister company

Actions: First in market with J2EE enterprise software application suite for e-commerce. Devised

vision/strategy, hired executive team, designed
and commercialized first-mover software, signed
strategic partners and customers.

Results: 1) Company hired 100 people and went from $0 to
$4.9MM in revenues within 2 years; 2) Attracted
strategic acquirers though financial and technology
markets imploded in 2000 and company was unable
to complete acquisition/secure additional capital.

Company: Broadmore Marketing Solutions

Job Title: Senior Partner/COO

Dates Held: Month, Year – Month, Year

Problem: Take early stage, entrepreneurial consulting company to higher level business results.

Actions: Developed services to a high value/high margin
annuity stream. Instituted metrics in client and
employee satisfaction. Secured clients beyond initial single client to include fortune 500 companies
such as ABC, XYC, etc. Expanded focus to international. Substantially grew team of consultants.

Results: 1) Delivered a 300% increase in pretax profits on
revenue growth of 50%; 2) Instituted client satisfaction survey and results included 4.63 average rating
on overall satisfaction (scale of 1-5 with 5 best) over
multiple years/multiple clients; 3) Employee morale
and financial results were best in class.

Company: ABC Credit

Job Title: Director of Marketing/Chief of Staff/Area Plans and Controls Manager (de facto COO/CFO)

Dates Held: Month, Year – Month, Year

Problem: Identify and initiate $100MM of cost reductions.

Actions: Identified organizational and operational inefficiencies to take SG&A costs out.

Results: **Recommended and implemented closing of area organization I was running as it was redundant. Leadership actions resulted in President's Quality Award.**

Company: ABC Credit

Job Title: Division Manager of Financing Operations

Dates Held: Month, Year – Month, Year

Problem: Transform $1B divisional credit function and outsource specific responsibilities to new ABC Credit division without disrupting customer experience and affecting topline growth.

Actions: Identified program offerings, devised rules of engagement, codified new processes and established indemnification vehicle.

Results: **1) Helped launch ABC Credit into world-class financing organization while maintaining industry-**

best loss ratios and continuity in customer satisfaction and divisional revenue growth; 2) Recipient of Vice President's Excellence Award.

Company: ABC Credit

Job Title: Manager of Market Support

Dates Held: Month, Year – Month, Year

Problem: Startup ABC division with no processes, metrics and tools.

Actions: To support sales/marketing, hired new staff, gathered requirements and institutionalized business processes, tools and measurements.

Results: *Recipient of Vice President' Excellence Award and exceeded all divisional objectives ahead of schedule.*

Company: ABC Credit

Job Title: Branch Administration Manager

Dates Held: Month, year – Month, Year

Problem: Turnaround one of the bottom 5 performing branches (100+) in ABC division.

Actions: Identified new staffing plan, rebuilt culture, instituted new metrics for financial performance, employee and customer satisfaction.

Results: *1) Branch office became one of the top performers in nation consistently achieving financial, employee* *and customer satisfaction scores; 2) Recipient of ABC Regional Manager's Award and promoted to Assistant to Division CFO.*

PROFESSIONAL STRENGTHS AND DEVELOPMENT NEEDS

Strengths:

1) Execution – operationalize ideas, "move the ball" forward & "keep score"

2) Arranger – can handle many simultaneous moving parts (e.g., 7 portfolio companies)

3) Team/morale builder – hire "best athletes" with diverse/complementary backgrounds

4) "Un-ambiguous" and strong communicator – written/oral, 1-1, group, etc.

5) Partner/customer relationships – create multiple touch-stones and enduring respect

6) Quick study – able to "get it", process, analyze and solve multiple and disparate data points

7) Multidisciplined strategic planning - marketing, finance, operations, etc.

8) Resourceful and entrepreneurial – remove obstacles

9) "Laser beam" focus – high intensity to accomplish critical initiatives

Situations in which I perform well:

1) *Dynamic, lots of balls in the air*

2) *Intellectual challenges...working with smart, high-integrity people*

3) *Working on "big deals" with financial and timeline pressures*

Favorite tasks/duties:

1) *Hire/develop/mentor/grow teams*

2) *Create "victories" for customers, partners, employees*

3) *Drive many simultaneous initiatives/actions/tasks*

4) *Surround myself with "thoroughbreds"*

5) *Execute a vision*

6) *Create singleness of purpose in organizations*

7) *Instill culture rich with values*

8) *Work hard, but have fun*

Organizational preferences:

1) *Impeccable ethics...must occupy high ground--always*

2) *Flat, apolitical, with little protocol and no bureaucracy*

3) *Disciplined, focused, responsive and organized leadership*

4) *Nimble, adaptable, open and firm decision-making style*

5) *Equal partnerships*

Professional development needs, weaknesses, dislikes:

1) *Need additional manufacturing and international experience*

2) *Need additional experience in structuring complex financial transactions*

3) *Dislikes – politics, egos, gamesmanship, questionable ethics, incompetence*

As you can see, preparing your PVP is not a small task. Once you have honed your personal value proposition down to a 100 word summary and validated it with your trusted advisors, commit it to memory. I encourage you to keep a copy beside your computer, in your briefcase and in your car and read it before you go to bed every night. This is your "elevator pitch" and should be the lens through which you view every potential job opportunity. One of your goals is to make certain that it becomes the way the job market defines and relates to you.

The primary value of discovering your PVP is that it will change the way you approach the job market. These are not exercises in professional narcissism, nor an elaborate attempt to reshape your resume, although you might choose to do so. The exercise is designed to reshape your thinking by identifying and describing your professional genetic makeup. *Your PVP is the DNA of your career.* It tells you what kinds of problems you gravitate toward and solve, thus forming a powerful tool for sorting out where to direct your research and targeting efforts to a vast, highly fragmented job market. Once you have worked through the PVP exercises and crystallized your problem-solving skills, you are ready to look for the buyers of those skills; precisely the subject of the next chapter.

Chapter 6
TAKING AIM
Identifying Your Buyers

Your newly minted PVP answers the first of the three brutal questions: "What do I have to sell?" and establishes the first pillar of your foundation, which is "a clear knowledge of what you have to sell." Now let's move on to the next essential question: "What kinds of organizations have the types of problems I can solve?" This forms the second pillar of your foundation: *"A clearly defined market of buyers."*

A SPECIAL NOTE TO EXTROVERTS AND INTROVERTS

If you are an extrovert, you may feel like this step will slow you down. If you are patient and follow this process, it will actually speed your search. If you are an introvert, you will like this because it translates into fewer cold calls and more meaningful interaction with prospective employers.

"What kinds of organizations have the types of problems I can solve?" This is the ultimate marketing question, is it not? What industry sectors and specific organizations within those sectors desperately require your PVP? Remember, it's not about who likes you, or who knows you, but who needs you to solve their problems. *It's all about the buyer, not the seller.* Even in the most dismal job market conditions, organizations are screaming for problem-solvers like you. Your job is to find them.

The River Metaphor

At the end of the movie *A River Runs Through It,* while the camera pans an old man fly-fishing in a beautiful river in Montana, director and narrator Robert Redford concludes, "Eventually all things merge into one, and a river runs through it..." Please keep this scene and these words in mind so that we can use it as a metaphor. Imagine that your entire work experience with all organizations and industries is a river. Visualize standing on the banks of the river. Look upstream for a moment. This is where the river comes from-its past, its source. It probably connects upstream to other streams, creeks, lakes and reservoirs. Now look downstream. This is where the river is going, its future. It probably connects to larger rivers, lakes and reservoirs and eventually to the ocean. All of these places, upstream and downstream, past and future, are connected to the point at which you stand. Your place on this river actually connects you to a massive watershed well beyond what you may have seen and experienced thus far.

Business and economics are a lot like that river. Everything connects to a larger system. Now let's think about your experience:

Look upstream at the suppliers and service providers to your current and previous employers. They are somehow dependent on your place in the river. Stop right now and make a list of all the upstream suppliers, sub-suppliers and vendors that flow into your section of the river. They are interested in who you are and what you have done because it relates directly to *their* survival. Take a minute and write down all the organizations you can think of that directly or indirectly provide products and services to your section of the river.

Look downstream and apply the same analytical thought process to whatever services and businesses are downstream from your place on the river. They will be your customers (or your customers' customers) and represent all businesses and organizations that consume what you produce in order to provide for their own customers. Take a minute to identify all the companies or industries that directly or indirectly are customers of or derive benefit from your section of the river.

Look directly across to the opposite shore. Businesses over there will understand the possibilities of your section of the river because they share it as well. They are the competitors of your current or former employers. They will immediately grasp the significance of your place on the river and understand what you might be able to do for them. Make a list of all the competitors, or similar businesses, of which you are aware.

Diagram #5

THE RIVER METAPHOR

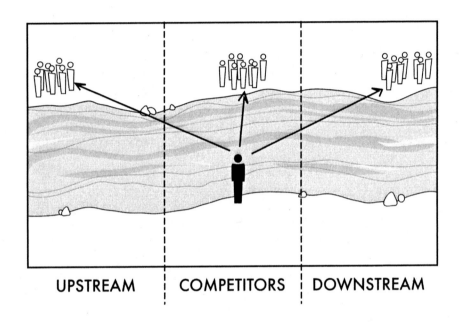

UPSTREAM   **COMPETITORS**   **DOWNSTREAM**

Now combine these three lists into a single master list of all businesses and organizations that are connected to your current and previous employment scenarios. It will be helpful if you can create subgroups within the master list based upon upstream, downstream or competitor status. Your goal is to have as many organizations on this list as you can think of. *This list will be substantially reduced later on, so it is extremely important that it contain at least 40 organizations, preferably more.* If you have fewer, go back and rework the river paradigm until your list reaches at least 40.

Sharpening your focus

It is my observation that most sellers (job hunters) are unaware that they can distinguish themselves from other sellers by becoming knowledgeable about the issues that matter to the buyer. A seller who is knowledgeable and interested in the buyer's problems is more impressive than a seller who is only knowledgeable about himself. With this in mind, take this comprehensive target list you just compiled and sharpen your focus by doing some more homework. Your objective is to determine which of these organizations have the greatest need for your problem-solving skills. How do you accomplish this? Three words: research, research, research. Go to your local public library and consult with the librarian, or fire up the Internet browser on your computer and begin. If you would like to see some specific resource recommendations, please visit www.kissyourresumegoodbye.com on the World Wide Web, and look over the "Useful Resources" section. Your goal is to identify all organizations that you have competed against or been connected to upstream and downstream through your work with current or past employers. You need to learn as much as you can about these organizations. Begin by answering the following questions:

- ✦ How does the stock market value them compared to peers? Why?

- ✦ What are the major industry trends shaping the competitive environment for these companies?

- ✦ What are the notable successes and failures for each company during the past 12 months?

- ✦ Have there been key personnel changes lately? Why?

- ✦ Note all technology breakthroughs, innovations or process improvements that will affect this company.

- ✦ Have they sold off any divisions or subsidiaries in the past two years?

- ✦ Have they acquired any other businesses during the past two years?

- ✦ Can you learn why these acquisitions or divestitures were made?

The above questions are often easiest to answer for publicly-traded companies because of SEC requirements, Sarbanes-Oxley and other mandatory disclosure regulations. If, however, some of your target companies are privately held, you will need to be more creative. Begin with the company Web site, and move methodically to news services and industry publications to research all stories and public relations announcements during the past two years.

For both public and private companies, researching suppliers and customers can yield valuable information.

Once you have the answers to these questions for your target companies, I'm going to ask you to do something very unusual: pretend that you are seriously considering buying each of these companies, sort of like Warren Buffet. Why? So that you will look beyond the issues that relate just to you and take a long-term, marketplace view of each company. If you were going to buy the company, what questions would you ask senior management? What would you want to know about its future plans, inherent strengths, weaknesses and opportunities for improvement? Are there technology or industry challenges that threaten the company or position it for growth? Be sensitive to gaps in company product lines or services and issues regarding distribution. The objective is to identify and list as many problems for each company as possible, and then put a check mark by those that your PVP indicates you are qualified to help solve. Remember, your focus is on *them* and solving *their* problems.

For each company, consolidate your research onto a single sheet of paper containing all the critical information you have learned. From this, you must narrow your targets to not more than 30: 10 upstream, 10 downstream and 10 competitors. If your refined master list has less than 30 companies, return to the river paradigm and expand your research until you have at least 30.

Once you have accomplished this, the next step is to prioritize and further refine your master list of target organizations and companies. Put your list through the following five edits:

71

◆ Edit #1: Make certain every company is a competitor or has a clear upstream or downstream relationship to your primary industry or company experience and has problems that you can solve.

◆ Edit #2: Arrange your master list into three subgroups: 10 competitors, 10 upstream and 10 downstream organizations.

◆ Edit #3: Break each subgroup of 10 into the top five and bottom five, *ranked according to your ability to pinpoint problems they have that you can solve.* Additionally, you may prioritize around factors important to you such as location of the company, business processes or reputation.

◆ Edit #4: Create two new lists, the first consisting of your top 15 organizations (five from each of three sub lists) and the second consisting of the bottom 15.

◆ Edit #5: Develop 10 questions specific to each of your top 15 organizations. These questions will be used when you are in front of the right people and will demonstrate your understanding about each company and its problems.

Once you have developed a summary sheet for each of your top 15 target organizations, you are ready to take the next step. What follows is an example of how a target company worksheet might appear.

TOP 15 TARGET ORGANIZATIONS

Company #1 Name: XYZ Corporation

Financial summary: revenues, profits, stock price, etc.

Brief Description of Business: divisions, subsidiaries, quick recap of products, services with which you would be involved.

Brief Description of function: department size, manager, how it is viewed within the company or by customers.

Brief summary of your 10 research questions:

Brief summary of your strategic 'Warren Buffet' questions:

Before we proceed, let's review where we are in this process right now. The work done in chapter five developed your PVP statement and supporting information, which establishes your first pillar: a clear knowledge of what you have to sell. The work you just completed in this chapter produced a target list of 30 organizations -15 of which you have designated as your top priority. This is the marketplace for your PVP and establishes your second pillar: a clearly defined set of buyers.

The next chapter will tackle the formation of your third, and final, pillar: developing a clear game plan linking you, the seller, with buyers.

Chapter 7
TAKING CHARGE
Fixing the Ineffective Network

When it comes to overused, misunderstood and ineffective concepts for job changers, *networking* is near the top of the list. Networking is a discipline, so whether you are an introvert or an extrovert, it is crucial to develop a network as part of the process of finding your next job. Most job seekers credit their network with finding their next job and for this reason most successful job changers reverently vow "never to let their network grow cold again." But a fresh look at the subject of networking reveals a hidden flaw: it works best for sellers who already know what they have to sell and who wants to buy it. Therefore, I commend to you **The Network Rule**: *the objective of developing a network is to build a bridge that connects your PVP with your target marketplace.*

Why would job hunters or career changers abandon their old networks? When they function contrary to your goal of finding a better job fast. Bear in mind, a network is neither good nor bad. Its value is determined by how you construct and use it.

THE NETWORK RULE

The objective of developing a network is to build a bridge that connects your PVP with your target marketplace.

Most job seekers and career changers define their network so broadly that it includes anyone with a pulse who might help them find a job. If this sounds like your definition, then your network probably consists of three categories of people: people you know that cannot help you; people you know that want to help you; and people you know that can help you. It is this third category, people who can help, that most job hunters do not properly define and focus on. If your definition of those who can help is limited to people you already know, you overlook the vast potential of a much larger group: those who can help you that you don't know yet. *Your task is to identify and focus on those who can help, whether they know you or not.* Unfortunately, most job seekers become sidetracked by sympathetic acquaintances that want to help but are not in a position to do anything useful. This approach to networking may *feel* productive because you are speaking with lots of people, but in reality you are wasting your three most valuable resources: time, contacts and personal energy. You are directing your energy outward in an unfocused manner and any engineer will tell you that this will accomplish much less than directing your energy toward specific targets. This old networking paradigm is visually depicted by Diagram #6 on the following page.

Diagram #6

TRADITIONAL APPROACH TO NETWORKING

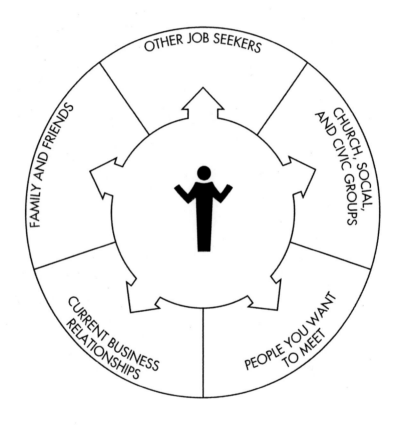

So what *should* a productive network look like? According to *Merriam-Webster's Collegiate Dictionary,* a network is "a fabric or structure of cords or wires that cross at regular intervals and are knotted or secured at the crossings; a system of lines or channels … interconnected or interrelated…." Note that the definition conveys a sense of similarity, patterns and firm connections rather than random connections and accidental meetings, a critical distinction when applying this definition to networks of people.

If you integrate Webster's definition of network into your value proposition and research, here is what you get: *Your job hunting network should consist of people who can lead you to people and organizations that need to solve the kinds of problems that you can solve.* You may want to form a secondary network to serve as a source of encouragement and support, but *the network leading to your next job must be stacked with people who comprehend and can communicate your PVP to your target marketplace.*

Networks come in all shapes and sizes, but it is important to be particularly sensitive to the level of the people in your network. Practically speaking *your network contacts should lead directly to people who are one or two levels above the level at which you will be hired,* because that is where the decision to hire you will be made. This means if you are looking for a CEO spot you should target board members and investors; for VP spots you want to reach the SVP, EVP and COO levels, and so on depending on the organization and its structure. Beware of limiting your network to peers and subordinates who may lack the authority and vested interest in solving buyers' problems.

A network is a means to an end, not an end in itself. It does not matter if your new network consists of old friends or new, your brother-in-law or complete strangers. *You must first define what you have to sell and who you want to sell to, and then build a network that gets you to the people in your predefined target market.* The message to communicate through your new network needs to be simple and clear: "These are the kinds of problems I solve, and these are the companies that have those problems." Once your network participants comprehend your PVP and lead you to the correct people at buyer organizations, you both will look like winners.

Your new network is a market driven one. Visualize yourself burrowing through your large, unfocused network to progressively smaller more focused networks until you reach those people who will lead you to your target market. In contrast to Diagram #6 which demonstrates how traditional networking radiates outward and has no target, Diagram #7 on the following page shows the new networking paradigm focusing in progressively tighter and more intentional circles. The largest circle represents everyone who could be in your network, and each progressively smaller circle represents the statistical reality that relatively fewer people will actually understand your PVP and be helpful. An important benefit of having a finely honed PVP is that it allows you to discern who ought to be in this inner circle where you will be concentrating your energies.

Diagram #7

MARKET-DRIVEN APPROACH TO NETWORKING

PEOPLE WHO MIGHT BE ABLE TO HELP
PEOPLE WHO WANT TO HELP
PEOPLE WHO CAN HELP

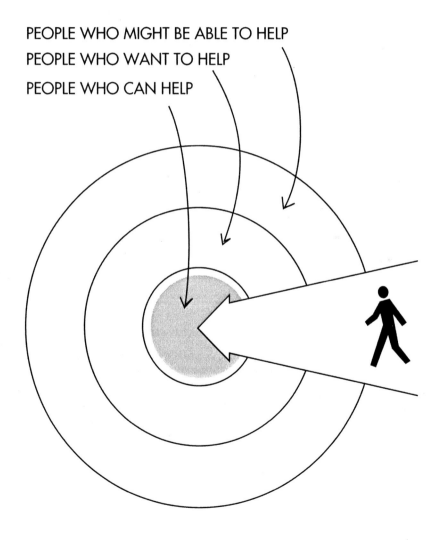

Building A Market Driven Network

Now that you have the theoretical framework for a market driven network, you are probably wondering how to begin building one. As with the previous two pillars of your foundation, the third one must also be established with research. Take out your target list of 15 companies; for each one you will now develop a second sheet of information, listing key contacts and referrals that will expand your network into that organization. Please keep two goals in mind as you do this: 1) your objective is to obtain direct contact information and, if possible, a door opening referral one or two levels above the level at which you would work, and 2) the clearer you communicate how your PVP addresses real problems at the target company, the more likely it is that your network will be helpful. If you already know people at your target companies, then write their names down. But this will rarely produce enough contacts for you, so here are some suggestions to expand your network of those who can help:

1. List all the consultants, attorneys, accountants and other vendors with established relationships at each target company (annual reports often list some of this information.) Focus on service providers assisting each company in the area of your functional and proven problem-solving expertise, because they will understand how you can benefit this company and might provide you with the appropriate introduction. Identify all engagement partners and key managers in these organizations, since they may have a vested interest in referring you into a situation that will help their client and make them look good.

2. Examine the professional associations to which you belong. Ascertain if any employees of your target companies are also members of these associations. If so, approach them during an association event and ask to speak with them privately. Share your insights into the problems your PVP addresses at their company and ask whom you should speak with about these issues.

3. Use your research tools to identify the key people at each company that, by virtue of job title and function, are likely to be responsible for the problems your PVP addresses. Ask all your contacts in service organizations, suppliers and competitors of your target company if they are personally acquainted with the person you have identified and could introduce you. It is not always possible to obtain a personal referral or introduction to all key people within the target company. If you lack a network contact, try this: send a brief introductory email to the correct person briefly mentioning the problems you have identified and your interest in discussing them. Follow up with a written letter the next day and with a direct phone call three days later.

Prior to your initial discussions with your target organizations let me offer a word of caution: although insiders may feel the freedom to criticize their company, outsiders (that's you) must be respectful and use great care. Don't appear to be presumptuous, be curious. I call this the "Colombo approach," in honor of the famed detective character played by Peter Falk. Detective Colombo's unassuming, yet persistent, questioning always triumphed over the arrogance and shallow thinking of his opponents. Similarly, the power of your insightful, probing questions will impress most buyers far more than criticism that makes you look smart but embarrasses them. Never forget, it's all about them.

The Network Payoff

Many conscientious job seekers are concerned with how to reward their networks for assisting them. While this is a valid concern in an era when few people take the time to say thank you, it is important to realize that *the market driven network built around your PVP is doing itself a favor by helping you.* It works because it is in the best interest of those in your network to facilitate your movement into an organization in which you can solve problems. Service providers and employees of your target companies will be helping themselves by helping the company identify and acquire good talent. In fact, many large law firms and accounting firms regard such referrals as an important way to strengthen existing client relationships and build new ones. If you execute this strategy properly, everyone in the network will increase marketplace credibility by helping you, which in turn strengthens future business relationships for all participants. Also note that a network built on your PVP will provide numerous opportunities for you to reciprocate to your network participants. The first opportunity might be to share the *Six Rules that Rule the Job Market* with them so that all participants can become more focused and effective.

Chapter 8
WHAT GOES AROUND
Perpetuating the Process

The old saying, "What goes around, comes around," rings true when one reflects upon the potential for role reversal in the relationship between buyers and sellers in the job market. That is to say, the seller is likely to become a buyer at some point in the future, and the buyer may become the seller. With this in mind, buyers might consider two possible conclusions:

1) *To be humble is to be smart.* Treat sellers the way you want to be treated when you become one. It is a very small world, indeed.

2) *Use the* Six Rules that Rule the Job Market *to increase your job security.* Below are two immediate practical applications that can be put into effect by most senior management executives in their current jobs.

   a. Identify your PVP and actively pursue situations within your organization where you can focus on your problem-solving expertise.

b. Challenge your organization to use problem-solving criteria to drive job definitions, hiring requisitions and recruitment. You can vastly improve upon job descriptions defined by obscure titles, vague or irrelevant requirements and empty boxes on an organization chart. This is simply good business.

For sellers, I recognize that the previous seven chapters are brief, yet they suggest you do a lot of work to benefit from all the exercises. Remember that discovering your PVP and applying the *Six Rules That Rule the Job Market* is a process, not an event. The payback for investing in this process is the qualitative improvement of your interactions with your target market of prospective employers, discussing their problems and your unique ability to solve them. This is what will result in a better job, one that corresponds with your proven strengths and areas of contribution.

At this juncture a few words about timing and serendipity are in order. First, it is only reasonable to expect some of your top 15 target organizations will not recognize, or be in a position to address, the problems you identified in your research. It logically follows that such organizations may not see the need for your problem-solving skills or will not be able to pursue a meaningful dialogue. Often you will not discover this until you have used your new network to make the appropriate contact and have had your first discussion. If you discover this, do not take it personally and make sure you do not appear overbearing or negative. If for any reason they aren't able to realize, or take advantage of, your problem-solving skills, just move on to the next organization on your list. In the consumer marketing world it is often noted that you cannot sell what the consumer is unwilling to purchase. Similarly, pressing your PVP on an unwilling buyer will not get you far. On the other hand, you may discover that one of your target organizations has recently awakened to a specific issue or problem, and you may be perceived as the answer. Particularly at very senior levels, organizations have been known to create new jobs to accommodate the timely arrival of valuable problem solvers. But this happens at the buyer's initiative and you cannot force it to happen as an outsider.

Finally, after you have successfully applied this process and made the transition to a new job, you will want to stay sharp and focused in anticipation of your next job change. Here are some final pointers.

+ Regularly review and refine your PVP as you grow and develop. This needs to be done on an annual or semiannual basis.

+ Expand and deepen your PVP-based network. Seek creative ways to strengthen your affiliation with professionals grappling with the kinds of problems you love to solve. Try these suggestions:

  ✧ Join an existing professional association and volunteer to form a subcommittee that is committed to researching and building a knowledge base directly related to your PVP and the issues addressed by your problem solving strengths.

✧ Start your own informal association of like-minded people. Meet quarterly to exchange ideas and industry developments.

✦ Share the wealth. Help someone else out of the traditional job change rut and show them how to build the three pillars for successful job change. Don't be surprised if you end up leading a small group of interested people who want to walk this path together.

When you put this approach into practice you will be able to navigate in the twenty-first century job market efficiently and effectively. If you diligently follow this path, you will never return to the old ways because it is clear that they empower others rather than you.

As we conclude the second section of **Kiss Your Resume Goodbye,** you now have the tools to discover what you have to sell, identify who the buyers are, and you have a method for constructing a network that will connect the two. But there is more to it than this. You have learned five of the *Six Rules that Rule the Job Market* and if this were a theoretical book, we would end here. But experience suggests that there are several dangerous pitfalls awaiting most executive job hunters and career changers that might cause you to discount or ignore your PVP-based approach. These issues and some other valuable tips are the subject of the last section.

SECTION III

WATCH YOUR STEP

Chapter 9
BRAVE NEW WORLDS
Changing Industries, Functions and Life

This chapter is for you brave job hunters and career changers who feel compelled to move far beyond changing employers or job titles. Experienced professionals who want to change the very function they perform or the industry in which they perform it must do so with careful deliberation and planning. Let me begin by acknowledging three things: first, I have great empathy for those who pursue this course in their lives; second, based upon the thousands of people I have interviewed there appears to be much bad advice dispensed on this topic, usually offered by people who do not possess the buyers' perspective; and third, there is not enough space to squeeze all my suggestions into this chapter. So, in keeping with the brevity of this book, we will only touch on important practical highlights.

Most of the people I interview indicate that they have considered pursuing a radically different type of work at some point in their career. Such private musings seem to be common among high achievers. Some are enticed by the prospect of better opportunities elsewhere, such as the recent boom of Internet-based businesses and telecom gear markets that lured thousands of seasoned professionals out of their traditional industries and functional roles. There are those for whom career change is mandated by unexpected illness or the need to accommodate caring for loved ones. Others may reach a point in life where they decide to put family and quality of life considerations above job and career. Finally, there are those who have an epiphany or personal revelation that reorders their vision and mission in life.

All of these reasons are legitimate. But although the reasons for career change are as unique as the people making them, the types of changes can be put into three categories: those changing industries, those changing job functions and those making quality of life changes. Chapter 10 focuses on quality of life changes while the remainder of this chapter is dedicated to industry and functional changes.

Changing Industries

After watching many successful professionals shipwreck their careers while attempting to change industries, some practical advice could help you avoid significant and unnecessary pain and angst. Those seriously considering changing the industry in which you work must answer two questions: 1) Do my functional job skills translate easily to other industries? And 2) Which ones? The risk of changing industries will vary depending upon your functional job skills. For example, sellers with expertise in finance and accounting generally move easily between industries because functional knowledge is usually more valuable to the buyer than industry knowledge. But with many other functions these changes must be made with great care, always focused on whether or not your PVP addresses the problems of the hiring organization or of the industry in general. To guide you in sizing up a change of industry, consider the following check points:

+ *The sanity check* is critical. If you have concluded that your PVP has limited value in your current industry, ask your trusted advisors to review your thought process and conclusion before moving on. Make careful note if they do not agree, or raise questions you cannot answer.

+ *Research* other industries with similar processes, products, customers and markets to the ones you already know. For example, the automotive industry and the financial services industry might have similar financial and marketing functions, but very different sales and distribution functions. *The objective is to target industries that are similar to your current one in your area of functional expertise.*

+ *Narrow your focus* to three industries and target three companies in each based upon your assessment of their need for your problem-solving expertise (remember, it's all about them) and personal criteria you establish, for example, location or company reputation.

+ *Revisit* chapters 5 and 6. Rewrite your PVP and supporting documentation into the language of each new industry you are targeting, making sure that you purge all irrelevant language, industry labels and processes. In the process of rewriting, you are likely to become more convinced that this change makes sense, or you will begin to realize that you are stretching your credibility beyond what buyers will tolerate.

+ *Building a new network* may be required. Revisit Chapter 7 and draft a plan to build a network that will lead you to your target companies in your new industry that require your problem-solving skills.

Changing Functional Roles

The late Groucho Marx once said, "I don't care to belong to a club that accepts people like me as members." While we may laugh at the absurdity of this statement, we also recognize its profound truth: many people don't respect and value who they are and what they do. A fortune 500 CEO once confided to me, "Nothing happens around here unless somebody sells something, so I have never understood people who lament 'Oh, I'm just a salesman.'" In fact, I have met financial executives who wished they were in sales and successful sales leaders who wanted to be engineers. If this sounds like you, before you go back to school or plunge into some new functional role that you have never worked in before, try the following:

+ *Always start with problem-solving.* Review your work in chapters 5 and 6 and determine if you have clearly defined your PVP. Do your past accomplishments correspond with your current or recent functional roles and job assignments?

+ *Are you striving to fulfill your dreams or someone else's?* Make certain your perception of yourself is not mixed up

94

with parental expectations echoing in the back of your mind, or the demands of a spouse or another significant person in your life. If you suspect this might be the case, you would be wise to seek out a licensed psychologist with whom you can work through these issues. In fact, you may eventually need to rework your PVP.

✦ *Reality check*: Don't plunge into a completely new functional role until you have reviewed the idea with your trusted advisors. Do others confirm the misfit that you believe exists between you and your job?

✦ *Testing and career counseling*: We all need advisors who can offer us rational, objective advice regarding changing functional roles. Testing to determine your appropriateness for a job is a complex and controversial topic. Those seeking career guidance via psychological testing, interest inventories and skills assessment tools should ask the test-giver to provide hard evidence that these assessments correlate with real world job requirements and reliably predict job success and satisfaction.

The above reasons are the basis for recommending **The Experience Rule** to those contemplating a job change outside of their functional or industry expertise. **The Experience Rule** states that you should *focus your job hunting on the industries and functional areas in which you have your greatest expertise unless:*

1. *There is overwhelming, objective evidence that your industry holds little or no future for your problem-solving skills, or*

2. *There is substantial, objective evidence that you are not well-*

95

THE EXPERIENCE RULE

Focus your job hunting on the industries and functional areas in which you have your greatest expertise unless:

1. *There is overwhelming, objective evidence that your industry holds little or no future for your problem-solving skills, or*

2. *There is substantial, objective evidence that you are not well-suited to your current function and are clearly better suited to a specific functional alternative.*

suited to your current function and are clearly better suited to a specific functional alternative.

In summary, when considering either an industry or functional job change it is absolutely critical to develop a clear and compelling PVP for each new industry or function that you pursue. Do not expect the job market or buyers to do this interpretation for you: it's your job, not theirs.

Chapter 10 discusses life change considerations and related issues that often side-track experienced professionals along the road to your next job.

Chapter 10
COMMON PITFALLS
Potholes and Detours Along the Way

In the clever comedy film, *Lost in America*, actor Albert Brooks shows us what can happen when a very talented executive makes a major career decision in an emotionally charged atmosphere. The film follows Brooks, playing the role of a frustrated advertising executive, and his wife as they quit their corporate jobs, liquidate all their assets, buy a Winnebago and literally drive off into the sunset in pursuit of their dreams. The story offers several compelling messages about the risks associated with pursuing major lifestyle or career changes.

While there is nothing wrong with professionals pursuing their dreams, it is important to realize that confusion can result when job changing and dream chasing are combined. Equally important is the knowledge that there are certain times and circumstances when you should *not* make big decisions combining jobs and dreams. After hundreds of interviews with people who have chased both their dreams and jobs across the country and around the world, the following suggestions may save you heartache, financial loss and stress.

+ Never commit to changing jobs or careers while on vacation.

+ Never make significant job or career decisions in the midst of or immediately following divorce, death of a family member, or other life-changing event.

+ Never make job or career changes during an episode of depression.

+ Never change careers solely because of unhappiness with your boss, your company or a management change.

+ Make sure the desire to *run toward* a new opportunity is *twice as strong* as the desire to *run away* from your current opportunity.

+ Never attempt to turn your hobbies into viable employment unless you are surrounded by objective advisors who loudly applaud the idea and promise (preferably in writing) to be your customers for life.

Generally speaking, I have observed that baby boomers, those currently ranging from their mid-30s to mid-50s, are more focused on quality of life issues and less willing to relocate for career advancement than their parents were. When faced with employer-driven relocation, baby boomers often choose to leave the organization. Therefore, it is not surprising that as a group they experience more job change than the generation of loyal corporate foot soldiers who preceded them. But such quality of life transitions still need to be based upon your PVP and pursued methodically.

What follows are three common detours that I observe sellers frequently making on the road to their next job. Each can sidetrack you from your PVP, and deserves special attention.

The Good Guy Detour

Many professionals who are both talented and caring become involved in nonprofit organizations during their careers. Churches, synagogues, chambers of commerce, school systems and other charitable organizations require the time and expertise of generous professionals like you. These worthwhile organizations often provide you with intellectual stimulation and a sense of purpose far beyond what your *real* career offers. Yet these very attributes can become a snare to the unwary professional. Sellers who are between jobs or rethinking their careers often feel drawn to charitable or civic organizations. But if you are not careful, your free time can be gobbled up by such organizations until a board member or volunteer suggests that you consider working there full-time. Before you accept the offer and plunge into a full-time job with a charitable or civic organization ask yourself these questions:

+ Does this organization have the kinds of problems that I can solve according to the work I did as illustrated in Chapter 5?

+ Did this organization surface as a prospective employer on any of the lists I generated in Chapter 6? Why or why not?

✦ Do I understand the culture and work environment of this organization on a day-to-day basis?

✦ Would I still feel passionate about joining this organization if I discovered a better job opportunity more closely aligned with my industry and functional expertise?

✦ Can this organization afford to pay for my services, or am I willing to make the trade-off between mission and money?

✦ If you are financially secure, searching for a new mission and relate well to a religious perspective, find a copy of *Half Time* by Bob Buford. He covers this subject quite well.

The Consulting Detour

For many professionals, nothing seems quite as tantalizing as the possibility of consulting. It appears to be a superb course of action because it allows you to leverage all your industry and functional expertise, yet avoid all the hassles of bosses and bureaucracies. I need to pause for a moment here, and differentiate between interim consulting and launching a career in consulting. Interim consulting work, while you are hunting for your next full-time job, is an excellent way to bring in cash, provide valuable service to former and future employers and a savvy way to further develop your PVP-oriented network. If, however, you are seriously considering consulting as a career, that is quite different. Your first choice, and one that is often overlooked, should be to join an established consulting firm that has clients needing your problem-solving skills. They will have valuable selling and service delivery processes already in place and an established infrastructure that should allow you to focus on your area of expertise. If you are considering launching your own consulting business, however, you may want to consider these points before you do so:

1. *It's all about selling.* No matter how good you are and despite the euphoria of landing your first consulting assignment, you will spend more time selling than you could have imagined. This becomes painfully obvious in economic downturns. Therefore, consulting rarely fits most professionals who lack a strong, direct sales background.

2. *Big brands rule.* You may be cheaper and better than big name consulting companies, but over time they win. They are selling machines and have the luxury of separating those who sell from those who deliver; you must do both.

3. *Beware the franchise.* Some people choose to partner with consulting franchises or networks offering brochures and affiliation in exchange for a piece of your revenue and access to your customers. Beware of three things:

   a) There is often a product or service you are expected to sell;

   b) This appeals most to those who desire the connection with something bigger than themselves

   c) These affiliations rarely ease your selling burden.

4. *You've really got something.* You may really have something special going if the above points don't scare you off. A truly unique consulting niche that leverages your PVP and

lacks serious competition is a rare, but precious, find. If you think you have what it takes, and your personal advisers concur, it may be worth a 90-180 day trial after which you might want your advisers to help you review and determine the next steps.

The Entrepreneurial Detour

Trying to launch a business, other than temporary consulting, has always been tough and is not an advisable undertaking while trying to find another job. Recent years have been particularly unkind to high-tech entrepreneurs. When the economy heats up again, however, they will be evident once more in great numbers. It takes tremendous tenacity to launch a viable company. At a bare minimum, you must possess a unique and defensible concept or technology, a sustainable cost or delivery advantage and have demonstrated implementation expertise. If you have all this and remain determined to become an entrepreneur, I suggest you take the following steps in the order listed:

1. Draft a detailed business plan (there are books, software and online templates readily available).

2. Develop a list of all the Venture Capital funds (VCs) and Small Business Investment Corporations (SBICs) in your area.

3. Shop the plan aggressively to all of them, *and listen carefully to any and all feedback you receive.*

4. Interview four entrepreneurs: two who succeeded and two who failed. Prepare specific questions for them about what

they have learned about building businesses, teams of people and capital markets. Take detailed notes. The wisdom you gain from these veterans might mean the difference between success and failure for your venture.

After all this research, if you still feel you must do it, then try. You may be that one in a million.

Chapter 11
EMOTIONS, LOVED ONES AND YOU
Dealing with Your Feelings and Family

It is necessary to explore the emotional impact of changing jobs on you as well as your immediate family and close friends. In 1965 Simon and Garfunkle penned one of their legendary, melancholy hits containing this memorable refrain:

> "I touch no one and no one touches me
> I am a rock, I am an island!"

This poetic line may resonate with your feelings at times, but it is simply not reality for most people. In fact for most seasoned professionals, changing jobs and careers is a family affair because our lives are so intertwined with family and friends. Top recommendations and suggestions from counselors plus your fellow job hunters and career changers who have borne the pain and emerged intact on the other side follow.

The Stress of Job Loss

Few things match the stress of job loss. Even if you initiated the change, there is anxiety. Every year hundreds of thousands of jobs are eliminated, often for reasons beyond anyone's control. And if that's not enough, your family, loved ones and dependents can sometimes feel wounded too or, even worse, irrationally believe you have let them down. The reality is that everyone is affected. Your friends and family can either become your biggest assets or your biggest liabilities, depending on your ability to communicate with them and enlist their support. Depending upon their experience and background, you may decide to include them among your trusted advisors, or simply ask them to be sounding boards when developing your PVP.

The Roller Coaster

Looking for another job or changing careers is by definition an emotional roller coaster. You soar to the top of the world after a promising interview, and then plunge into despair when a second interview or an offer doesn't materialize. During times of self-doubt you wonder how someone with your abilities ever managed to make it as far as you have. To make matters worse, you can be easily seduced into the comparison trap. Your neighbor may have bought a new boat or built an addition onto his house. Why does everyone seem to be better off than you are? Then the phone rings or an email arrives. Some company appears to recognize your true value, and you soar to the peaks of limitless possibilities. No, you are not crazy. This is the experience of most job seekers and career changers. As any top-notch salesperson will attest, prospecting for customers is tough and there is a high rejection rate even under the best circumstances. This is why it is so crucial to clearly define your PVP and your target market, because they will dramatically cut down on the volume of rejections you experience since you will be talking the language and issues of the buyer. And remember, this is what buyers want to talk about so your interaction is usually positive and stimulating.

Physical Health

Think of job hunting like training for a marathon -you want to be at your peak. Therefore, if you are already taking good care of yourself it is imperative that you keep up this discipline during job transition. If you have not been taking good care of your body, consider this an excellent reason to start. Schedule a visit with your doctor and involve him/her in launching a regimen to improve your physical well-being. Between the stress of job loss and the ups and downs of job seeking you need to be as healthy as possible. Do not dramatically alter your diet unless your physician recommends it. Eat sensibly, exercise regularly, get plenty of sleep and eliminate or cut back on alcoholic consumption during this transition period. Remember, you are the seller; you are the product.

Mental and Emotional Fitness

Just like physical fitness, mental and emotional fitness are crucial to making a successful transition. The main culprits here are grief, anxiety and depression. Unhelpful thinking about the ups and downs of a prolonged job search can produce anxiety, depression or both. Watch carefully and give your trusted advisors such as spouse, clergy, family physician or honest friend, the permission to point this out to you without fear of offending you. If you have any concerns, or they raise concerns, you should discuss them immediately with your family doctor or a licensed mental health practitioner. Grief is a normal reaction to job transition, and anxiety and depression are widespread in our fast-paced world. Usually, emotions are manageable, but if one ignores more serious symptoms and refuses to deal quickly and appropriately with them, the consequences could be serious.

Include Family and Friends

How to involve your family and friends in your job hunting or career changing activities amounts to balancing your tendency to shield those close to you with your understandable need to feel supported by them. If you are married, I believe your spouse should always know what's going on. If you have children, though, what should you tell them? As a general rule, the older your children are, the more aware and involved they can be. There is no magic age at which to begin discussing a job loss with a child, but the focus should always be to help the child make sense of only those aspects of the job loss he/she actually experiences. For example, explain why dad or mom suddenly starts staying at home during the day, or if finances necessitate canceling music or karate lessons. Younger children should probably not hear about a parent's unseen psychological symptoms -loss of self-esteem or concern about whether a job will ever turn up. Of course, if a parent is depressed, then a professional should help the family through the process of making sense of the depression to both the parent and the children.

Letting your spouse, children and extended family ride the roller coaster with you can be humbling, but also helpful for two reasons: first, you will be surprised by how insightful and supportive the people close to you can be; second, you are setting an example and blazing a trail that most of your friends and loved ones will likely follow at some point in their lives. So share the wealth and pain, welcome their support when they offer it and let them learn and grow with you.

Chapter 12
CONCLUSION

The mission of **Kiss Your Resume Goodbye** is simple: to revolutionize the way experienced professionals approach the process of changing jobs. The game plan for achieving this is equally simple: equip yourself with the tools, skills and abilities to purposefully navigate between jobs and/or careers. Let's be honest, changing jobs is rarely painless and often fraught with difficulty even when you know and apply the *Six Rules that Rule the Job Market*. But you can certainly reduce the length of time between jobs and avoid moving into the wrong job by having a clear knowledge of what you have to sell, a clearly defined market of buyers and a clear game plan linking you, the seller, to your target audience of buyers.

The objective of applying the *Six Rules that Rule the Job Market* is to make your job transition process efficient, effective and predictable, just like any well-conceived business process. Once you have mastered the process, you will be able to repeat it as often as necessary, to the betterment of you, your family and the organizations wise enough to grab hold of a problem-solver like you.

It's time to abandon the old ways and kiss your resume goodbye.

Appendix I
THE FOUNDATION

The foundation of successful job hunting and career changing has three pillars:

1) A clear knowledge of what you have to sell

2) A clearly defined market of buyers

3) A clear game plan linking you, the seller, with buyers

(Page 10)

Appendix II

SIX RULES THAT RULE THE JOB MARKET

1. **THE MARKET RULE**

   The job market is like any other marketplace driven by buyers, sellers and their agents. Understand the marketplace and you will avoid five classic misconceptions. (Page 14)

2. **THE RESUME RULE**

   Resumes are overused and ineffective tools for both buyer and seller. (Page 20)

3. **THE HIRING RULE**

   People get hired to solve the problems of the hiring organization. (Page 31)

4. **THE PVP RULE**

   You are responsible for clearly defining what you bring to the marketplace. This is your Personal Value Proposition (PVP). (Page 38)

5. **THE NETWORK RULE**

   The objective of developing a network is to build a bridge that connects your PVP with your target marketplace. (Page 76)

6. **THE EXPERIENCE RULE**

   Focus your job hunting on the industries and functional areas in which you have your greatest expertise unless:

   1. There is overwhelming, objective evidence that your industry holds little or no future for your problem-solving skills or

   2. There is substantial, objective evidence that you are not well-suited to your current function and are clearly better suited to a specific functional alternative. (Page 96)

Appendix III

YOUR PVP DEVELOPMENT WORKSPACE

JOB

INDUSTRY EXPERTISE
(Focus this as much as possible.)

_____
_____
_____
_____

COMPANY EXPERTISE
(Group similar employers.)

_____
_____
_____
_____

FUNCTIONAL EXPERTISE
(Less is more. Stay focused.)

_____
_____
_____

What kinds of problems do I solve?

_____

_____

_____

_____

_____

_____

_____

_____

What kinds of organizations have these problems?

_____

_____

_____

_____

_____

_____

_____

What would compel an organization to hire me to solve its problems?

_____

_____

_____

_____

_____

_____

_____

_____

PERSONAL VALUE PROPOSITION (PVP)

Your 100 word statement of marketplace value

_____

_____

_____

_____

_____

_____

_____

_____

_____

_____

_____

_____

_____

_____

_____

_____

_____

_____

_____

_____

_____

_____

_____

_____

_____

_____

_____

_____

_____

_____

ABOUT THE AUTHOR

For the past 20 years corporations have called upon on Ron Evans to find, evaluate and hire seasoned business leaders and executives. Ron's in-depth understanding of hiring organizations and individual candidates has allowed him to successfully fill hundreds of senior management positions including CEO and COO as well as heads of finance, marketing, sales and information technology. His clients range from international consulting firms to software and services companies, from Fortune 500 concerns to small, high growth startup companies.

Prior to founding ESearch Group, Ron worked as a consultant with several large professional services firms including Korn/Ferry International, Ernst & Young and Ward Howell International. His early career with IRM included designing and implementing field information systems for Miller Brewing, Mattel Toys, General Motors and Johnson & Johnson. Ron began his professional life with UCAC developing management training seminars to minimize unemployment tax liability for corporations.

A graduate of the University of Connecticut, Ron has been active in numerous business, civic and church organizations in Connecticut and Texas. With the publishing of **Kiss Your Resume Goodbye**, Ron fulfills a life-long desire to provide executive job hunters what they need most: a market oriented strategy that works.

To learn more about ESearch Group visit
www.esearchgroup.com

Burma's Economy in the Twentieth Century

At the beginning of the twentieth century, Burma was among the most prosperous territories in the East. Yet since gaining independence in 1948, its economy has struggled. Burma's developmental failure has often been attributed to gross mismanagement of the economy by the military who took power in March 1962 but in this illuminating book, Ian Brown, one of the leading economic historians of Southeast Asia, provides a fresh examination of the country's economic past, setting that failure in the context of the colonial period. For the first time, a review of Burma's economic experience in the final decades of British rule is integrated with an analysis of its economy since independence, providing a detailed understanding of the complex origins of Burma's economic failure in the second half of the twentieth century. This is a compelling introduction to Burma's political and economic history for students in Southeast Asian history, development studies and political science.

IAN BROWN is a research professor in the economic history of Southeast Asia at the School of Oriental and African Studies, University of London. He has published extensively on the modern economic history of Southeast Asia, initially focusing on Thailand but, since the early 1990s, turning his attention to Burma.

Burma's Economy in the Twentieth Century

IAN BROWN

School of Oriental and African Studies, University of London

CAMBRIDGE
UNIVERSITY PRESS

CAMBRIDGE
UNIVERSITY PRESS

University Printing House, Cambridge CB2 8BS, United Kingdom

Published in the United States of America by Cambridge University Press, New York

Cambridge University Press is part of the University of Cambridge.

It furthers the University's mission by disseminating knowledge in the pursuit of education, learning and research at the highest international levels of excellence.

www.cambridge.org
Information on this title: www.cambridge.org/9781107680050

© Ian Brown 2013

First published 2013

Printed in the United Kingdom by TJ International Ltd. Padstow Cornwall

A catalogue record for this publication is available from the British Library

Library of Congress Cataloguing in Publication data
Brown, Ian.
Burma's economy in the twentieth century / Ian Brown.
  pages cm
Includes index.
ISBN 978-1-107-01588-3 (hardback) – ISBN 978-1-107-68005-0 (paperback)
1. Burma – Economic conditions – 21st century.   2. Burma – Economic policy – 21st century.   3. Burma – Social policy – 21st century.   4. Burma – Politics and government – 21st century.   I. Title.
HC422.B76   2013
330.9591'4 – dc23   2013030073

ISBN 978-1-107-01588-3 Hardback
ISBN 978-1-107-68005-0 Paperback

Andrew and Alasdair
their footsteps, once heard behind,
are now seen far ahead

Contents

Illustrations

Tables

Note on names

In June 1989, the recently created State Law and Order Restoration Council decreed that the rendition into English of the official name of the country in Burmese script be changed from 'Burma' to 'Myanmar'. As the change was being imposed by a military government that many felt was illegitimate, opponents of the regime refused to accept this change and insisted on the continued use of 'Burma'. In this book, both terms are used without intended political implication: 'Burma' for the period prior to June 1989, 'Myanmar' for the subsequent period. As the country was called in English 'Burma' for most of the twentieth century, 'Burma' alone is used in the title. Similarly, 'Rangoon' is used for the main city before SLORC, but 'Yangon' thereafter.

The Burmese have no family names but only personal names, normally of one to four syllables. In different contexts, Burmese may also be given a designation: the most common are, for men, *U* (pronounced 'oo'), a term of respect that might be translated as 'Mr' or 'Uncle'; and the female equivalent, *Daw*, translated as 'Aunt'. Thus the name of the first prime minister of independent Burma, U Nu, is just Nu: the *U* is a term of respect.

With a number of the Burmese authors cited in this book, their name appears in their publications with a designation: thus U Tun Wai and U Thet Tun. With other Burmese authors, there is no designation: thus Maung Shein and Hla Myint. These two different formulations are retained here in the text and in the footnote references, but not in the bibliography, where designations are removed: thus U Tun Wai in the text and footnotes but Tun Wai in the bibliography.

Acknowledgements

This book is built principally on a reading of the substantial body of specialist research that has been published on the modern economic history of Burma. My debt is clearly evident in the book's footnotes and in its long bibliography, but it remains appropriate that I acknowledge it here. Returning to that body of work to write this book has enhanced still further my appreciation of the considerable achievements of numerous individual writers on Burma, from the scholar-officials of the colonial decades – J. S. Furnivall remains a very substantial presence – through to the academic specialists writing today. To refer to any one group is perhaps unjust. But I have come to re-appreciate above all the achievements of a remarkable generation of Burmese economists from the immediate post-independence decade, and their work on Burma's economic history that was published in the 1950s and early 1960s – notably U Tun Wai, Maung Shein, and Aye Hlaing. And to those three names I would add, from the same period, Hugh Tinker, whose study of the first years of Burma's independence, first published in 1957 and running to four editions, remains a remarkable achievement and an invaluable source.

Jonathan Saha and Sean Turnell read a number of my chapters in draft, and David Howlett and Robert Taylor read all in draft. I have hugely appreciated their comments and suggestions, even on those occasions when, after careful reflection, I rejected them. I am particularly grateful to Bob Taylor, a colleague and close friend for more than three decades, for his invaluable advice and encouragement. I also wish to thank Tharaphi Than for bringing a number of sources to my attention, John Okell for translating and commenting on the original Burmese-language captions for a number of the illustrations, and Damien Bove, for drawing the map. Of course, I am responsible for all the errors that remain.

I am pleased to acknowledge the generous financial support of the School of Oriental and African Studies that made it possible for me to consult the papers of Louis Walinsky, held at Cornell University, Ithaca, NY in April 2011, and of the ASEASUK Research Committee, which funded my research visit to Myanmar in early 2012.

Some passages in the conclusion to this book were first published as part of an article, 'Tracing Burma's economic failure to its colonial inheritance', *Business History Review*, 85, 4 (Winter 2011). I am grateful to the editors of *BHR* for permission to reuse that material here in revised form.

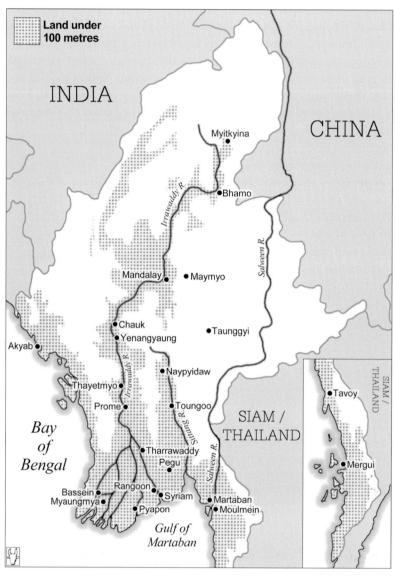

Map of Burma/Myanmar

Introduction

In 1987, Burma applied to the United Nations for classification as a Least Developed Country (LDC), a status that would make it eligible for relief on its international debt as well as eligible for additional financial assistance from UN agencies.[1] The application was successful. But although clearly impoverished, Burma was in fact strikingly rich in natural resources, including teak, jade, rubies, oil and natural gas, lead, zinc, tin, but above all rice, cultivated in the vast, extremely fertile delta of the Irrawaddy River. Moreover, in the first decades of the twentieth century, Burma, if judged by the production and trade statistics, had been among the most prosperous territories in the East. Yet now, towards the close of the century, it was classified among the poorest nations in the world, grouped by the United Nations with, for example, Lesotho, Burkina Faso, and Rwanda. It was a humiliation.

It was not difficult to identify what, or rather who, was responsible for Burma's economic failure. Freed from British colonial rule in January 1948, Burma had had a parliamentary civilian government for the first decade and more of independence, save for a brief military caretaker administration at the end of the 1950s. But then on 2 March 1962, the military had seized power, and for the following quarter of a century had pursued an isolationist-nationalist, doctrinaire-socialist economic strategy – 'infantile disorder', in the later words of a group of Burmese economists – that eventually brought the country to ruin.[2]

---

[1] Tin Maung Maung Than, *State Dominance in Myanmar: the Political Economy of Industrialization*. Singapore: Institute of Southeast Asian Studies, 2007, p. 222. There were three main criteria for LDC status: a per capita income below $200; a manufacturing sector contributing 10 per cent or less to GDP; and a literacy rate of 20 per cent or less. Burma clearly met the first two criteria: *Far Eastern Economic Review*, 22 October 1987, p. 101.

[2] Khin Maung Kyi, Ronald Findlay, R. M. Sundrum, Mya Maung, Myo Nyunt, Zaw Oo, et al., *Economic Development of Burma: a Vision and a Strategy*. Stockholm: Olof Palme International Center, 2000, p. 210.

1

The dominant political figure in this period was General Ne Win, autocratic and politically ruthless but also unpredictable and capricious, and who, it is said, sought the advice of astrologers on important government decisions.

That military mismanagement and ideological error brought ruin to a potentially prosperous economy is the common public understanding of Burma's tragic failure. This was stated with notable clarity in an editorial in *The Times* in August 2012.

Burma is a pre-eminent example of a nation ruined by the force of bad ideas and the brutal expedients needed to implement them. On gaining independence from Britain in 1948, its economic prospects appeared as bright as any nation's in South East Asia. With plentiful oil reserves, Burma grew rapidly in its early years of independence, on the strength of exports of primary products. Yet its per capita GDP is now about one eighth that of its neighbour Thailand. The difference is attributable largely to malign ideology.

Instead of openness to the global economy, Burma practised autarky and import substitution under a tyranny that shut itself off from the world. The fruits of the dictatorship of General Ne Win, who seized power in a military coup in 1962 and held it till 1988, were penury and repression. This peerless crank used astrology to guide his erratic and brutal policies.[3]

This approach to understanding Burma's economic failure – but of course developed with detail and nuance – is also found prominently in the scholarly literature. For example, reviewing the state of the economy in 2010, Sean Turnell declared that: 'The dismal state of Burma's economy is the product of nearly 50 years of wilfully inept economic management under a military regime that took power in a coup in 1962 and soon after, instigated a program known as the "Burmese road to socialism."'[4] Or again, Anne Booth, in the final sentence of a comparative study of economic development in East and South East Asia, focuses firmly on General Ne Win. His failure to pursue growth-promoting policies, she argues, was a reflection of his own personality and predilections: 'other [Burmese] leaders could well have chosen different policies, with different results, not just for

---

[3] *The Times*, 21 August 2012, p. 2.
[4] Sean Turnell, 'Finding dollars and sense: Burma's economy in 2010', in Susan L. Levenstein (ed.), *Finding Dollars, Sense, and Legitimacy in Burma*. Washington, DC: Woodrow Wilson International Center for Scholars, 2010, p. 21.

economic growth but also for the welfare of [Burma's] citizens'.[5] And as a final example, the group of Burmese economists who were to refer to 'our years of infantile disorder with socialism', unsurprisingly saw that period, 1962 to 1988, as 'undoubtedly . . . the most disastrous in the entire modern economic history of Burma'.[6]

This book is built on the argument that Burma's development failure in the second half of the twentieth century is more fully understood, not by focusing on the mismanagement of the economy by the military from 1962 and the misjudgements of the Burmese road to socialism, severely damaging though they undoubtedly were, but by establishing a much longer historical perspective. Specifically, it requires an exploration of the legacies of British colonial rule in Burma, including, crucially, Burmese perceptions of their colonial inheritance.[7] There are two dangers in this approach.[8] The first is political. The more Burma's development failure is explained in terms of a colonial inheritance,

---

[5] Anne E. Booth, *Colonial Legacies: Economic and Social Development in East and Southeast Asia*. Honolulu: University of Hawai'i Press, 2007, p. 204. It might be added that in an earlier paper, Anne Booth had sought to determine whether the argument that the military regime led by General Ne Win was to blame for contemporary Burma's plight was 'an entirely accurate account of the Ne Win years': Anne Booth, 'The Burma development disaster in comparative historical perspective', *South East Asia Research*, 11, 2 (2003), pp. 141–2.

[6] Khin Maung Kyi et al., *Economic Development of Burma*, pp. 10, 210.

[7] Two earlier examples of this approach should be noted. Allen Fenichel and Gregg Huff, 'Colonialism and the economic system of an independent Burma', *Modern Asian Studies*, 9, 3 (1975), have argued that 'it was largely colonial-period factors, in particular the relatively weak economic sector left in the wake of colonial rule, that determined the framework within which independent Burma has had to operate. In order to understand the Burmese approach to post-colonial development, the limitations and imperatives imposed by that framework must be taken into account' (p. 321). Elsewhere they argued: 'The economic development problems Burma has had since gaining independence in 1948 are closely related to the impact of British rule': A. H. Fenichel and W. G. Huff, *The Impact of Colonialism on Burmese Economic Development*. Montreal: McGill University, Centre for Developing-Area Studies, 1971, p. 30. And Tin Maung Maung Than, *State Dominance in Myanmar*, ch. 2 and pp. 305–7, has explored the ways in which 'the historical experience of Myanmar's first encounter, under British rule, with modernity and the international political economy' – the Burmese perception of their colonial inheritance – strongly influenced the approach of the Burma-Myanmar ruling elite to the challenges of economic development (p. 305).

[8] The following is taken with minor adjustments from Ian Brown, 'Tracing Burma's economic failure to its colonial inheritance', *Business History Review*, 85, 4 (Winter 2011), p. 726.

the less the responsibility for that failure might be said to lie with its military rulers – an unpalatable conclusion for many observers and activists.[9] But then so be it. The second danger is the danger of historical determinism. Thus were it to be argued that a particular economic strategy pursued by Burma's military rulers was heavily influenced, even determined, by their perception of Burma's colonial experience, that argument easily slides into the assertion that no other economic strategy was possible. Bound as it was by the colonial inheritance, Burma's military had no alternative. The past imprisons the future. The danger of historical determinism is a serious one in the present context.

To adopt a longer historical perspective, as proposed here, also fits a broader agenda. With the violent suppression of anti-regime protests in 1988, the apparent failure of the military to honour the results of multi-party elections for a constitutional assembly held in May 1990, the near-constant reports that the regime had been committing serious human rights abuses, and the detention of Aung San Suu Kyi, the 1991 Nobel Peace Laureate, held under house arrest for a total of fifteen years between 1989 and 2010, from the early 1990s Burma-Myanmar emerged as a major focus of international concern and protest. But the dramatic nature of the events that suddenly brought Burma-Myanmar to worldwide condemnation, perhaps most notably the continuing detention of Aung San Suu Kyi, has led to the exclusion of the historical context from much of the public debate and understanding. In the eyes of most of the world, the history of Burma begins in 1988. Or as Thant Myint-U has commented, 'analysis of Burma has been singularly ahistorical, with few besides scholars of the country bothering to consider the actual origins of today's predicament'.[10] And essentially the same point has more recently been made by Michael and

---

[9] A conclusion made still more unpalatable by the fact that 'The colonial period is . . . cited [by the military] as the root cause of most of the problems facing the state.' David I. Steinberg, *Burma/Myanmar: What Everyone Needs to Know.* New York: Oxford University Press, 2010, p. 38.

[10] Thant Myint-U, *The River of Lost Footsteps: Histories of Burma.* London: Faber and Faber, 2007, pp. xiii–xiv. Indeed Thant Myint-U suggests a possible connection between the ahistorical nature of much analysis of Burma's contemporary 'predicament' and the fact that the 'myriad good-faith efforts' by the United Nations, individual governments, NGOs, and thousands of activists to bring about reform in Burma have, at best, produced disappointing results and may well, in his view, have unintentionally held back change.

Maitrii Aung-Thwin: 'the *external* perspective of Myanmar today is based on a single event – the "crisis" of 1988'.[11]

The central aim of the present book, therefore, is to explore that historical context, specifically to understand 'the actual origins' of Burma's development failure in the second half of the twentieth century. It begins with the economy of Burma at the opening of the century, prosperous – for some, possibly many – but with serious structural weaknesses, the legacies of which continue to haunt Myanmar a century later.

[11] Michael Aung-Thwin and Maitrii Aung-Thwin, *A History of Myanmar since Ancient Times: Traditions and Transformations*. London: Reaktion Books, 2012, p. 34. The emphasis is in the original.

1 | *The economy at the beginning of the twentieth century*

A jewel in the imperial diadem

In the preface to a 'comprehensive treatise' on Burma published in 1901, a former British official declared the territory to be 'one of the richest provinces of our Indian Empire', adding on a later page, rather more poetically, 'one of the brightest jewels in the Imperial diadem of India'.[1] There was much to sustain that view. To judge by the near-relentlessly rising production and trade statistics, the vast rural expanses under commercial cultivation, and the crowded wharves and hectic commercial streets of the capital, Rangoon, Burma at the beginning of the twentieth century was indeed a prosperous possession, a notably valuable component in Britain's eastern empire.

Colonial Burma's economic position was built mainly on the cultivation and export of rice. In the first decade of the twentieth century, Burma exported on average 2.17 million tons of rice and paddy (rice grain still in the husk) each year, making it by some distance the single most important rice-exporting country in the world. Just over one-third of those exports was sold in Europe, partly for use as food and fodder, in brewing, and in the manufacture of starch, but also for re-export, after re-milling, to Cuba, the West Indies, West Africa, and South America. A further quarter or more was shipped to India and Ceylon, for India, prone to scarcity and famine, had long regarded Burma as a granary from which any large or unexpected demand could at once be supplied. The final substantial markets for Burma's rice in the first decade of the twentieth century were China and Japan and, more importantly, South East Asia. Rice shipped to South East Asia – Singapore was an important initial destination – fed the populations of immigrant Chinese and Indians in the Malay States, Straits Settlements,

---

[1] John Nisbet, *Burma under British Rule–and Before*. Westminster: Archibald Constable, 1901, vol. 1, pp. v, 453.

and the Netherlands East Indies engaged in the production, processing, and shipping of those territories' principal commodity exports,
tin, tobacco, sugar, and rubber.[2]

Burma's rice was cultivated across the vast deltaic plain of the
Irrawaddy and Sittang rivers. With an annual rainfall of between
80 and 130 inches (brought largely on the south-west monsoon
between May and September), the high temperatures of those lati-
tudes, extremely fertile soils (the land being constantly replenished by
fresh silt brought down by the rivers), and the unending flatness of the
landscape, this is a region ideal for the cultivation of rice.[3] Exploiting
that marked comparative advantage to the full, in the first decade of
the twentieth century, around seven million acres, and rapidly rising,
were under rice in lower Burma.[4]

This most important of colonial Burma's industries was built on
the labour of tens of thousands, if not hundreds of thousands, of
Burmese agriculturalists.[5] In reclaiming vast tracts of the delta from
nature, preparing the land for cultivation, and then planting, tending,
and harvesting the crop, they were the foundation of the industry, the
ultimate creators of Burma's wealth from rice. But other communities,
immigrant communities, also had important roles in the industry. First
there were labourers from India, tens, even hundreds of thousands
entering Burma annually in this period. Each year, gangs of Indian
labourers moved through the rice districts to assist in the planting and
then harvesting of the rice crop, their presence clearly important during
these few weeks when the demand for agricultural labour soared. But
Indian labour was still more important in the subsequent processing
and shipping of the crop. The majority of the unskilled and skilled
labourers in the rice mills were Indian. In the big mills at the ports,
notably Rangoon, it was overwhelmingly so. The Indian presence was
still more pronounced on the Rangoon docks: in this period, dock
labour work was quite simply an Indian preserve.

[2] Cheng Siok-Hwa, *The Rice Industry of Burma 1852–1940*. Kuala Lumpur:
   University of Malaya Press, 1968, pp. 201, 203–4, 211, 213–14, 222.
[3] Ibid., pp. 21–2; Charles A. Fisher, *South-East Asia: a Social, Economic and
   Political Geography*, 2nd edn. London: Methuen, 1966, pp. 52, 422–4.
[4] Cheng, *The Rice Industry of Burma*, pp. 241–2.
[5] This broad description of the racial structure of colonial Burma's rice industry
   draws on Cheng, *The Rice Industry of Burma*, and Michael Adas, *The Burma
   Delta: Economic Development and Social Change on an Asian Rice Frontier,
   1852–1941*. Madison, WI: University of Wisconsin Press, 1974.

Figure 1.1 The steam-powered rice mills at Pazundaung Creek, Rangoon, in the early twentieth century
Source: Scenes in Burma: an album of 125 views depicting the principal features of interest in Rangoon, Lower Burma, Upper Burma and the Shan States. Rangoon: Whiteaway, Laidlaw, n.d.

Far fewer in number among the Indians arriving in Burma, but of comparable economic importance, were Chettiar moneylenders from Madras. The Chettiars had been involved in commercial lending for centuries, and in the final decades of the nineteenth century, their operations extended into many parts of South East Asia. They were a major presence in British Burma, where they lent on a very substantial scale to the Burmese rice cultivators, both directly but also indirectly – that is, the Chettiars lent to local Burmese moneylenders who, with those funds, then provided loans to the cultivators. Chettiar capital financed, in long-term loans, the reclaiming of the delta and the preparation of the land for cultivation: and then, in short-term loans it financed each rice crop, from planting through to harvesting. There were also significant Indian interests in rice milling and, more importantly, in the rice trade. Perhaps not surprisingly, the substantial trade in Burma's rice to India came to be transacted almost entirely by Indian merchants. It should be added that there were also Chinese moneylenders, rice mill-owners, and rice merchants, although they were fewer in number than the Indians, and less economically significant.

European commercial interests in colonial Burma's rice industry were concentrated in milling at the ports and in the export trade, where indeed they were dominant at the beginning of the twentieth century. Among the European rice interests, just four firms dominated – Steel Brothers, the Anglo-Burma Rice Company, Ellerman's Arakan Company, and Bulloch Brothers. In addition, Burma's rice was shipped mainly by British lines, including notably the British India Steam Navigation Company, the Asiatic Steam Navigation Company, Bibby Line, and the Ellerman Hall Line.

In the first decade of the twentieth century, rice and paddy accounted for around three-quarters of the total value of Burma's seaborne exports, a remarkable degree of domination by a single commodity.[6] Burma's second most valuable export in this period, accounting for around one-tenth of the total value of seaborne exports but rising, was petroleum products, principally kerosene but also paraffin wax and candles. The main oilfields were in the southern part of Burma's dry zone, some 300 miles north of Rangoon, at Yenangyaung, Chauk, and Yenangyat.[7] Oil had been drawn from the ground in this part of Burma possibly for centuries but the modern industry, using capital-intensive technology in both extraction and refining, had been established only from the late 1880s. The modern industry in colonial Burma was a preserve of foreign interests – the Indo-Burma Petroleum Company (a joint initiative between Steel Brothers and Abdul Kadar Jamal, an immigrant from India who, arriving in rags, had in time built an important Rangoon merchant firm), the British Burmah Petroleum Company, the Asiatic Petroleum Company (a merger of the Royal Dutch and Shell and the Paris Rothschild oil marketing agencies in the East), and, dwarfing all others, the Burmah Oil Company. Formed in 1886, in the first decade of the twentieth century Burmah Oil was producing,

---

[6] Calculated from Maung Shein, *Burma's Transport and Foreign Trade (1885–1914) in Relation to the Economic Development of the Country*. Department of Economics, University of Rangoon, 1964, pp. 218–19.

[7] The following draws on Maung Shein, *Burma's Transport and Foreign Trade*, pp. 165–76; 'Oilfields of Burma', in Arnold Wright, H. A. Cartwright and O. Breakspear (eds), *Twentieth Century Impressions of Burma: its History, People, Commerce, Industries, and Resources*. London: Lloyd's Greater Britain Publishing Company, 1910, pp. 207–12; and T. A. B. Corley, *A History of the Burmah Oil Company 1886–1924*. London: Heinemann, 1983.

on average, almost 90 per cent of Burma's total output.[8] It had refineries at Dunneedaw and, more importantly, at Syriam, both close to Rangoon, the crude oil from the company's wells to the north being pumped to these installations through a 275-mile pipeline. In 1904 Burmah Oil employed more than 7,500.[9] Of that total, over 80 per cent were Indians and just 14 per cent were Burmese. In the refineries, the Indian domination was greater still. Less than 3 per cent of the staff was European or Eurasian, presumably Burmah Oil's senior managers, engineers, and technicians.[10] And finally it should be noted that over the first decade of the twentieth century, the volume of Burma's exports of kerosene, its most important petroleum product by far, rose ten-fold.[11] Burma's kerosene exports were, bar a tiny proportion, exclusively for India.

The third most valuable of Burma's seaborne exports in the first decade of the twentieth century, accounting for around one-twentieth of total export value but falling, was teak.[12] Although it was also cut by Burmese lessees and by the Burma Forest Department, often employing small-scale Burmese contractors, in this period the extraction, milling, and export of Burma teak was largely and increasingly dominated by just five British concerns – Steel Brothers, Macgregor and Company, Foucar and Company, T. D. Findlay and Son, and, most importantly, the Bombay Burmah Trading Corporation.[13] The companies held important leases at this time in the Chindwin, Shwebo, and Pyinmana forests, towards and in the north, but in fact worked concessions in many different parts of Burma. After being felled, the teak was

---

[8] Maung Shein, *Burma's Transport and Foreign Trade*, p. 168.

[9] Corley, *A History of the Burmah Oil Company 1886–1924*, pp. 149–50.

[10] As a final comment here on Burmah Oil, in 1909 it established the Anglo-Persian Oil Company, later British Petroleum, later still BP. In other words, Burmah Oil was the parent company of that eventual giant, and indeed, together with the British government, long held the bulk of Anglo-Persian's ordinary shares.

[11] Calculated from Maung Shein, *Burma's Transport and Foreign Trade*, p. 269.

[12] Calculated from Maung Shein, *Burma's Transport and Foreign Trade*, pp. 218–19.

[13] The following draws on Raymond L. Bryant, *The Political Ecology of Forestry in Burma 1824–1994*. London: Hurst, 1997; F. T. Morehead, *The Forests of Burma*. London: Longmans, Green, 1944; E. J. Foucar, 'Teak', in Wright et al., *Twentieth Century Impressions of Burma*, pp. 184–93; Maung Shein, *Burma's Transport and Foreign Trade*, pp. 160–5; and A. C. Pointon, *The Bombay Burmah Trading Corporation Limited 1863–1963*. Southampton: Millbrook Press, 1964.

Figure 1.2 Oilfield worker, Burmah Oil, 1930
Source: H. S. Bowlby photographs, Centre of South Asian Studies, University of Cambridge

dragged through the forest by elephants and buffaloes to a near creek, from where it was floated out, often with considerable difficulty, to the main rivers, the Irrawaddy, the Sittang, and the Salween. At major measuring stations on the rivers, for example, at Mandalay, Pakokku, Prome, and Toungoo, the trees were then lashed together into vast rafts, and navigated, through rapids and past sandbanks, small craft, and river ferries, down to Rangoon and Moulmein. As the more southern Burma forests had been worked through in the final decades of the nineteenth century and the companies had moved further and further north, the journey for the teak rafts had become longer, potentially more hazardous, and certainly more expensive. At Rangoon and Moulmein the teak was delivered into timber-yards, where it was stacked, commonly by elephants, or directly into the steam-powered sawmills. There it was cut into squares, planks, decks, and scantlings for shipment. In the first decade of the twentieth century, around two-thirds, by volume, of Burma's teak exports was shipped to India.[14] The India trade, in poorer-quality teak, was mainly for building construction, the railways, and for making tea-boxes and pipe staves. A further fifth or more of teak exports went to Britain. This was the best-quality timber, used principally in shipbuilding and in the construction of railway carriages. The labour force engaged in the extraction, processing, and shipping of Burma's teak was substantial. In the first decade of the twentieth century, the Bombay Burmah alone was said to employ about 10,000 – and nearly 2,000 elephants.[15] Burmese worked in the forests and on the rivers, as girdlers, fellers, and raft-men. But the labour in the sawmills in this period, as in the oil refineries and the rice mills, was largely Indian.

Foreign commercial interests, most often British interests, were as important in other parts of colonial Burma's modern economy as they were in rice, oil, and teak. For example, the Irrawaddy Flotilla Company, reincorporated in 1876 and with its head office in Glasgow, had a near monopoly of passenger services on Burma's rivers, channels, and creeks, and also carried substantial goods traffic.[16] Its double-decked paddlers, said to be the largest shallow-draught side-paddle steamers in the world, worked a rapid service between Rangoon and

---

[14] Calculated from Maung Shein, *Burma's Transport and Foreign Trade*, p. 267.
[15] Foucar, 'Teak', p. 189.
[16] This paragraph draws on Alister McCrae and Alan Prentice, *Irrawaddy Flotilla*. Paisley: James Paton, 1978.

Mandalay. But the company also served the upper Irrawaddy to Bhamo and Myitkyina, the Chindwin, the rivers that converged on Moulmein, and towns across the delta. In the early twentieth century, the Irrawaddy Flotilla Company fleet comprised close to 200 powered vessels, from the large paddlers down to modest launches, and perhaps 300 rafts (known as 'flats') and cargo barges. The deck and engine crews were from Chittagong, 'natural watermen of the rivers and creeks of Bengal'. In this same period, the company also owned four construction and repair yards, at Rangoon, Moulmein, and Mandalay, to build and maintain its fleet.

As a further example, foreign banks, specifically the British exchange banks, dominated the financing of colonial Burma's foreign trade. In the first decade of the twentieth century, there were branches in Rangoon of, for example, the Chartered Bank of India, Australia, and China (established in Burma in 1862), the Hongkong and Shanghai (1892), and the National Bank of India (a British bank with its head office in London, the Rangoon branch being opened in 1885).[17] By far the major part of the business of these branches in Burma was in financing the province's foreign trade through the provision of short-term bills of exchange. And of course the merchant houses and trading concerns for whom they provided that finance, not least the four major rice firms noted earlier, Steel Brothers, Anglo-Burma Rice, Ellermans, Bulloch Brothers, but in fact many others were also foreign. The strong foreign presence in the modern economy of colonial Burma, in crucial sectors the overwhelming foreign presence, raises a number of highly important issues which will be taken up later in this chapter. Meanwhile this opening survey of Burma's economy at the beginning of the twentieth century now turns briefly from the province's exports to its imports.

In the first decade of the century, textiles, notably cotton piece-goods, accounted for more than 40 per cent of the total value of Burma's seaborne imports.[18] The high level of piece-goods imports

---

[17] M. F. Gauntlett, 'Finance', in Wright et al., *Twentieth Century Impressions of Burma*, pp. 159–63; U Tun Wai, *Burma's Currency and Credit*. Calcutta: Orient Longmans, revd edn, 1962, pp. 23–39; Sean Turnell, *Fiery Dragons: Banks, Moneylenders and Microfinance in Burma*. Copenhagen: NIAS Press, 2009, pp. 104–17.

[18] Calculated from Maung Shein, *Burma's Transport and Foreign Trade*, pp. 219–22.

reflected the specialization of Burma's rural population in the cultivation of rice for export, that is the abandoning of household spinning and weaving, and indeed many other domestic occupations, to focus on the cultivation of rice. But it may also have indicated increasing prosperity, as Burma's cultivators spent rising incomes on a range of foreign textiles. Foodstuffs, notably sugar, spices, dried fish, and wheat-flour, accounted for a further 15 per cent and more of the total value of Burma's imports by sea. Again this reflected the specialization in the cultivation of rice and perhaps indicated an increasing prosperity. Substantial imports of spirits, beers, and tobacco too might have indicated rising consumption, at least for some. In this period there were also very substantial imports of machinery, including drilling equipment and refining plant for the oil industry, electricity generators, steam engines, husking and polishing plant for the rice mills, and sawing machinery for the timber mills. Together with wrought iron and steel, machinery accounted for towards one-fifth of the total value of Burma's seaborne imports in the early twentieth century, evidence of major investment being made in the construction of the modern export economy. There are two final points to be noted on Burma's imports in this period. The first is that the total value of seaborne imports was increasing very rapidly, evidence of the economy's vigorous expansion. It effectively doubled between 1890–2 and 1910–12. But second, despite that remarkable rate of increase, the total value of imports remained far below the total value of exports, just half in 1910–12. In other words, in the early twentieth century, Burma was running a huge trade surplus. This is a further important issue, to which, again, the chapter will return.

Burmese, Indians, and Europeans

The ethnic divisions of occupation and economic function briefly described above – the rice cultivators were Burmese, moneylenders were Indian, senior commercial managers were Europeans – were far from absolute. For example, there were in fact far more Burmese moneylenders than Indian, although since Burmese lenders generally worked on a much smaller scale, it is probable that the Chettiars, far fewer in number, accounted for the major part of the lending to

Burma's cultivators at the beginning of the twentieth century.[19] In the same way, more than half the rice mills in Burma in this period were in fact owned by Burmese.[20] But since the Burmese mills were generally small up-country concerns, it was the European-owned mills, comparatively few in number, which still accounted for the largest share of milling capacity. Therefore these references to the Burmese presence in moneylending and milling do not detract from – indeed they reinforce – the central observation that at the beginning of the twentieth century, foreign interests dominated colonial Burma's modern economy. That 'stranglehold', to use an emotive word appropriate for this context, was to provide a potent grievance for Burma's nationalists in the final decades of British rule, and, crucially, its legacy continued to be powerfully felt long after independence was regained. In other words it was (and remains) a central issue in Burma's modern economic experience. It is therefore important to explore in some detail the origins of the ethnic divisions of occupation in colonial Burma – the foreign domination of the modern economy – or, perhaps of greater interest, the different ways in which those origins might be understood, and in particular the way in which they were understood by Burmese themselves. In doing so it should be noted that domination of the modern economy by foreign interests, both Western and Asian, was of course not unique to British Burma. It was a highly prominent feature across colonial South East Asia – in the Malay States and Straits Settlements, the Netherlands East Indies, French Indo-China, the Philippines, and in Siam – although inevitably the precise configuration and circumstances differed in each territory. In a later chapter it will be valuable to compare the ways in which foreign economic dominance was understood and, in particular, resolved in Burma with the understandings and resolutions elsewhere in modern South East Asia.

The ethnic divisions of occupation and economic function in colonial Burma – and elsewhere – can be explained in terms of the proposition that each ethnic community, through, for example, historical experience, social structure, or cultural attitudes, came to possess considerable economic or commercial advantages in certain occupations and roles. This argument is most clearly demonstrated in one explanation

---

[19] Adas, *The Burma Delta*, p. 112.
[20] Cheng, *The Rice Industry of Burma*, pp. 82–6.

for the Chettiar domination of lending to Burma's rice cultivators. As noted earlier, when the Chettiars began to move into the rice districts in strength from the 1880s, they had behind them many centuries of experience in commercial lending. Those centuries had not only allowed the community to build and refine its formidable commercial skills, but had also profoundly shaped its social organization and social values, in ways that enhanced still further the community's commercial drive. This last point was explained in detail by Michael Adas in his study of the Burma delta, published in 1974, and is worth quoting at length.

The homelife and upbringing of a Chettiar child inculcated values of thrift and self-reliance and prepared him for a position in a Chettiar firm when he came of age. Chettiar parents were expected to set aside a certain amount of money at the birth of each son. The money with accumulated interest was later used to finance the boy's education. Although Chettiar families normally resided in joint households, each married member cooked and ate his meals separately. Fixed allotments of food and other provisions were divided among married members of the family annually, and they were expected to use their supplies judiciously so that they would not be caught short. The wives of even the most wealthy Chettiars dressed simply, performed menial household tasks, and wove baskets or spun thread to help pay household expenses. When a Chettiar visited his relatives, he received only his first meal free. If he stayed longer, he would be 'quietly debited' the cost of the rest of his stay. Until the age of ten or twelve Chettiar boys studied in Tamil schools, where they learned bookkeeping techniques and the caste's special counting system. At the age of twelve they went to work as apprentices for Chettiar firms.[21]

The Chettiars had further substantial advantages. Because they worked as members of established firms, never as individuals, their lending operations were almost invariably firmly structured, well informed, and precisely resourced. Moreover, the Chettiars maintained strong communal networks in Burma, through which each firm could be supported, advised, and, as necessary, sanctioned. In the main Chettiar temple on Mogul Street in Rangoon, according to Michael Adas, 'Chettiars held periodic meetings, determined current interest rates, settled disputes, formed common opinions regarding important political issues . . . and exchanged gossip.' In brief, the Chettiars

---

[21] Adas, *The Burma Delta*, p. 115. This discussion of the Chettiars draws on Adas, pp. 113–18.

possessed both superior organization and communal solidarity. And finally, through centuries of dealing with European traders in the East, the Chettiars were able to form close relations with the Western banks established in Burma from the final decades of the nineteenth century, and thus secure working capital from them.

Burmese moneylenders had none of these advantages. Most worked as individuals; few if any had ready access to the branches of the Western banks in Rangoon; and most importantly, the Burmese had not had centuries of extensive experience in commercial lending – with the influence that experience might have had in refining lending practices and fostering a single-minded commercial attitude – or centuries of close dealing with European merchants in the East. In view of those competitive disadvantages against the Chettiar, it may seem surprising that Burmese moneylenders still far outnumbered the Indians in this period. But the Chettiars lent only to reliable borrowers with good security, including some Burmese moneylenders, and left the more risky business to those Burmese.

There are many other examples that might demonstrate the ways in which in colonial Burma particular ethnic groups came naturally – through the influence of historical experience, social structure, economic circumstances, or cultural attitudes – to dominate particular occupations. Thus the Indian domination of the labour force in the big rice mills at the ports, notably Rangoon, can be explained principally by the fact that Indian labour, recruited from some of the most desperately impoverished districts in India, was willing to work long hours for little pay.[22] In contrast Burmese labourers would not accept the appalling working conditions being imposed in the rice mills at the ports, and certainly not for the low wages being offered. In fact, with strong demand for labour in the rice districts, Burmese labourers were under little pressure to accept. Other factors might further explain the Indian domination. The mill owners apparently found the Indian labourers to be docile and submissive, perhaps a further reflection of their economic desperation. The big mills at the ports housed their labourers in barracks and lodging houses, sleeping twenty-five to thirty to a room. That accommodation met the circumstances of the Indian labourers, single males whose families had remained in India during the few months or years in which they worked in Burma, but not the

[22] Cheng, *The Rice Industry of Burma*, pp. 131–4.

Burmese who, if moving into Rangoon, were apparently reluctant to be separated from their families. The owners of the big mills secured their workforce through an Indian *maistry* (labour contractor) who, naturally, engaged labourers from his own community, indeed often from his own village in India. And finally, once established, Indian domination of the labour force would tend to be self-perpetuating. The mill owners would continue to recruit Indians, since a relatively homogeneous workforce was perhaps less troublesome to manage: and over time, Burmese labour would become ever more reluctant to enter this Indian preserve.

Just two further brief examples of a naturally created ethnic domination will suffice. Colonial Burma's modern oil industry was a preserve of foreign interests, in effect a preserve of the Burmah Oil Company, because those interests alone possessed the extraction and refining technology and experience, as well as the access to substantial capital, organizational structure, and market connections that were essential in that industry. No Burmese concern could possibly compete. And the cultivation of rice, by far the most important of colonial Burma's export industries, was naturally dominated by Burmese, because they had had centuries of experience in cultivating the crop in Burma's distinctive climate, soils, and topography. As an additional considerable advantage, the Burmese cultivator alone in Burma had access to family labour. In summary, each of the ethnic structures noted above – the Chettiar domination of lending to Burma's rice cultivators, Indian control of the labour force in the big rice mills at the ports, Western control of the modern oil industry, the Burmese domination of the cultivation of rice – reflected the advantage possessed by that community in that occupation as a result of historical experience, social structure, economic circumstances, or cultural attitudes. These ethnic-occupational allocations were not deliberate, planned, or manufactured. In the words of the British official-scholar, J. S. Furnivall, 'it just happened'.[23]

But there were alternative explanations for the ethnic divisions of occupation and economic function in colonial Burma. One such explanation was that in important areas, the colonial administration had in fact consciously acted to promote British commercial interests and

---

[23] J. S. Furnivall, *Colonial Policy and Practice: a Comparative Study of Burma and Netherlands India*. New York University Press, 1956, p. 119.

exclude Burmese concerns. A prime example, it was alleged, was in the distribution of teak forest leases. In detail, in 1907 the Forest Department allocated the working of the most important teak forests in Burma to the European timber firms under a system of long-term, renewable leases, an arrangement that, according to a later observer, 'effectively eliminated the possibility that Burmese firms would ever be able to compete on equal terms with their European counterparts'.[24] Thus in 1925, the European firms held leases covering an area of 56,926 square miles, Burmese concerns just 1,614 square miles. Moreover, most of the leases allocated to Burmese firms were short-term and for the less valuable forests. And as a further demonstration of the colonial administration's promotion of British commercial interests against possible Burmese competition, the Irrawaddy Flotilla Company, which had a near monopoly of passenger services on colonial Burma's rivers, channels, and creeks, received substantial government subsidies.[25]

A final perspective on the ethnic divisions of occupation and economic function in colonial Burma also focused on the colonial administration. But here the colonial government was criticized on quite different grounds. If the Burmese were unable to compete effectively against the Chettiar moneylender, the Indian rice-mill labourer, the British oil company, for the reasons outlined earlier, then unless the colonial administration intervened, the Burmese would inevitably be excluded from the modern economy. However the colonial administration, committed to belief in the efficiency and effectiveness of the market, would not intervene. It saw its role, apparently, as being to create and then maintain 'a fair field and no favour'.[26] But then a contest between the advantaged and the disadvantaged was not a fair contest.

In this line of argument, there were three principal forms of action that the British colonial government might have taken to secure a greater Burmese engagement in the modern economy. The first was to

---

[24] Bryant, *The Political Ecology of Forestry in Burma*, p. 149.

[25] Aung Tun Thet, *Burmese Entrepreneurship: Creative Response in the Colonial Economy*. Stuttgart: Steiner Verlag Wiesbaden GmbH, 1989, pp. 65, 78–9; Maung Shein, *Burma's Transport and Foreign Trade*, pp. 98–9.

[26] G. E. Harvey, *British Rule in Burma 1824–1942*. London: Faber and Faber, 1946, p. 52. The quotation in full: '"A fair field and no favour", as the elephant said when he danced among the chickens.'

restrict Indian immigration, not only to create greater opportunities for Burmese directly but also, possibly, to push up wages to levels that would attract rural Burmese labourers into urban jobs. The second was to adapt jobs in the modern sector to match the skills, experience, and attributes of the Burmese. Crucial here would be the creation of access to the modern world for those Burmese who, of course, spoke Burmese but not English or Hindi.[27] And the third was to provide the vocational, technical, and professional education, in English, that would enable the Burmese to compete effectively against at least the Indians in the modern colonial economy.

But the colonial government did not take these actions, perhaps because of its commitment to a laissez-faire economic administration but also, in each case, for practical reasons. Because Burma was simply a province of British India between 1886 and 1937 – a point to be considered below – presumably it was not possible in that period to restrict immigration into Burma from India 'proper'. In filling administrative jobs, including the lowest grades, it was inevitably cheaper and less troublesome to recruit Indians, familiar with the practices of British administration and commerce, than to adapt those positions to the skills and experience of the Burmese, or indeed to train the Burmese in those modern practices. And to provide the Burmese with vocational, technical, and professional education in English, in effect from scratch, would be hugely expensive. But crucially, by failing to take such action, the argument runs, the British colonial administration effectively excluded the Burmese from modern economic life.

The domination of colonial Burma's modern economy by foreign interests had a further important consequence. It created a substantial and continuous drain of income from Burma, in the remittance of the foreigners' earnings in the province to their home countries. The drain included the meagre savings of hundreds of thousands

---

[27] With the overwhelming presence of Indians, access to much of colonial Burma's modern sector, either for employment or as a customer, was restricted to those who spoke English or Hindi. A notable example was the telephone system, predictably an Indian preserve. According to Furnivall, into the 1930s it was not possible to use the telephone in Burma without some command of Hindi, much less secure employment in the telephone department. Furnivall, *Colonial Policy and Practice*, p. 121.

of Indian labourers from their pitiful wages, the profits made by Chettiar firms, Indian merchants, and Chinese shopkeepers, and dividend payments and profit transfers by Burmah Oil, Steel Brothers, and the Irrawaddy Flotilla Company, for example. But it also included the substantial savings of British commercial managers and British and Indian civil servants, their pension contributions, and their home-leave allowances. There are no figures for these remittances and transfers, no balance of payments data, certainly not for this period. But given the number of individuals and commercial concerns involved – the domination of British Burma's modern economy by foreign interests – and the size of the colonial establishment, the drain was clearly very substantial, sufficient to account for the major part of Burma's huge trade surplus.[28]

These remittances and payments can be understood in different ways. It might be argued that the foreign presence – the Indian capital and labour, the British capital, technology, and market networks – contributed hugely to the creation of wealth in colonial Burma, and that the remittances and transfer payments were no more than the foreigners' due return, not least because, it would be said, a substantial part of the newly created wealth remained in Burma with the Burmese. An alternative view would argue that the remittances and transfers in fact far exceeded a due return for the foreigners, and the substantial dividends paid by British firms in Burma, even in bad times, was important evidence in support of that opinion.[29] And a third perspective would simply focus on the huge drain of wealth from colonial Burma, paying little attention to the contribution of foreign capital and labour to its creation. Needless to say, nationalist opinion strongly favoured these last perspectives.

---

[28] The meagre savings of labourers from their pitiful wages would of course produce a considerable total, given the numbers involved. It has been estimated that in the late 1930s, roughly Rs 30 million were remitted by Indian labourers in Burma to India each year by money order alone. To that estimate should be added the funds sent in other ways, not least Indians returning to India and carrying their remaining savings with them. J. Russell Andrus, *Burmese Economic Life*. Stanford University Press, 1948, p. 182.

[29] According to one source, in some of the interwar years, Steel Brothers returned dividends of 40 per cent, indeed 50 per cent in 1929, although the dividend could also be much lower. Cheng, *The Rice Industry of Burma*, p. 233.

Burma and India

At the beginning of the twentieth century, there were some 550,000 Indians in Burma, out of a total population at the 1901 census of 10.5 million.[30] The Indian population was extremely fluid, for it consisted mainly of single male labourers who worked in Burma for just a few months or for two or three years before returning to India.[31] It was also geographically concentrated, notably in Rangoon. In 1901 the Indian population of the capital was roughly 120,000.[32] In other words, one in five of the Indians in Burma lived and worked in that city. More striking still, the 120,000 accounted for just over half of Rangoon's total population, most living in the central districts, close to the rice and teak mills, warehouses, and wharves in which so many Indians worked. In brief, Rangoon, the commercial and financial as well as the political and administrative capital of British-ruled Burma, was an Indian city. However, the demographic and, as established above, economic prominence of the Indians was part of a much broader relationship between British India and Burma under British rule. And that broader relationship too had important political and administrative dimensions.

The British seizure of Burma in the nineteenth century occurred in three stages, the outcome of three wars between Britain and the Burmese kingdom.[33] The first took place in 1824–6, at the end of which Burma was forced to cede to Britain the border territories of Arakan, on the west, and Tenasserim to the south-east. Following the second war in 1852–3, Britain annexed the province of Pegu, the territory of lower

---

[30] Nalini Ranjan Chakravarti, *The Indian Minority in Burma: the Rise and Decline of an Immigrant Community*. London: Oxford University Press, 1971, p. 15.

[31] The statistics are far from precise, but Cheng's figures suggest that at the beginning of the twentieth century, perhaps around 175,000 Indians were arriving in Burma each year, while 135,000 were returning to India. Cheng, *The Rice Industry of Burma*, p. 122. Hidden within these figures was a substantial proportion of repeat migrations, although for many, in time repeated migration led to established settlement in Burma.

[32] Calculated from Donald M. Seekins, *State and Society in Modern Rangoon*. London: Routledge, 2011, pp. 6, 39.

[33] The following provides the briefest summary of these complex events. For Burma in the nineteenth century see, for example, Thant Myint-U, *The Making of Modern Burma*. Cambridge University Press, 2001; and John F. Cady, *A History of Modern Burma*. Ithaca, NY: Cornell University Press, 1958.

Burma. In 1862, the British administration of Arakan, Tenasserim, and Pegu was amalgamated to form British Burma. The final war took place in late 1885, at the end of which, on 1 January 1886, Britain annexed the remaining territories of the kingdom. On 26 February 1886, Burma, consolidated under British rule, became a province of British India.

India was a critical factor in the British forward movement in Burma, in that it was British determination to protect India's north-east border, first against an aggressive Burma and then against the prospect of intervention in Burma by France, which provoked the first and, to a degree, the third war. But more important in the present context was the profound influence of British India on the administration of Burma once it came under British rule. From the first, British-ruled Burma was administered under the authority of Calcutta – initially the seat of the East India Company and then, from 1858, that of the government of India – with Burma's commissioners being drawn from the Indian service. The authority of the Indian government was fully confirmed with the establishment of Burma as a province of British India in February 1886. Burma was now part of India. The establishment of Burma as an Indian province immediately following the final war had huge consequences, and for that reason, it is important to establish the circumstances that resulted in that decision to incorporate Burma into India.

As a broad proposition, a colonial administration will seek to govern not directly but through the local political structures. It is perhaps less disruptive of the social order, and therefore less troublesome and less costly. Thus the early administration of British-ruled Tenasserim was 'based in large measure on the Burmese pattern', although in contrast British administration in Arakan 'paid little deference to traditional Burmese institutions'.[34] But when the British seized the final part of the Burmese kingdom in the mid-1880s, the option to rule indirectly did not exist, because Burma's political-administrative structures, for long increasingly fragile, now imploded on the final British occupation. The king, Thibaw, had been exiled to India as the British took his capital, Mandalay, in 1885, and although there remained a number of individuals of royal descent, one of whom the British might place on the throne, the pool of appropriate candidates had been greatly

---

[34] Cady, *A History of Modern Burma*, pp. 81, 84.

diminished by bouts of bloodletting at the Burmese court in earlier years.[35] But perhaps more seriously, Burma's political-administrative institutions and individuals, the *Hluttaw* (Council of State) and the instruments of district administration, were broken. They had been destroyed not simply by the immediate British intervention but also internally, by the decades-long strains created by the presence, often aggressive, of the British in Arakan, Tenasserim, and Pegu and, perhaps more importantly, by the inevitable process of dynastic decline. Thus it was evident to the British newly established in Mandalay that the territory – Burma as a whole – could not be governed through Burmese institutions. Those institutions, in effect, no longer existed. There was no choice. Burma would be directly ruled.

This still left, at least in theory, decisions to be made as to the precise form of direct administration to be erected. In broad terms, there were two options. The first was simply to extend the British India administration – its administrative structures, bureaucratic practices, and indeed its personnel – to Burma. The second was to construct a British administration in Burma quite separate from British India, to take structures, practices, and personnel from across the imperial territories to fashion in Burma an administration perhaps more responsive to local circumstances. But in practice, there was no choice. To extend the British India administration to Burma, rather than create anew, was obviously a less challenging prospect and far less expensive. More importantly, the decision to extend had, in effect, already been taken decades earlier. As noted above, from the 1820s, Arakan, Tenasserim, and then Pegu, under the authority of Calcutta, had broadly taken the administrative structures, bureaucratic practices, and certainly the personnel of British-ruled India. The establishment of Burma as a province of British India in February 1886 thus merely reinforced an existing integration.

As stated earlier, the establishment of Burma as a province of British India had huge consequences. Four stand out. First, over the following decades, tens of thousands of Indians were recruited in India to fill positions in the Burma administration and in the province's public services, positions from the lowest to among the most senior. To recruit those Indians, rather than employ Burmese, was clearly much

---

[35] This passage to the end of the paragraph draws on Thant Myint-U, *The Making of Modern Burma*, pp. 193–8.

easier and possibly cheaper in some circumstances. The Indians came with a sufficient command of English for their work and grade, or their British senior officials, often with long service in India 'proper', had sufficient grasp of the relevant Indian language to communicate and command. In addition, Indians recruited in India had long experience of the procedures, practices, standards, and jargon of British administration. Of course, some adjustments would be required of them to work in the Burma administration, but the essentials were familiar. In sharp contrast, far fewer Burmese had sufficient command of English and, inevitably, there was no long Burmese experience of British administration and its procedures. Far better to recruit police constables for Burma from the ranks of the police in India, to take an obvious example, than to educate, instruct, and train Burmese. Thus Indians ran vast swathes of colonial Burma's administration and public services. For example, the warders in British Burma's prisons were Indians, recruited mainly from the United Provinces: in the mid-1920s, several attempts were made to appoint Burmans to these positions, but with little success.[36] In addition, the railways, the Public Works Department in part, the medical establishment (other than nurses), and the post and telegraph services were also Indian preserves.[37] And in all government departments, the great majority of the subordinate staff – the messengers, watchmen, and attendants – were again Indians. There was, of course, a substantial number of Burmese officials, in the lower but also more senior grades. Indeed there were some departments – the Forest Department, the Land Records Department – in which Burmese apparently dominated. But to the extent that positions in the Burma administration and the province's public services were filled by Indians recruited in India, the opportunities for Burmese to secure the education, training, and experience to run a modern society were clearly diminished.

A second important consequence of the establishment of Burma as a province of British India was that in important respects, British Indian administration was extended to Burma with little or insufficient

---

[36] Ian Brown, 'South East Asia: reform and the colonial prison', in Frank Dikötter and Ian Brown (eds), *Cultures of Confinement: a History of the Prison in Africa, Asia and Latin America*. London: Hurst, 2007, p. 242.

[37] F. S. V. Donnison, *Public Administration in Burma: a Study of Development during the British Connexion*. London: Royal Institute of International Affairs, 1953, p. 66.

reference to Burmese circumstances. Fully part of British India in a legal-constitutional sense from early 1886, Burma was inevitably seen as such in most other aspects too. A striking example of that perspective was evident in a major reform of the structure of local administration that took place just after the third and final war. The pivotal official in the pre-colonial administrative structure was the *myothugyi*, the head of the district. The *myothugyi*, a local man whose family had held the position for generations, was responsible for keeping peace and order in his district, and for ensuring that the district met the requirements and requisitions of the central government. He was the pivotal link between the government and the people.[38] The major reform of the structure of local administration that followed the final war was driven principally by Sir Charles Crosthwaite, the Chief Commissioner from March 1887. Sir Charles had had nearly thirty years of executive and judicial experience in the North-West Provinces and Central Provinces. On his appointment to Burma he came to believe, incorrectly, that the *myothugyi*, taking advantage of Burma's recent disturbed state, had usurped the position of village leaders, and his reform sought to restore the latter to their rightful authority, as he saw it. The reformed local administration that was brought in from the late 1880s designated the village as the pivotal point in the structure, and the village headman, with powers as revenue collector, police officer, and magistrate, as the pivotal official. The British Indian mindset that drove the reform was well caught in an account written by a British official of a later generation, F. S. V. Donnison. The reform, Donnison argued

proceeded on the assumption that the village, or group of hamlets within sight or hail of each other, was in Burma, *as in India*, the basic social and political unit... It admitted the existence of *myothugyis*, *taikthugyis*, and other such officers but they were considered, *on the basis of Indian experience*, to have over-shadowed and usurped the rightful power of the village headman.[39]

A crucial point to add is that Donnison, and indeed other later observers, saw this British Indian imposition as highly damaging, as a

---

[38] A standard text on Burma's pre-colonial administration is Mya Sein, *The Administration of Burma*. Kuala Lumpur: Oxford University Press, 1973. Chapters IV and V consider the appointment, succession, functions, and remunerations of the *myothugyi*.

[39] Donnison, *Public Administration in Burma*, p. 31. Emphasis added.

prime cause of the social disorder that was such a prominent feature of rural Burma under British rule in the following decades. For the reform driven through in the late 1880s had destroyed 'the largest indigenous social and political unit' – the *myothugyi*: while the pivotal institution and official to replace it, the 'restored' village and village headman, was in fact 'no organic growth but a mechanical contrivance . . . an artificial administrative unit.'[40]

In 1900, according to one source, 'nearly a third of the service [senior officials] in Burma had spent the formative years of their career in India.'[41] Undoubtedly that over-powerful India connection, cemented when Burma became a province of British India after the final war, explains in large part, as noted above, the unreflective and unaware manner in which British Indian administration was extended to Burma. In the minds of British officials, in general, Burma was simply a part of India. But there was a further factor that might explain that unreflective extension of British Indian administration. Until 1897 and the estab-lishment of a legislative council in Rangoon, Burma's laws were made in India. In practice, when legislation was required, a bill was drafted by the local administration and submitted to the Legislative Council of India.[42] When passed by the Council and then having received the consent of the Governor-General-in-Council, it was published in the *Burma Gazette* and became law in the province. But even after 1897, British India influence remained powerful, not least because Burma's newly created Legislative Council initially had just nine members, four officials and five nominated non-officials, and its powers were strictly limited. Most importantly, legislation with a financial dimension was reserved to the central government, that is to Calcutta and then, from 1911, to Delhi.[43]

The third consequence to be noted is that a substantial part of the revenue raised in Burma was remitted to the central government, the government of India, which in turn took responsibility for important

[40] Ibid., p. 32; Furnivall, *Colonial Policy and Practice*, p. 76.
[41] Harvey, *British Rule in Burma*, p. 77. Harvey further noted that of the eighteen governors of Burma from 1862 – presumably to the end of British rule – sixteen were members of the Indian Civil Service. More importantly, of those sixteen, only four had previously served in Burma.
[42] Mya Sein, *The Administration of Burma*, p. 80.
[43] Donnison, *Public Administration in Burma*, p. 38.

areas of state expenditure in Burma.[44] These financial transfers had been taking place from the early decades of British rule, but in the late nineteenth century, as Burma became a province of British India, they were governed by a five-year Provincial Contract (or Provincial Settlement). Thus the contract that came into force in April 1897 secured for the central government, for example, one-third of the receipts from the land revenue and one-half of the receipts from excise, the Burma administration retaining the remaining two-thirds and one-half respectively. In the subsequent Provincial Contract, from April 1902, the central government's share of the land revenue was increased to one-half, and of the excise to two-thirds, the shares of the Burma administration falling in proportion. And with respect to expenditure, the central government was responsible for, inter alia, the railways, military works, and the senior political administration: and the provincial government was responsible, inter alia, for the police, prisons, education, health, irrigation, and general administration. In the official year 1900/01, the central government's revenue receipts from Burma exceeded 37 million rupees, while its expenditure in Burma was only a little over 10 million rupees. However that apparent surplus of 27 million is misleading, for a major part of it represented Burma's contribution to the expenditure of the government of India on, for example, the army, pensions, and home charges. Even so, there was a strong perception in Burma that the province paid substantially more to the central government than it received in return, and certainly that the revenues being remitted to Calcutta and then Delhi would be far better spent in Burma itself. In other words, it was held that the revenue remittances to and local expenditure by the government of India were a substantial element in Burma's colonial drain. That perception was justified, as will be demonstrated in the following chapter.

And finally in the context of the integration of Burma into British India, there is evidence that more senior British officials were often psychologically or emotionally distant from Burma, indeed on occasion simply disliked the place. For example, in a memoir published in 1913, Sir Herbert Thirkell White reported that

---

[44] This paragraph draws on Alleyne Ireland, *The Province of Burma: a Report Prepared on Behalf of the University of Chicago*. Boston, MA: Houghton, Mifflin, vol. 2, 1907, pp. 553–68. See also John Nisbet, *Burma under British Rule–and Before*. Westminster: Archibald Constable, 1901, vol. 1, pp. 260–2.

no doubt Burma was regarded as a place of banishment, a dismal rice-swamp (or, as was once said, a howling paddy-plain), where the sun never shone. I remember, while still in London, the commiseration expressed with one of our seniors whose deportation to this dreary land was announced.[45]

In turn, Burma's dismal reputation lowered the quality of the British officials sent to the province. Men were sent to Burma, White noted, 'for their sins, either permanently or for a term of years. A Chief Commissioner's wife is said to have told one of these young men that other Provinces [of British India] sent their worst men to Burma'.[46] There is also evidence of psychological or emotional distance on the part of senior British officials in the attitude towards those few who did in fact engage with Burma and the Burmese. In another Burma memoir, Maurice Collis noted that if a British official mixed socially with Burmese, that alone was sufficient to identify him as pro-Burmese. And that was a very damaging charge indeed:

it meant that you had for the Burmese a greater feeling of sympathy and fellowship than was sanctioned by British opinion [in Burma] at that date... The implication was that you were lowering British prestige; the Burmese would think less of us if we did not treat them as inferiors.[47]

Material circumstances may at times have shaped those attitudes. In the late nineteenth and early twentieth centuries, British officials saw Burma as an expensive posting and the prospects for promotion within the senior ranks of the local administration as being poor, naturally given the fact that there had been a flood of young appointments immediately following the final annexation in the 1880s.[48] In addition, in this period – perhaps throughout the decades of British rule – Burma had a reputation for rebellion and disorder. Following the final annexation, there were serious risings in every district in the recently

---

[45] Herbert Thirkell White, *A Civil Servant in Burma*. London: Edward Arnold, 1913, p. 8. This was certainly not White's own view. 'I found Burma a bright and pleasant land... its people singularly human, cheerful, and sympathetic.' But then White was an exception, spending 'his entire career, thirty-two years, in the service of Burma': Edith L. Piness, 'The British administrator in Burma: a new view', *Journal of Southeast Asian Studies*, 14, 2 (September 1983), p. 374.

[46] White, *A Civil Servant in Burma*, p. 7.

[47] Maurice Collis, *Into Hidden Burma: an Autobiography*. London: Faber and Faber, 1953, p. 44.

[48] White, *A Civil Servant in Burma*, p. 8; Nisbet, *Burma under British Rule*, vol. 1, p. 228.

seized northern Burma and indeed through much of the southern territory under established British administration.[49] The savage British response – the initial policy was to execute all men captured and in possession of arms – undoubtedly fuelled Burmese hostility still further, and it was several years later and only after the deployment of a substantial force of troops and Indian police that a measure of order was restored. In the final years of the nineteenth century, Burma would not have been an attractive prospect for the ambitious Indian Civil Service officer fresh from Britain.

And perhaps the psychological or emotional distance of senior British officials reflected directly the integration of Burma into British India, secured with the final annexation in the mid-1880s. This is a speculation, although the logic is persuasive. Burma was an outpost of British India both geographically (it occupied the furthest eastern extent, across the Bay of Bengal) and temporally (it was a very late addition).[50] Although of substantial economic and financial importance, it was a merely peripheral element in the government and administration of British India. Burma was indeed, in the words used by Sir Herbert Thirkell White, 'a place of banishment' to which British officials were sent 'for their sins'. Seen in these terms, it is little wonder that senior British officials kept their distance and that so few embraced Burma and the Burmese.

The impact of psychological or emotional distance can be seen in a number of the colonial administration's most important measures. One example was noted earlier. The major reform of local administration undertaken just after the final war betrayed a serious misreading on the part of the British authorities of the Burmese structures the reform was to replace, a disregard of Burmese circumstances. A still more striking disregard of Burmese interests was evident in British Burma's land legislation from the 1870s, to be considered in the following section. In both cases – local administration and land legislation – the socio-economic impact on the Burmese through the remaining decades of British rule was to be immense.

---

[49] For a brief account of the 'pacification' of Burma between 1886 and 1890 – note the striking euphemism – see John F. Cady, *A History of Modern Burma*. Ithaca, NY: Cornell University Press, 1958, pp. 132–7.

[50] 'Burma is a sort of recess, a blind alley, a back reach': Sir J. G. Scott, *Burma: a Handbook of Practical Information*. London: Daniel O'Connor, 1921, p. 1.

The creation of the modern economy: the cultivation of rice

Colonial Burma's modern economy was created in just a few decades. When the British annexed lower Burma in the early 1850s, the vast deltaic plain of the Irrawaddy and Sittang rivers had relatively few people and was largely abandoned to nature, while Rangoon was a 'labyrinth of hovels [and a] wilderness of mud'.[51] Half a century later, huge tracts of lower Burma's deltaic plain had been cleared and were now occupied by great numbers of cultivators and by vast expanses of rice, while Rangoon was established as one of the great port-cities of the East, British Burma's administrative, financial, and commercial capital. This final section of this chapter is concerned with that extraordinary economic transformation, focusing on by far its most important element, the expansion of the cultivation of rice for export across the final decades of the nineteenth century. That focus places the Burmese themselves centre stage, and thus balances this chapter's earlier concentration on foreigners and foreign interests.

The expansion of rice cultivation and of rice exports in the second half of the nineteenth century is caught in the following two tables. These are striking figures. Between the 1850s and the first years of the twentieth century, the area under rice in lower Burma increased almost seven-fold: and between the late 1860s and the 1900s, the volume of rice exports increased over five times. The end of this period saw the most substantial increases, in absolute terms. Over a million acres were added to the area under rice in lower Burma in the decade from the mid-1890s: and around three-quarters of a million tons were added to the average annual export of rice, comparing the 1890s with the first decade of the new century.

The reclaiming from nature of the vast Irrawaddy-Sittang deltaic plain, the preparation of the land for cultivation, and then the planting, tending, and harvesting of the crop, was undertaken by Burmese agriculturalists in their hundreds of thousands.[52] The Burma delta was thinly populated when it was annexed by the British in the early 1850s, and thus inevitably the vast force of agriculturalists who reclaimed it

---

[51] This was the assessment of pre-British Rangoon by the Prince of Wales: Donald M. Seekins, *State and Society in Modern Rangoon*. London: Routledge, 2011, p. 30.

[52] This section rests heavily on Adas, *The Burma Delta*; and Cheng, *The Rice Industry of Burma*.

Table 1.1: *Annual average acreage of paddy land in lower Burma, 1845 to 1900–1904*

	Thousands of acres
1845	354
1855	993
1860	1,333
1863–64	1,412
1865–69	1,627
1870–74	1,965
1875–79	2,704
1880–84	3,402
1885–89	4,011
1890–94	4,865
1895–99	5,765
1900–04	6,832

Source: Cheng Siok-Hwa, *The Rice Industry of Burma 1852–1940*. Kuala Lumpur: University of Malaya Press, 1968, p. 25.

Table 1.2: *Annual average exports of rice and paddy from Burma, 1860s to 1900s*

	Thousands of tons
1865/66–1870/71	399
1871/72–1880/81	810
1881/82–1890/91	981
1891/92–1900/01	1,463
1901/02–1910/11	2,169

Source: Cheng Siok-Hwa, *The Rice Industry of Burma 1852–1940*. Kuala Lumpur: University of Malaya Press, 1968, p. 201.

and put it under rice in the following decades included many tens of thousands of migrants from other parts of Burma, mainly from Upper Burma, the Burmese kingdom until the final war of 1885. A rough indication of the scale of the migration into the delta in this period is provided by data from the 1901 census. In a lower Burma population of a little over four million in that year, more than 400,000 (10 per cent) had been born outside the delta.[53]

The reclaiming of the delta by the Burmese agriculturalist in the second half of the nineteenth century was an immense achievement: in the words of J. S. Furnivall, an 'epic of bravery and endurance'.[54] To bring a tract in that frontier wilderness into cultivation was indeed a punishing task.[55] The pioneer agriculturalist commonly had to fell an extensive stand of forest, burn off the undergrowth, and hack out the tangle of thick, deeply embedded tree-roots. Such were these demands in clearing a tract that it could be several years before the land was ploughed and planted with rice. In addition, this was an extremely hostile environment. The cultivator was always vulnerable to the debilitating diseases, notably malaria and dysentery, which could take hold in areas of new settlement. He could lose his work animals to rinderpest, anthrax, or foot-and-mouth. And he could lose his crop, to excessive flooding, as monsoon-swollen rivers broke through embankments, and to the ravages of rats, wild pigs, crabs, birds, worms, and beetles, which devoured young shoots and attacked the maturing crop. There were also human predators. All too often the pioneer agriculturalist, having spent years bringing some frontier tract into production, found himself dispossessed by a land speculator who, much earlier and in certain anticipation that at some point the area would be settled, had filed with the local administration a provisional claim for possession. Or the pioneer was simply driven from his land by intimidation and thuggery. Of course, by no means all cultivators fell victim to malaria, wild pigs, or land-grabbers. But many did. And for all, there was the risk that they might. At the same time there was the absolute certainty of back-breaking labour. This raises an interesting question. With those

---

[53] Adas, *The Burma Delta*, p. 42.
[54] Furnivall, *Colonial Policy and Practice*, p. 116.
[55] This and subsequent paragraphs are a reworking and substantial reduction of Ian Brown, *Economic Change in South-East Asia, c.1830–1980*. Kuala Lumpur: Oxford University Press, 1997, ch. 8.

risks and that certainty, why did hundreds of thousands of Burmese agriculturalists embark on this 'epic of bravery and endurance'?

A major part of the explanation must be that the large-scale cultivation of rice for export offered the agriculturalist the prospect of a substantial improvement in material well-being. Over the second half of the nineteenth century, the price of rice more than doubled, from 45 rupees per hundred baskets in 1855 to 95 rupees in 1900.[56] Undoubtedly a substantial proportion of that price was taken by intermediaries – local traders, millers, the export merchants – but the strength of the international demand for rice in these decades suggests that the Burmese cultivator too received a considerable return. Thus as prices rose and as larger tracts were brought into production by employing seasonal labour, the cultivator's cash income increased. And crucially, with British-ruled Burma open to the world's manufactures, there were many opportunities to spend that income. Well before the end of the nineteenth century, an impressive range and volume of imported manufactures had reached even the most distant rural settlements. Some were, in the circumstances of the time, modest luxuries – clocks, glassware and crockery, metal safes and chests, mirrors. But most were essentials – textiles, corrugated-iron roofs, soap, kerosene lamps.

The argument that the Burmese agriculturalist was drawn into the delta in the second half of the nineteenth century by the prospect of substantial material gain would be decisively confirmed if it could be demonstrated that the material circumstances of the rice cultivator did indeed improve over those decades. However the evidence of improvement, while suggestive and indeed often persuasive, is not absolutely decisive. In large part the evidence consists of the observations made by senior rural officials at the time, either their broad characterization of the rice-cultivating population as being 'solvent and prosperous', or their references to specific examples of consumption – the use of wood, rather than bamboo, in the construction of dwellings, corrugated-iron roofs rather than thatch, and the common sight of imported furniture, Lancashire textiles, canned milk, imported biscuits, kerosene lamps, soap, and imported crockery. In a striking example of the latter, quoted by Michael Adas, in the first years of the twentieth century, one rural

---

[56] Cheng, *The Rice Industry of Burma*, p. 73. In 1912 the price hit 160 rupees. These are wholesale prices of paddy in Rangoon.

official reported seeing a rice cultivator 'smoking a French briar pipe and suckling his motherless babe with an English nursing bottle containing Swiss condensed milk'.[57]

Adas drew out further evidence to support the conclusion that the material circumstances of the rice cultivator improved substantially over the second half of the nineteenth century. He recounted the experience of a particular agriculturalist, Maung Kyaw Din, who, having migrated into the delta from northern Burma in the 1870s to clear a wild tract and establish a smallholding, in the following decades, using his rising income to add repeatedly to his land, became a major landlord.[58] By the first decade of the twentieth century, he owned 750 acres, thirty work animals which he rented out, and a house worth 5,000 rupees. In addition he had financed the construction of a Buddhist monastery and temple in his settlement, at an estimated cost of 23,000 rupees. Michael Adas concluded: 'Maung Kyaw Din was only one of thousands of diligent cultivators who achieved positions of wealth and local importance on the Delta frontier' in the second half of the nineteenth century. And finally, Adas constructed, from the official reports of the time, the cultivator's cash balance sheet – the income from the cultivation of rice set against the cost of living, the cost of cultivation, and capitation and land taxes – for selected districts in the delta at different times in the final two decades of the nineteenth century and the first decade of the twentieth.[59] In each case, the constructed cash balance produced a substantial surplus – that is, the cultivator's income from rice substantially exceeded his core expenditures.

An important weakness in the evidence above is that it fails to capture the distribution of prosperity – or of economic failure and impoverishment – across the rural population. Senior officials in the rice districts could report sightings, even frequent sightings, of corrugated-iron roofs, Lancashire textiles, and Swiss condensed milk, but these alone did not establish that the consumption of such articles was widespread. Moreover the cultivator's substantial cash balances constructed by Michael Adas are averages and therefore hide, for the individual cultivator, much smaller surpluses, or indeed cash deficits. And Maung Kyaw Din and his ascent from pioneer cultivator to major landowner was surely exceptional, despite the assertion by Adas that

---

[57] Adas, *The Burma Delta*, p. 76.   [58] Ibid., pp. 71–2.   [59] Ibid., pp. 74–5.

there were thousands like him. This is not to dismiss the evidence. Rather it is to argue, again, that the evidence of an improvement in the material circumstances of the Burmese rice cultivator over the second half of the nineteenth century, while suggestive and indeed often persuasive, is not absolutely decisive.[60] This in turn suggests that more than material incentives brought the Burmese cultivators in their hundreds of thousands into the delta. In other words, they were pushed as well as pulled.

Burma's northern dry zone, from which so many of the pioneer cultivators migrated, was, as the name indicates, an area of scanty and uncertain rainfall, and therefore prone to drought, food shortages, and occasional famine. Therefore, with the opening of the delta frontier under British rule from the mid-nineteenth century, desperate cultivators and their families in the north could escape to the south, for there a vast expanse of cultivable land and strong demand for labour offered a prospect of relief. It is interesting to note that the numbers migrating into the delta at any particular point in these decades often reflected the food position in the north. Thus when the local rains failed in 1896, the railway and roads leading south were crowded with cultivators and their families in search of land and work in the delta. It might also be noted that those districts in the north with irrigation works, and therefore the more secure production of food, supplied fewer migrants to the rice frontier. It is also possible that cultivators and their families were driven from the north by the social disorder and administrative disintegration that accompanied the final years of the Burmese monarchy, and that followed its abolition in the mid-1880s.

There remains one final important aspect of Burma's rice economy in the final decades of the nineteenth century to be considered. It was a flaw, a failure, and it was to have severe consequences for the Burmese. '[T]he main object of the agricultural policy' of the British colonial administration in Burma in the final decades of the nineteenth century, wrote J. S. Furnivall at the beginning of the 1930s, was 'the creation of a body of peasant proprietors', for it was widely held that 'cultivators would be more industrious and law-abiding if they owned the land they

---

[60] Perhaps the reality – that not all prospered and that many failed – was less important than each pioneer's belief and hope that, irrespective of the failure of others, he surely would become prosperous. In other words, hundreds of thousands of Burmese cultivators were drawn into the delta by *the prospect* of substantial material gain.

cultivated'.[61] British land legislation and administration in Burma certainly encouraged the occupation and ownership of agricultural land by the cultivator. The great expansion in the delta's cultivated area in the final decades of the nineteenth century was achieved principally through squatting – the pioneer agriculturalist clearing and bringing into cultivation a tract of vacant wilderness on the frontier. Under the Lower Burma Land and Revenue Act of 1876, a squatter who continuously occupied a plot of land and paid the revenue on it for twelve successive years acquired title to that land.[62] Provided the annual land revenue then continued to be paid, the cultivator had secured a permanent, heritable, and transferable right in the land. It was now his private property. But there was a further provision. During the initial twelve years, years in which the squatter could be evicted by the authorities but rarely was, the land was accepted as security for loans. In other words, even though the cultivator had yet to secure landholder's right, as it was known, if he defaulted on a loan and his lender foreclosed, the land would be transferred to the latter, to the moneylender. This was a crucial provision, for it provided the foundation upon which, from the 1880s, the Chettiars began to move into the rice districts and to lend on a large scale to the rice cultivators.

The fact that squatter-occupied land was readily accepted as security for loans can be interpreted in two opposing ways. On the one hand it can be seen as strengthening the position of the pioneer agriculturalist by giving him access to the substantial funds needed to clear his wilderness, prepare the land for cultivation, and then plant, tend, and harvest the crop. It made more possible the establishment of a thriving new holding, and the fulfilment of the British administration's aim to create a 'body of peasant proprietors'. On the other hand it might be seen as making the position of the pioneer cultivator more vulnerable, in that, presumably, it encouraged high levels of borrowing, which in turn made the consequences for the cultivator of even a modest setback potentially more damaging. One poor harvest and the rice cultivator, heavily in debt, could so easily default

---

[61] J. S. Furnivall, *An Introduction to the Political Economy of Burma*. Rangoon: Burma Book Club, 1931, p. 49. This and subsequent paragraphs are a reworking and reduction of Ian Brown, *A Colonial Economy in Crisis: Burma's Rice Cultivators and the World Depression of the 1930s*. London: RoutledgeCurzon, 2005, pp. 17–22.

[62] Cheng, *The Rice Industry of Burma*, pp. 138–40.

and lose his land, thus thwarting the colonial administration's aim of creating a population of owner-cultivators. But here there is a further, absolutely critical point. There was nothing in British land legislation and administration to prevent individuals normally resident outside Burma – the Chettiar – from owning agricultural land in the province. In other words, not only would the defaulting rice cultivator lose his land, but ownership of that land would pass to an alien. In the first years of the twentieth century, fully one-tenth of agricultural land in the thirteen principal rice-growing districts of lower Burma was owned by 'non-resident non-agriculturists', in effect the Chettiar moneylenders.[63]

In the early 1890s, Burma's Financial Commissioner, Donald Mackenzie Smeaton, had argued that the rice cultivator would keep hold of his land only if he were prevented from borrowing too freely from the moneylender, and that this could be achieved only by sharply restricting the use of land as security for loans.[64] Legislation was drafted in 1896. This stipulated that a revenue officer, who maintained the land register for his district, would sanction the sale of an agriculturalist's land only to another agriculturalist. Furthermore, it recognized only usufruct mortgages, that is loan agreements which allowed the cultivator-borrower who defaulted to remain on the land as a tenant of the lender, in this case for up to fifteen years. The legislation was not enacted. A decade later, in 1906, a further attempt was made to introduce legislation that would curb the loss of agricultural land to non-agriculturalists, an attempt driven by the Lieutenant-Governor himself, Sir Herbert Thirkell White. White too wished to recognize only usufruct mortgages: and he sought to revive the traditional Burmese practice that gave those who sold a piece of land the right to repurchase it after a number of years. But there was considerable opposition to the proposed legislation from 'articulate opinion' in both the colonial administration and commerce. There were three main objections. It was not practicable to define 'agriculturalist', it

---

[63] Ibid., p. 145. Almost certainly the figure of one-tenth does not fully reflect the rate at which Chettiars were foreclosing. Reluctant to own land, the Chettiar would attempt to sell on – to a cultivator – any holding he had been forced to seize on the failure of a loan.

[64] This discussion draws on Cady, *A History of Modern Burma*, pp. 166–67. See also Nicholas Bayne, *Burma and Tudor History: the Life and Work of Charles Bayne 1860–1947*. Bideford: Edward Gaskell, 2008, chs 7 and 10.

was said.[65] Revenue officers, required to sanction or reject each proposed sale of land by an 'agriculturalist', would be administratively
overburdened. And most importantly, it would oust the Chettiar from
the Burma delta – since the Chettiar would lend only against land as
security – and therefore severely disrupt the provision of credit to the
rice cultivator. That in turn would sharply reduce the rate at which the
area of cleared-cultivable land was increasing and could well leave a
substantial proportion of existing holdings uncultivated. Burma would
produce less rice.

White failed to enact his Land Alienation Bill. His successor, Sir
Harvey Adamson, abandoned it. White's memoirs, completed soon
after his departure from Burma, captured his disappointment.

I had much at heart the enactment of legislation for restraining the alienation
of land . . . I was unsuccessful in effecting [this object] before my retirement.
I have no doubt that gradually but surely the Burman is being squeezed off
the land, and that if, as seems likely, the proposed legislation is abandoned,
the land will fall into the hands of non-agriculturists and natives of India.
Free trade in land as in other things may be good. From an economic point
of view the position is probably sound. More rice will be grown for export;
more land revenue and customs duty will be garnered. But there are other
considerations. The standard of living will be lowered. The deterioration of
the Burmese race which will inevitably accompany their divorce from the
land will be a subject for regret when it is irremediable.[66]

In other words, the most rapid expansion of rice production and
exports – and therefore government revenue and the earnings of rice
traders, millers, lenders, import merchants, and shipping lines – was
set against the creation of a population of industrious and law-abiding
owner-cultivators. And the former took precedence.

---

[65] For a number of reasons it was in fact difficult to distinguish between
agriculturalists and non-agriculturalists. For example, it would appear that on
occasion, landowners decided themselves how their occupation was recorded
in the village register of holdings. And as colonial officials were prone to treat
non-agriculturalist landowners sternly, for example with regard to tax
remissions, it was advantageous for the large landowner to record himself as an
'agriculturalist'. For a detailed discussion, see Asuka Mizuno, 'Identifying the
"agriculturists" in the Burma Delta in the colonial period: a new perspective
on agriculturists based on a village tract's registers of holdings from the 1890s
to the 1920s', *Journal of Southeast Asian Studies*, 42, 3 (October 2011).

[66] White, *A Civil Servant in Burma*, p. 296.

It is important to note that not only the British in Burma but other colonial administrations in South East Asia too had to trade economic gain, principally for foreign interests, against maintaining the local social order. However the latter often came to a quite different conclusion, and, in contrast to the British administration in Burma, sought to protect the social order by imposing legal restrictions on the ownership of agricultural land. The Federated Malay States provides a prime example.[67] In the late 1900s, the British administration in the FMS became concerned that the rural Malays were selling substantial areas of their land to European companies, for with the price of rubber soaring, the companies were extremely eager to expand their plantation acreage. The Malays were presumably securing an attractive price. But they were also losing their land – not simply a critical economic resource but the very foundation of Malay rural society – and the British administration thus concluded that it was now vital 'to protect Malays against themselves'. The Malay Reservations Enactment of 1913 gave the British Resident in each of the Federated Malay States the authority to declare any specified area in the state a Malay Reservation: and Malay reserved land could not be sold, leased, or otherwise disposed of, to a non-Malay, in practice to a Chinese, Indian, or European. In the following years, a substantial area was gazetted, such that by the end of 1923 there were almost 2.8 million acres of Malay Reservations in the Federated Malay States, a little over 15 per cent of the total area. The Netherlands East Indies provides a further example. It was a central principle of Dutch colonial administration through the nineteenth century and into the twentieth that 'native land should not be alienated to foreigners'.[68] Foreign economic interests – European and Chinese planters – could rent native land or lease waste land from the state, and the terms upon which that renting and leasing took place was an important concern of the Dutch administration. But throughout, the local population remained in control of its land in accordance with custom.

---

[67] The following draws on Lim Teck Ghee, *Peasants and their Agricultural Economy in Colonial Malaya 1874–1941*. Kuala Lumpur: Oxford University Press, 1977, pp. 106–16, 165.

[68] Furnivall, *Colonial Policy and Practice*, p. 224: with further detail from J. S. Furnivall, *Netherlands India: a Study of Plural Economy*. Cambridge University Press, 1944, pp. 47, 178–81.

There are perhaps three main considerations that might explain this contrast between the willingness of the colonial administrations in the Netherlands East Indies and the Federated Malay States to intervene, and intervene to substantial effect in the market for cultivable land, and the failure of the British administration in Burma to do so. The first is that intervention in the Malay States and the East Indies did not have significant economic costs for the foreign interests there. The creation of Malay Reservations does not appear to have restricted the expansion of European rubber acreage – it rose from 6,000 acres in 1900 to well over one million in 1920 – and it did not prevent the emergence of British Malaya as by far the most important exporter of cultivated rubber in the world in those same decades.[69] In the Netherlands East Indies, it seems clear that through its renting and leasing provisions, in time colonial land legislation and administration gave foreign commercial interests there the access to the land they sought, and over the nineteenth century and into the twentieth, the Dutch colony became a major exporter of a range of agricultural commodities, including sugar, coffee, tobacco, and rubber. In contrast, if the British administration in Burma had acted to prevent the ownership of agricultural land passing to non-resident non-agriculturalists, or even to resident non-agriculturalists, the expansion of the economy would have greatly slowed. At the centre of Burma's colonial economy was the initiative and resources of the Burmese rice cultivator, and among his resources, critically so, was access to Chettiar capital. To oust the Chettiar, as legislation to prevent the alienation of land to non-agriculturalists might well have achieved, would have slowed substantially the expansion in rice production and exports, and therefore government revenue and the earnings of rice traders, millers, lenders, import merchants, and shipping lines, as noted earlier. In brief, in British Burma, maintaining the rural social order would come only at a substantial economic cost, notably to foreign interests.

The second consideration is that, with the exception of the Punjab, no major province of British India introduced legislation to prohibit the alienation of agricultural land to non-agriculturalists, although the issue was debated at great length across the subcontinent in the late

---

[69] J. H. Drabble, *Rubber in Malaya 1876–1922: the Genesis of the Industry.* Kuala Lumpur: Oxford University Press, 1973, pp. 216, 220.

nineteenth and early twentieth centuries.[70] Provincial administrations feared that such a restriction would harm the revenue. As Burma was a province of British India – and as many of its most senior officials had spent the formative years of their career in India 'proper' – inevitably British Indian practices and approaches, in land legislation and administration as well as in many other matters, was a powerful influence.

The third consideration was Burma's paradoxical position with respect to British India. As noted earlier, the territory was seen as an outpost both geographically and temporally, but at the same time a very considerable economic, commercial, and financial asset, in other words a political-administrative appendage but a rich economic quarry. In the context of the present discussion – the British administration in Burma setting the most rapid expansion in rice production and exports above the creation of a body of law-abiding owner-cultivators – this characterization is important in two respects. The recognition of Burma as an economic quarry accounts for the very considerable influence of commercial interests, exercised through the Burma Chamber of Commerce, through the Chamber's representative on the Legislative Council, and through the businessman's social-personal contacts with senior officials, in opposing legislation that would restrict the alienation of land to non-agriculturalists.[71] And second, the perception of Burma as a political-administrative appendage can be seen as underpinning the opposition of many in the Burma administration itself to such legislation, even against the ambitions and warnings of its most senior figures, Donald Mackenzie Smeaton and then Sir Herbert Thirkell White. Here perhaps was a further reflection of the psychological or emotional distance of many senior British officials from Burma and the Burmese, suggested earlier. That distance,

---

[70] Dietmar Rothermund, *An Economic History of India from Pre-Colonial Times to 1986*. London: Croom Helm, 1988, p. 46; Neil Charlesworth, *Peasants and Imperial Rule: Agriculture and Agrarian Society in the Bombay Presidency, 1850–1935*. Cambridge University Press, 1985, pp. 243–4.

[71] Cheng, *The Rice Industry of Burma*, pp. 148–9. The triumph of commercial interests in British-ruled Burma was brilliantly caught by the fictional Flory in Orwell's Burma novel: '"My dear doctor," said Flory, "how can you make out that we are in this country for any purpose except to steal? It's so simple. The official holds the Burman down while the businessman goes through his pockets."' George Orwell, *Burmese Days*. London: Penguin Books, 1989, p. 38.

ultimately an absence of engagement, was caught by G. E. Harvey, late of the Indian Civil Service, writing at the very end of British rule.

It was not for lack of information that nothing was done; we always had plenty of officers who were specialists in land revenue with enough information at their fingertips to settle the matter three times over. It was lack of will. Since 1875 there have been dozens of inquiries and bills, carefully drafted, discussed till everyone was tired of them, and dropped – the problem was not yet urgent, it was a difficult problem, there were arguments on both sides to be weighed [*sic*].[72]

For the Burmese, the socio-economic impact of this failure was to be immense, its legacy deep and long-lasting.

To return to the very first sentence of this chapter: at the beginning of the twentieth century, British-ruled Burma was described by a former colonial official as 'one of the richest provinces of our Indian Empire... one of the brightest jewels in the Imperial diadem of India'. The chapter has sustained that view. But it has also demonstrated that beneath the near-relentlessly rising production and trade statistics, and the sight of vast rural expanses under rice and crowded wharves and commercial streets in Rangoon, serious failings undermined the prosperous, as it was seen, colonial economy. In the first decades of the twentieth century, those failings would become ever more evident.

---

[72] Harvey, *British Rule in Burma*, pp. 51–2. The final word in this passage, [*sic*], appears in the original, indicating that Harvey did not believe that the arguments were finely balanced, but rather that the case for legislation to protect the rice cultivator in the ownership of his land was simply overwhelming.

2 | *Strains in the late colonial economy*

The closing rice frontier

The extraordinary increase in rice production and exports in the final decades of the nineteenth century, and the consequent establishment of Burma as the single most important rice exporting country in the world, was achieved through a huge expansion in the area under cultivation. Cultivation methods and inputs remained essentially unchanged but were now being employed on a vastly greater scale. This expansion was possible, of course, because when the British annexed lower Burma in the early 1850s, the great deltaic plain of the Irrawaddy and Sittang rivers was sparsely populated and largely abandoned to nature. There was a vast open frontier. But inevitably, in time, the frontier would begin to close and the pace of expansion would slacken. That time came in the first decades of the twentieth century.

Table 2.1 records the annual average acreage of paddy land in lower Burma in the first four decades of the twentieth century. It should be read alongside Table 1.1 in the previous chapter, recording paddy acreage in the second half of the nineteenth century. In the final three decades of the nineteenth century, some 3.8 million acres had been added to the area under rice in lower Burma. In the first three decades of the twentieth, the increase was around 2.7 million acres, considerably less although still substantial. It is important to add that this reduced expansion in the rice acreage in the early twentieth century also increasingly involved bringing into cultivation less productive land. As the prime districts came to be cleared and settled – local shortages were being reported from the final years of the nineteenth century – inevitably the pioneer agriculturalist was increasingly forced to turn to tracts with poorer soil, or those prone to excessive flooding.[1]

---

[1] Michael Adas, *The Burma Delta: Economic Development and Social Change on an Asian Rice Frontier, 1852–1941.* Madison, WI: University of Wisconsin Press, 1974, pp. 128, 131.

Table 2.1: *Annual average acreage of paddy land in lower Burma, 1900–1904 to 1940*

	Thousands of acres
1900–04	6,832
1905–09	7,532
1910–14	8,024
1915–19	8,362
1920–24	8,912
1925–29	9,582
1930–34	9,720
1935–39	9,865
1940	9,932

Source: Cheng Siok-Hwa, *The Rice Industry of Burma 1852–1940*. Kuala Lumpur: University of Malaya Press, 1968, p. 25.

Table 2.2: *Annual average exports of rice and paddy from Burma, 1900s to 1930s*

	Thousands of tons
1901/02–1910/11	2,169
1911/12–1920/21	2,176
1921/22–1930/31	2,676
1931/32–1939/40	3,141

Source: Cheng Siok-Hwa, *The Rice Industry of Burma 1852–1940*. Kuala Lumpur: University of Malaya Press, 1968, p. 201.

The reduced expansion in acreage and the increasing settlement of less productive land – the closing of the delta rice frontier – was reflected in a slower growth in exports. Table 2.2 records the annual average export of rice and paddy from Burma in the first four decades of the twentieth century. It should be read alongside Table 1.2 in the previous chapter, recording exports in the final decades of the nineteenth century.

In the final three decades of the nineteenth century, the annual average export of rice and paddy from Burma had increased by some 650,000 tons. In the first three decades of the twentieth, the increase was around 500,000 tons, again considerably less although still substantial. In other words, the impact of the closing rice frontier on exports was clear but relatively modest. The far more severe impact was on the material condition and prospects of Burma's rice cultivators, for the first decades of the twentieth century saw the material circumstances of, specifically, tenant-cultivators and landless labourers in the delta deteriorate markedly.[2]

During the decades of rapid expansion in Burma's rice economy in the late nineteenth century, the open frontier had provided the cultivator with a substantial prospect of upward socio-economic mobility. Given hard work and a measure of good fortune, the tenant or even the labourer, having accumulated some resources, could with relative ease locate an unoccupied highly fertile tract, clear it, and establish ownership. In time, with continuing commitment and fortune, he could, like Maung Kyaw Din in the previous chapter, add repeatedly to his land – the frontier was open – and become a major landlord.

But as the rice frontier closed, for tenants and labourers that prospect of upward mobility faded. In the long-settled rice districts of the delta, the most fertile tracts were now taken, and for ambitious tenants and labourers employed there working the lands of others, the nearest unoccupied fertile tracts were now impractically distant. And where unoccupied land *was* within practical reach, either the soil was of such poor quality as to be unprofitable to cultivate, or a substantial initial investment was required, for example in the construction of bunds to prevent excessive flooding, an investment far beyond the resources of a labourer or tenant. Nor could the ambitious tenant simply purchase an existing local holding, for with the most fertile tracts now taken, sale prices were rising beyond the resources of all but the most substantial

[2] The following draws on Adas, *The Burma Delta*, ch. 6: and Ian Brown, *A Colonial Economy in Crisis: Burma's Rice Cultivators and the World Depression of the 1930s*. London: RoutledgeCurzon, 2005, pp. 22–5.

existing landowners.[3] Thus the extension in the area under rice that did take place in the first three decades of the twentieth century – as noted above, a further 2.7 million acres, roughly, were brought into cultivation in this period – was undertaken primarily by large landowners and land speculators. The solitary labourer and his family clearing and occupying a tract on the frontier, common in the late nineteenth century, was now relatively rare.

The closing of the delta rice frontier not only sharply restricted the opportunities for labourers and tenants to move up into the ranks of the owner-cultivators and even in time to become a large landlord. It also, in numerous ways, led to a marked deterioration in the terms upon which, held in their existing positions, tenants rented land and labourers secured work. To consider tenants first: as fewer tenants moved on to become owners; as owner-cultivators lost their lands – for reasons to be noted below – and began to search for tenancies; as the agricultural population grew; and of course as the expansion in the cultivated area slowed; for all these reasons the competition for tenancies became more intense, and consequently landlords could impose considerably harsher terms.[4] Rents rose substantially. Until the late 1880s, commonly the rent on rice land had been about one-tenth of the holding's output, although most tenants also paid the land revenue.[5] However, from the final years of the nineteenth century, the proportion of output taken in rent rose, at first moderately but, from the mid-1910s, far more sharply. By the mid-1920s, the rent on even the least fertile tracts could approach one-fifth, and in the most fertile districts of the delta, landlords were commonly taking one-half of the output in rent. Indeed a government inquiry in the mid-1920s found landlords in a part of Tharrawaddy, one of the most densely populated rice districts, demanding rents on first class land of some five-eighths of

---

[3] For example, the price of land in Hanthawaddy District in the lower delta rose from about Rs 20 per acre around 1900 to Rs 70 in 1910, and then to Rs 105 in the early 1930s. Adas, *The Burma Delta*, p. 129.

[4] The population of the thirteen rice districts increased by almost half a million between the census in 1911 and that in 1921. T. Couper, *Report of Inquiry into the Condition of Agricultural Tenants and Labourers*. Rangoon: Central Press, 1966 (reprint), p. 6.

[5] Adas, *The Burma Delta*, pp. 79, 148.

output.[6] Many landlords then extracted still more from their tenants than had been agreed, simply by using baskets larger than the standard government size – one-fourth as large again, the Tharrawaddy inquiry noted – to measure out their tenants' rent deliveries. In addition, many tenants were required to cart their rent to the landlord's storage sheds, often a considerable distance, at their own expense.

In other ways too, landlords were now imposing harsher terms. In the late nineteenth century, most had granted remissions on rent when the harvest had been poor – because of inadequate rains, flooding, or attacks from wild pigs, rats, or various paddy-devouring grubs and beetles. Now, in the first decades of the twentieth century, many land-lords refused rent remissions, even when the tenant was in a desperate position. Moreover, tenancies were almost invariably for just a sin-gle year, a practice that not only encouraged the landlord to fix the rent higher each year, but also put pressure on the tenant to accept all the landlord's conditions in the hope of securing a renewal. And finally, on occasion a landlord would take a failing tenant to court and threaten imprisonment, a procedure that undoubtedly encouraged other tenants to meet the landlord's demands. However the tenant was not entirely helpless in such circumstances. For example, if a landlord did indeed go to court to secure his rent in full, the tenant, who for a time had physical control of the paddy on the threshing-room floor, could spirit away much of the crop before the law could act. In other circumstances, because he had control of the recently harvested paddy, the tenant could surreptitiously sell a major part to a broker before delivering the rent to the landlord, to give the impression that the crop, and therefore the rent due, was much smaller than was really the case. And finally, for the tenant on a single-year lease, with no established dwelling and few ties, it was psychologically and physically easy to abscond as the harvest was brought in, with the rent not delivered and loans left unpaid. But even with such defensive stratagems, there is little doubt that by the 1920s, indeed earlier, the terms of tenancies in the rice districts had shifted decisively in favour of the landlord.

The terms on which the labourer secured work similarly deteriorated in this period, as was noted earlier. As fewer labourers moved on to become tenants or owners; as owner-cultivators lost their lands and

---

[6] Couper, *Report of Inquiry into the Condition of Agricultural Tenants and Labourers*, pp. 30–1.

tenants failed to secure tenancies, and were therefore forced to seek labouring work; as increasing numbers of Indian labourers moved into the rice districts in search of work during the slack months for the rice mills and on the docks; as the agricultural population grew; and of course as the expansion in the cultivated area slowed, for all these reasons the competition for labouring work became more intense and consequently employers could impose considerably harsher terms. Writing at the beginning of the 1930s, J. S. Furnivall cautiously estimated that agricultural wages – that is nominal wages – had fallen by about 20 per cent since the 1870s.[7] Of course, once rises in living costs are taken into account – and there were pronounced price rises in the late 1910s and into the 1920s – the decline in the *real* wage of agricultural labourers would have been substantially greater. Moreover, as wages were driven down, the labourer was often forced into greater debt. Paid less and therefore unable to support his family through to the next harvest, he had no choice but to borrow further from shopkeepers or the landowner, often on harsh terms that left him with even less for the following year. Until the 1910s, Michael Adas concludes, the labourer working in the rice delta could break even, given reasonable health and modest fortune.[8] If other adults in the family secured work, he might accumulate enough to secure a tenancy or even to become an owner. But by the 1920s, even if all the adults worked, often the family could not survive, or could survive only by finding additional work, perhaps as carters, by drifting into the towns, or through robbery, house-breaking, and theft. The landless labourer in the rice delta was impoverished.

A number of further damaging strains were evident in Burma's rice economy in the first decades of the twentieth century. Among the most serious was a decline in the fertility of the land. Undoubtedly there was substantial variation in yield by district, and also by year, reflecting local cropping conditions. But one recent calculation indicates that the paddy yield per hectare fell from a little over 1.6 tons in the 1900s to just over 1.4 tons in the 1920s.[9] Part of the explanation for this fall in

---

[7] J. S. Furnivall, *An Introduction to the Political Economy of Burma.* Rangoon: Burma Book Club, 1931, p. 77.
[8] Adas, *The Burma Delta*, p. 153.
[9] Teruko Saito and Lee Kin Kiong (comp.), *Statistics on the Burmese Economy: the 19th and 20th Centuries.* Singapore: Institute of Southeast Asian Studies, 1999, p. 80.

yield was noted earlier – as the frontier closed, further expansion of the area under rice increasingly involved clearing and settling tracts with poorer soil, or those prone to heavy flooding. But in addition, yields in long-settled districts were now declining, inevitably so, for year-after-year, over many decades, crops had been taken from the land with little replenishment, except when flood water brought in deposits of silt.[10] Moreover, single-year tenancies gave tenants no incentive to maintain the holding: thus damaged field bunds were not repaired, leaving the most fertile top soil to drain away. At the same time, few cultivators used either natural or manufactured fertilizer on their main fields (although the nurseries were often manured). And even at the end of the 1920s, less than 2 per cent of the area under rice was planted with improved varieties.[11]

Three further serious strains in Burma's rice economy, clearly evident in the 1920s, should be noted. The first was a substantial rise in the cost of cultivation – in the price of, for example, plough bullocks, harrows, ploughs, and sickles: but then also important items of food and clothing – between the mid-1910s and the mid-1920s.[12] The second strain was price-fixing among paddy-brokers and speculators and, more potently, between the major milling and exporting firms in the ports.[13] From as early as the 1870s, the big European millers and rice merchants had at frequent intervals sought to agree among themselves the maximum price at which they would purchase paddy. The aim, clearly, was to reduce or indeed eliminate competition between the firms, and thus keep paddy prices low and their profits high. However, such agreements easily disintegrated, as a result, for example, of a lack of trust between the participating firms, or greed, or through the entry of a new firm offering a slightly higher price for paddy. Even so, over time the agreements appear to have become more robust. The most powerful, certainly the most notorious combination was the Bullinger Pool, formed in 1921 by four of the largest milling and exporting firms in Burma – Steel Brothers, Bulloch Brothers, Ellerman's Arakan Rice

---

[10] Couper, *Report of Inquiry into the Condition of Agricultural Tenants and Labourers*, pp. 4–5.

[11] Adas, *The Burma Delta*, p. 131.

[12] In many cases, prices had doubled or more. Couper, *Report of Inquiry into the Condition of Agricultural Tenants and Labourers*, pp. 7, 66. (The first column on p. 7 should presumably be 'March 1914', not 'March 1924'.)

[13] The following draws on Cheng Siok-Hwa, *The Rice Industry of Burma 1852–1940*. Kuala Lumpur: University of Malaya Press, 1968, pp. 64–8.

and Trading, and the Anglo-Burma Rice Co. As the Bullinger Pool accounted for a third and more of the rice milled for export, it was widely believed, certainly by nationalist opinion, to be depressing the price received by Burma's cultivators for their crop.[14]

And the third serious strain in the rice economy: borrowing by Burma's agriculturalists, short-term to finance the year's crop and to cover failures of income but also longer-term for investment, increased substantially in the first decades of the twentieth century. In fact, by the late 1920s, for many rice cultivators, the burden of debt-servicing and debt-repayment had become crippling. A government enquiry in 1929–30, the Burma Provincial Banking Enquiry, reported that at the close of the agricultural year, a mere 14 per cent of cultivators were clear of debt, had not been forced to sell their work-animals in settling their liabilities, and had sufficient paddy to take them through to the next harvest.[15] In contrast, 22 per cent had debts that were equivalent to half or more of the value of their land; and 11 per cent of cultivators had debts that exceeded the value of all their property. Among tenants cultivating rice, in an ordinary year, just one in four was in a position to pay the rent, clear all debts, and put aside enough paddy to feed the family through to the next harvest.

The impact of each of these four factors – the decline in the fertility of the land, the rising cost of cultivation, price-fixing on the part of major millers and exporters, and the rising burden of agricultural debt – was clearly to squeeze the cultivator's return, if not eliminate it entirely. The tenant and the labourer, the marginal owner-cultivator, but almost certainly many others too, now struggled to survive.

The most explosive issue for the colonial rice economy, and a central legacy for Burma on independence, was the dispossession of the Burmese rice cultivator of his land. As was noted in the previous chapter, 'the main object of the agricultural policy' of the British colonial administration in Burma in the final decades of the nineteenth century, in the words of J. S. Furnivall, was 'the creation of a body of

---

[14] The allegation that the Bullinger Pool was impoverishing the rice cultivator while enriching itself – and also other allegations, for example that it was driving small millers and traders out of business – is closely examined in Maria Serena I. Diokno, 'British firms and the economy of Burma, with special reference to the rice and teak industries, 1917–1937'. PhD, University of London, 1983, ch. 4.

[15] B. O. Binns, *Agricultural Economy in Burma*. Rangoon: Government Printing and Stationery, 1946, p. 40.

peasant proprietors', for it was widely held that 'cultivators would be more industrious and law-abiding if they owned the land they culti-vated'. And yet, again as noted earlier, in the first years of the twentieth century, fully one-tenth of agricultural land in the thirteen principal rice-growing districts of lower Burma was owned by 'non-resident non-agriculturists', in effect the Chettiar moneylender. In subsequent years, the situation deteriorated further. By the late 1920s, towards one-quarter of agricultural land in the principal rice-growing districts was owned by 'non-resident non-agriculturists'.[16] And tenancy levels soared. Between the mid-1900s and the end of the 1920s, the propor-tion of occupied land in the delta let to tenants at full rent rose from 30 per cent to almost 46 per cent.[17] At the same time there was con-siderable variation between districts, with the highest levels of tenancy occurring in the lower delta. Thus in Pyapon and Hanthawaddy, the proportion of the occupied land being worked by tenants was already above 50 per cent by the mid-1920s. In certain parts of those districts, the proportion was over 60 per cent, even 70 per cent.[18]

By the mid-1920s the Burma government was sufficiently concerned to assign Thomas Couper, a senior official with long experience in the province's land administration, to enquire into the condition of ten-ants and labourers in lower Burma, to discover whether 'the land is passing out of the hands of the agriculturists, what protection, if any, tenants have, whether landless men can get land and, if remedies are required, what those remedies should be'.[19] Couper's report, published in 1924, established clearly that the material condition and security of tenants and labourers in the rice districts had indeed deteriorated sharply: Couper's evidence and argument have in fact informed the discussion above. Burma's rice economy was facing a deepening crisis. But the response of Couper to that crisis – his proposed 'remedies' – was weak: and the weakness was very revealing. Among his ten chief recommendations were: 'the paddy measuring basket should be stan-dardized at nine gallons and...after five years the possession of baskets differing substantially from the standard should be a penal offence'; 'the imprisonment of an agriculturist for debt be abolished';

[16] Cheng, *The Rice Industry of Burma*, p. 145.
[17] Adas, *The Burma Delta*, p. 150.
[18] Couper, *Report of Inquiry into the Condition of Agricultural Tenants and Labourers*, p. 27.
[19] Ibid., p. 1.

'areas where rents are unfair should be notified and in these a landlord should not be permitted to replace one tenant by another so long as the tenant treats him fairly'.[20] This was merely tinkering. No remedy was proposed for a number of the major underlying failings that Couper himself had identified in his report, for example, the decline in the fertility of the land. Crucially, no remedy was proposed here for the most explosive failing, the dispossession of the Burmese rice cultivator of his land. However a brief, guarded reference was made to this issue in the Burma administration's initial response to Couper's report, in the Resolution by the Governor in Council published with it: 'whether the time has come to place any restriction on the transfers of land' is a question which calls 'for most anxious and careful consideration and on which the Government reserves its opinion'.[21]

But perhaps the colonial administration could do little. Its hands were tied. This is not simply a reference to the power of the interests opposed to legislation to prevent the alienation of agricultural land, the rice traders, millers, moneylenders, import merchants, and shipping lines, as well as officials concerned to secure the most rapid expansion of the government's revenue. It is also to suggest that by the 1920s, the colonial administration was almost instinctively tied to an economic tenet that had, it would certainly argue, created a prosperous Burma over the previous half century. No restrictions on the ownership of agricultural land had secured heavy Chettiar investment in the rice economy and thus an unparalleled expansion in rice acreage and exports. But that perspective had remained entrenched in the official mind even when that same economic tenet – no restriction on the ownership of agricultural land – had left the Burmese rice cultivator buried in debt and dispossessed of the land.

The 1930s depression

And then the 1930s world economic crisis hit Burma.[22] In the rice economy, the crisis was felt not in a fall in demand and contraction in

---

[20] Ibid., pp. 59–60. With respect to the final recommendation, defining 'unfair' and 'fairly' would surely be extremely difficult in practice.

[21] Resolution by the Governor in Council: T. Couper, *Report of Inquiry into the Condition of Agricultural Tenants and Labourers*. Rangoon: Central Press, 1966 (reprint), p. 3.

[22] This section draws on Brown, *A Colonial Economy in Crisis*.

Figure 2.1 Transplanting paddy in Pyapon in the early 1930s
Source: C. L. Lorimer photographs, Centre of South Asian Studies, University of Cambridge

production – indeed the volume of rice exports reached record levels in the first half of the 1930s, while the area under rice, after an initial dip, was maintained across the decade – but in a massive fall in price. In normal trading times, the final months of each calendar year would see the local price of rice slip back, as that year's crop reached the ports for shipment. But in the final months of 1930, it collapsed. Between August 1930 and February 1931, the price of Big Mills Specials at Rangoon fell over 40 per cent.[23] The rice price then continued to fall through the early 1930s, though with fluctuations within each year, reflecting the annual cultivation and trading cycle, and broken by the occasional short-lived recovery, reaching its lowest point of the depression years in early 1934, when the price for Small Mills Specials at Rangoon was barely one-third its mid-1930 level.[24]

From the final decades of the nineteenth century, cultivators across the great deltaic plain of the Irrawaddy and Sittang rivers had created an extreme dependence on the production of and trade in a single crop, rice. Vast resources of land, labour, and capital had been committed almost exclusively to the growing of that crop: and from the income earned by selling the surplus production, cultivators had been able to

[23] Brown, *A Colonial Economy in Crisis*, p. 116.   [24] Ibid., p. 41.

purchase all their other material needs, for clothing, shelter, food, and much else besides. Thus they had come to depend to an extraordinary degree on the market, on the world market for rice. It might therefore be anticipated that when the price of rice, and therefore the money income from the sale of the crop, collapsed from the final months of 1930, the rice cultivator's ability to meet his material needs from the market, to purchase clothing, shelter, food, cooking and lighting oil, pots, lamps, hoes, knives, also collapsed. Highly dependent on the market, Burma's rice cultivators, it would seem, would be cruelly exposed when it gave way. However, the reality was rather different, for as the price of rice collapsed, Burma's cultivators found or created a number of strategies to mitigate, to a degree, the threat to their material circumstances.

One action open to the rice cultivator to protect his money income as the price of rice collapsed was to increase the volume of paddy he put on the market. And indeed, as noted earlier, the volume of rice exports reached record levels in the first half of the 1930s. In more detail, Table 2.2 indicates that the annual average volume of exports of rice and paddy from Burma was towards one-fifth higher in the 1930s compared to the 1920s. A second defence for the cultivator was to repudiate the claims made by the landowner, moneylender, and tax collector against his income or against his production. Resistance was effected at different levels of intensity, from surreptitious evasion to violent confrontation, and it took many forms. Tenants secretly sold a major part of the recently harvested crop to a discreet, no-questions-asked trader, to mislead the landlord into thinking that the year's production, and therefore the rent due, was much smaller than was really the case. Or they just paid what they could afford, or said they could afford. In the same way, landowners, having borrowed heavily, repaid the Chettiar what they could afford, or said they could afford. Landowners also resisted, by petition but often more violently, demands for the payment of the land revenue. Or the colonial administration, recognizing reality, reduced the rate at which the revenue was levied and granted remissions and postponements. With the capitation tax too, the rural population defaulted on a substantial scale. And the colonial administration was more lenient.

The cultivator's third defence when the rice price collapsed was found in the subsistence economy. Even an overwhelming commitment of land, labour, and capital to the production of rice for the market could still leave the cultivator meeting a significant part of his material needs from his own resources or from the generosity of nature. Fish were taken from local streams and flooded fields, vegetables were cultivated and chickens raised on higher ground, and simple building material was at hand in nearby stands of bamboo. Perhaps the cultivator had used those resources only fitfully when the rice market had been strong. But when the market collapsed in the early 1930s, he could turn to subsistence more consistently, and in this way defend his material circumstances. Finally, the cultivator found protection in the depression years in a fall in the prices of articles of common consumption, including, notably, the local price of imported cotton piece-goods. In other words, the reduction in the cultivator's money income as the rice price collapsed was compensated, to a degree, by a fall in the cost of living.[25]

But there was no defensive action that could significantly mitigate, let alone prevent, the great wave of landowner loan defaults, then foreclosures and land seizures, that took place across the Burma delta during the depression. Two factors account for the scale of default and dispossession that occurred. The first was that by the late 1920s, for many rice cultivators the burden of debt-servicing and debt-repayment had already become crippling. As noted earlier, the Burma Provincial Banking Enquiry of 1929–30 reported that at the close of the agricultural year, 22 per cent of landowners had debts that were equivalent to half or more of the value of their land, and 11 per cent had debts that exceeded the value of all their property.[26] Clearly it would take only a modest reversal to tip these landowners into default, foreclosure, and dispossession. The second factor was the extent of the fall in the rice price. Again as noted earlier, at the lowest point of the depression, in early 1934, the price for Small Mills Specials at Rangoon was barely one-third its mid-1930 level. With Chettiar loans designated in rupees, and payment of interest and repayment of the principal made only in cash, the greater the fall in the rice price, and in the cultivator's money income, the greater the increase in the real burden of debt servicing and settlement. When the price of Big Mills Specials at Rangoon fell over 40 per cent between August 1930 and February 1931, the real burden of agricultural debt soared, and landowners defaulted and lost their

---

[25] For an assessment of the effectiveness of the rice cultivator's survival strategies in defending his material circumstances, see Brown, *A Colonial Economy in Crisis*, ch. 4.

[26] Binns, *Agricultural Economy in Burma*, p. 40.

land. In the late 1920s, towards one-quarter of agricultural land in the principal rice-growing districts had been owned by 'non-resident non-agriculturists', in effect the Chettiars. For the first half of the 1930s, the annual average proportion of the land owned by the 'non-resident non-agriculturist' had risen to 35 per cent. Towards the end of the decade, it was 42 per cent.[27] Between 1930 and 1937, almost 1.9 million acres in lower Burma passed into Chettiar hands.[28] Burma's cultivators had come to own less than half Burma's rice land.

As the long-gathering crisis in Burma's rice economy was brought to a head by the world economic depression in the first years of the 1930s, the social order came under severe strain. In early May 1930, Indian dock-labourers in Rangoon went on strike for improved wages.[29] Burmese labourers were brought in to break the strike, although, apparently, they were poorly suited to the work and the port rapidly became congested with ships waiting to clear their cargo. Towards the end of May, the Indian dock-labourers settled for a slight increase in wages, and as they returned to work, the Burmese strike-breakers were immediately dismissed. The situation was extremely tense, and when the returning Indian labourers jeered at the dismissed Burmese, it erupted into violence. For two days or more, Burmese mobs, reinforced by roughs from the districts who rushed into the capital, hunted down terrified Indians, most of whom sought to barricade themselves in their tenements, with some finding shelter in the Rangoon lunatic asylum. The police were overwhelmed and order was restored to Rangoon only when the British regiment then stationed in the capital, the Cameron Highlanders, was deployed. Contemporary reports suggested that between 300 and 500 had been killed, almost all Indians, and 1,000 or more injured, again mostly Indians. Then towards the end of the following month, on 24 June 1930, a riot broke out at the Rangoon Central Gaol – where an almost exclusively Indian staff administered

---

[27] Cheng, *The Rice Industry of Burma*, p. 145.

[28] Calculated from J. S. Furnivall, *Colonial Policy and Practice: a Comparative Study of Burma and Netherlands India*. New York University Press, 1956, p. 111.

[29] The following draws on Nalini Ranjan Chakravarti, *The Indian Minority in Burma: the Rise and Decline of an Immigrant Community*. London: Oxford University Press, 1971, pp. 132–3; John F. Cady, *A History of Modern Burma*. Ithaca, NY: Cornell University Press, 1958, p. 305. Maurice Collis, *Trials in Burma*. London: Faber and Faber, new edn, 1945, chs 5 and 6 provides an excellent first-hand account.

a prison population of roughly 2,000, the majority Burmese – that left 34 convicts dead or dying, mainly from gunshot wounds, and some 60 or more wounded.[30]

But by far the most severe fracture in colonial Burma's social order in this period occurred from the final days of that same year. On the night of 22 December 1930, rebels attacked villages in the south-west of Tharrawaddy District, seizing guns and, in two villages, killing the headman. In the days that followed, the rising spread to Insein District to the south, where again villages were attacked, headmen killed, and guns seized. There were also attacks on a railway station and on a military police post, assaults on police stations, an attempt to blow up a railway bridge, and the killing of several isolated British officials. On 31 December, a battalion of the Burma Rifles attacked the rebel head-quarters deep in Tharrawaddy. The rebels fled and their headquarters, a bamboo and thatch construction, was destroyed. But this action failed to check the rebellion and during the first half of 1931 there were serious disturbances across much of the delta and even, at one point, a rising in the Shan States to the north-east. The last major rising took place, in Pegu District, in late September 1931, although it took government forces, strengthened by two imported divisions, well into 1932 finally to restore order to the province. According to an official count, the number killed during the rebellion was 1,688, including 1,332 rebels. Over 1,300 rebels were captured, tried, convicted, and imprisoned. A further 126 went to the gallows, including the alleged leader of the rebellion, Hsaya San, captured north-east of Mandalay in August 1931, tried, convicted, and then hanged in the November.

The Hsaya San rebellion was the most serious armed challenge to British rule in Burma since the 1880s, and indeed one of the most serious rural risings to occur in South East Asia during the colonial period. The causes and character of the rebellion have been much explored, by contemporaries – a government report, *The Origin and Causes of the Burma Rebellion (1930–32)*, was published in 1934 – and in a now-substantial scholarly literature.[31] Hsaya San has been

---

[30] For an account and analysis of the riot, see James Warren, 'The Rangoon jail riot of 1930 and the prison administration of British Burma', *South East Asia Research*, 10, 1 (2002).

[31] The principal contributions include: James C. Scott, *The Moral Economy of the Peasant: Rebellion and Subsistence in Southeast Asia.* New Haven, CT: Yale University Press, 1976; Michael Adas, *Prophets of Rebellion: Millenarian*

understood, by British officials at the time, as an impostor, a plausible impostor, who preyed upon an ignorant, gullible, and superstitious peasantry; as a self-styled *Setkya-min*, a powerful ruler who, according to Burman tradition, would prepare the world for the restoration of the moral order; as a self-styled *minlaung*, the returning king; as a skilful political operator, building support and planning rebellion through modern nationalist organizations. The rebellion was the last gasp of traditional Burma: alternatively it was an early, rural, statement of modern Burmese nationalism.

However, the focus here is on the economic foundations of the rebellion, and specifically on the argument that the rebellion was a violent expression of the severe strains then being experienced within Burma's rice economy.[32] The weeks immediately preceding the outbreak of the rebellion in late December 1930 saw the initial, terrifying collapse in the price of rice, down over 40 per cent at Rangoon between August 1930 and February 1931. As the real burden of agricultural debt soared, landowners across the delta defaulted and lost their land, dropping down into the swelling ranks of tenant-cultivators or landless labourers, and driven to seek out a plot to rent, or manual work in what were now far harsher economic conditions. And if an owner survived that initial crisis and did not lose his land in the final weeks of 1930, he had every reason to fear that he soon would – the rice price was collapsing, he carried crushing debts, and Chettiar lending had been cut sharply. For decades the Burmese cultivator had been driven by the expectation and aspiration that with hard work and modest

Protest Movements against the European Colonial Order. Cambridge University Press, 1987; Parimal Ghosh, *Brave Men of the Hills: Resistance and Rebellion in Burma, 1825–1932*. London: C. Hurst, 2000; Patricia Herbert, *The Hsaya San Rebellion (1930–1932) Reappraised.* Clayton, Victoria: Monash University, Centre of Southeast Asian Studies, Working Paper 27, 1982; E. Sarkisyanz, *Buddhist Backgrounds of the Burmese Revolution.* The Hague: Martinus Nijhoff, 1965. And in an excellent study, Maitrii Aung-Thwin, *The Return of the Galon King: History, Law, and Rebellion in Colonial Burma.* Athens, OH: Ohio University Press, 2011, critically explores how the colonial reports relating to the rebellion, the foundation narrative for Scott, Adas, and Ghosh, indeed all earlier students of the rising, was constructed. See also Maitrii Aung-Thwin, 'Genealogy of a rebellion narrative: law, ethnology and culture in colonial Burma', *Journal of Southeast Asian Studies*, 34, 3 (October 2003), 393–419.

[32] This paragraph draws on Brown, *A Colonial Economy in Crisis*, ch. 5, where the argument is developed in substantial detail.

fortune he would rise from labourer to owner, even major landlord. That prospect had been weakening in the first decades of the twentieth century. It was finally destroyed by a terrifying collapse in the price of rice in the final weeks of 1930. Thus torn from his socio-economic moorings, Burma's rice cultivator turned to Hsaya San – impostor, returning king, political operator – and the prospect of a new order.

The previous chapter noted in passing J. S. Furnivall's description of the reclaiming of the delta by the Burmese agriculturalist in the second half of the nineteenth century as an 'epic of bravery and endurance'. It would now be appropriate to quote the passage in full.

Thus 'the epic of bravery and endurance' relating 'the greatest achievement in the history of Burma', the reclamation by Burmese enterprise of ten million acres of swamp and jungle, ends with a picture of imposing government offices and business houses in Rangoon, and gilded *chettyar* temples in Tanjore, while in the rice districts, the source of almost all this wealth, nearly half the land is owned by foreigners, and a landless people can show little for their labour but their debts, and, for about half the year, most of them are unable to find work or wages.[33]

Through the final decades of the nineteenth century, in that epic of bravery and endurance, the rural population of the Burma delta had committed itself to an extraordinary degree to the cultivation of rice for the international market. In so doing it had created a prosperous colonial Burma: and the delta population itself had shared in that prosperity, although not universally or consistently. And yet within just two or three generations, engagement with the international market had dispossessed the cultivator of his land, which was now in the hands of foreigners, and denied him work and wages. In brief, by the final full decade of British rule, the Burmese now had good reason to be wary of engagement with the market and with foreign economic interests.

Burmese beyond the rice field

Rice remained Burma's single most important industry through to that final full decade of colonial rule. Despite a closing land frontier, despite too the world depression, the area under rice in lower Burma increased without significant interruption through the first four decades of the

---

[33] Furnivall, *Colonial Policy and Practice*, p. 116.

twentieth century: in addition, as noted earlier, the volume of rice exports reached record levels in the first half of the 1930s, although of course the value of rice exports fell substantially during the depression years. That said, it is clear that by the 1930s, the rice industry, having almost alone created Burma's prosperous colonial economy in the late nineteenth century, was now badly stalled, its structures severely fractured. In the first place, the crop no longer overwhelmingly dominated Burma's exports. In the early years of the twentieth century, rice and paddy had accounted for around three-quarters of the total value of Burma's exports by sea. In the late 1930s, rice produced less than half of the province's total export income.[34] More seriously, as outlined immediately above, in the rice districts themselves, most labourers were living from hand to mouth, tenants had been reduced to a pitiable state, and landowners had, in their tens of thousands, lost their land. It was evident that the cultivation of rice for export would no longer sustain the Burmese, certainly not to the degree it had in the recent past. They would need to reach beyond the rice field.

But there were few such opportunities. As was established in some detail in the previous chapter, the modern economy of colonial Burma beyond the rice field was dominated by foreign interests. Among the large-scale enterprises of the modern economy, the rice millers-merchants, the shipping lines, the teak companies, banks, oil companies, there were none that were Burmese. Perhaps more importantly, there was relatively little Burmese employment in the modern enterprises brought to Burma by British rule. Indians dominated. The labour in the steam-powered rice mills at the ports, notably Rangoon, was overwhelmingly Indian; labour work on the docks at Rangoon was quite simply an Indian preserve; Burmah Oil recruited mainly Indians, notably so for its refineries; the deck and engine crews of the Irrawaddy Flotilla Company were from Chittagong, from across the Bay of Bengal. Of course there were exceptions, or partial exceptions. Again as noted in the previous chapter, there were in fact far more Burmese moneylenders than Indian, although since the Burmese generally worked on a much smaller scale, it is probable that the Chettiars, far fewer in number, accounted for the major part of lending to Burma's cultivators. In the same way, more than half the rice

---

[34] Calculated from J. Russell Andrus, *Burmese Economic Life*. Stanford University Press, 1948, p. 164.

mills in Burma in the early twentieth century were in fact owned by Burmese. But since the Burmese mills were generally small up-country concerns, it was the European-owned mills, comparatively few in number, which accounted for the largest share of milling capacity.

In the first decades of the twentieth century, the Burmese made inroads into a number of occupations with a heavy Indian presence. Perhaps most notably, at the beginning of the 1920s, Burmese accounted for 29 per cent of those employed in the province's oil refineries, compared to just 6 per cent (for Burmah Oil alone) less than a decade earlier.[35] Moreover, Burmese were prominent in many of the new concerns that were part of Burma's colonial modernity, including publishing and printing firms, film-making companies and cinemas, bus companies and taxi firms, and car-repair shops.[36] The number of cinemas in Burma, it might be noted, increased from 27 in 1921 to 137 in 1940. Burmese were prominent too in a number of the professions. At the beginning of the 1930s, well over 70 per cent of the lawyers in Burma were Burmese: and Burmese also accounted for around one-quarter of the doctors in the province practising Western medicine, and over three-quarters of the teachers (other than those teaching in religious institutions).[37] And finally, in this period Burmese made advances even in those government departments in which the Indians had long been deeply entrenched. In 1900 there had been just a single Burmese in the Public Works Department at executive or assistant engineer grade, out of a total of fifty-seven. In 1940 there were twenty-two Burmese at that grade, out of a total of 105.[38]

Nevertheless it is evident that the Burmese economic advance beyond the rice field in the final decades of British rule was extremely modest at best. To return to the Public Works Department, in 1900 and again in 1920, there were no Burmese at the level of superintending engineer or above: in 1940 there were just two, out of a total of thirteen. In 1940 there were no Burmese telegraph engineers in the Post and Telegraph Department, and just seven Burmese civil surgeons, out of a total

---

[35] T. A. B. Corley, *A History of the Burmah Oil Company 1886–1924*. London: Heinemann, 1983, p. 150. Burmese had long dominated employment in the oilfields.

[36] Aung Tun Thet, *Burmese Entrepreneurship: Creative Response in the Colonial Economy*. Stuttgart: Steiner Verlag Wiesbaden GmbH, 1989, pp. 97–9.

[37] Robert H. Taylor, *The State in Myanmar*. London: Hurst, 2009, pp. 139–40.

[38] Aye Hlaing, 'Trends of economic growth and income distribution in Burma, 1870–1940', *Journal of the Burma Research Society*, 47, 1 (June 1964), p. 133.

of fifty-one, in the Medical Department. And certainly, there were few opportunities for the vast numbers of Burmese labourers, tenants, and owner-cultivators struggling in the rice districts, or indeed for those cultivators who had already failed on the land. As was noted earlier, the Burmese who found work on the Rangoon docks in May 1930 were taken on then simply to break a strike by the long-established Indian dock-labourers, and were dismissed as soon as the Indians returned to work. Indian domination of the Rangoon labour market was barely dented. In Rangoon in 1931, 89 per cent of the unskilled and semi-skilled workers, and 70 per cent of traders and shop-assistants, were Indians.[39]

The creation of a substantial industrial sector beyond the process-ing of Burma's primary production for export – the rice mills, the oil refineries, the sawmills – but producing finished consumer articles for local consumption could have provided employment for Burmese beyond the rice field. But there was little progress in manufactur-ing in Burma in this period, principally because the economy was open to imports from the industrial world, including increasingly Japan, but also perhaps because a substantial part of the income of the well-paid foreign interests in Burma was remitted overseas rather than spent locally. At the end of the 1930s, manufacturing in Burma for local consumption was limited principally to the production of cement (the Burma Cement Company, a Steel Brothers subsidiary, met almost all Burma's needs and indeed exported to markets further east), rubber-soled canvas shoes and all-rubber shoes, matches, soap, beer, soda waters, and leather goods.[40] There were no cotton textile-weaving factories in Burma: there were, however, a few power looms installed in the prison at Insein and in other gaols. The total labour force in the manufacturing concerns listed was around 4,000 in 1940: for comparison, in the same year the rice mills alone employed over 40,000.[41]

The limited presence of the Burmese beyond the rice field, indeed their complete absence from major parts of the modern economy, was

[39] Ibid., p. 136, fn. 65.
[40] Details in Andrus, *Burmese Economic Life*, ch. 10.
[41] Calculated from Andrus, *Burmese Economic Life*, p. 142. The figures are for factory employment, a factory being defined as premises in which power was used in the production process and in which twenty or more were employed.

Figure 2.2 The Burmese, crowded out by the guests
Source: Thein Maung, *Immigration Problem of Burma*. Rangoon: New Burma Press, 1939

Taung-ka-chauk-lo, Myauk-ka-yu, Ah-lai-lu,
Ou-nai-haung-laung

Figure 2.3 As the Indians, Chinese, and British exploit Burma's wealth, the Burmese is left with an empty stomach
Source: Thein Maung, *Immigration Problem of Burma*. Rangoon: New Burma Press, 1939

a serious weakness in the economic but also the social and political structures of late colonial Burma. In the first place, and as suggested earlier, with the major sector of the economy in which Burmese labour and initiative was concentrated, the cultivation of rice, in serious crisis – the land frontier closing, labourers living from hand to mouth, tenants reduced to a pitiable state, and landowners losing their land – the absence of substantial alternative economic opportunities clearly threatened Burmese material circumstances and prospects. The fact that the alternatives were occupied by foreign interests – again, in Rangoon in 1931, 89 per cent of the unskilled and semi-skilled workers, and 70 per cent of traders and shop-assistants, were Indians – gave this failure in the economic structure its social and political dimensions. The Burmese-Indian riots in Rangoon in mid-1930 were just the first eruption.

But there are two further grounds on which the limited presence of the Burmese beyond the rice field can be seen as constituting a severe weakness in the economic, social, and political structures of late colonial Burma. Writing at the end of British rule, J. S. Furnivall observed that the Indian domination of colonial Burma's modern commercial and administrative structures 'erected a barrier between Burmans and the modern world that has never been broken down'.[42] The thrust of Furnivall's argument was that the barrier denied the Burmese an economic and administrative education, an education through hands-on experience in modern commercial and administrative practices. Even in the final decades of British rule, the Burmese remained on the periphery of Burma's modern commercial, industrial, and administrative world.

However, it is possible to see that barrier in a further way, as creating in Burmese minds the perception that the modern world was a foreign domain: and to the extent that foreign interests became wealthy through their domination of colonial Burma's modernity, while the Burmese became poorer, the perception of a firm association between the modern world as a foreign domain and Burmese impoverishment. In other words, it was not simply that under British rule the Burmese were denied engagement with the modern commercial and administrative world, but that the Burmese also became wary of that modernity. I will return later to this important argument.

---

[42] Furnivall, *Colonial Policy and Practice*, p. 46.

The limited presence of the Burmese beyond the rice field had one final damaging implication. If the foreign interests dominating colonial Burma's modern economy and administration were to leave, and specifically were the Indians to depart, it seems clear that the Burmese would have struggled to replace them, at least in some crucial occupations and at least immediately. Almost certainly Burmese would provide the workforce in the rice mills, the sawmills, and on the docks with relative ease, and Burmese moneylenders, small traders, and shopowners could take on businesses vacated by departing Indians. But denied economic and administrative experience, and too often denied advanced formal learning, there were too few Burmese to fill the more senior positions in Burma's commerce and administration. To return to the earlier figures for Burmese in senior positions in the government service in 1940: in the Public Works Department there were just two Burmese at the level of superintending engineer or above, out of a total of thirteen; there were no Burmese telegraph engineers in the Post and Telegraph Department; and there were just seven Burmese civil surgeons, out of a total of fifty-one, in the Medical Department. Were the remaining positions – the forty-four civil surgeon posts – then presumably held by Indians, to be vacated, there were few, perhaps no Burmese to fill them, certainly not immediately. This is not of course a comment on Burmese abilities. It is a comment on the near-exclusion of the Burmese from major parts of colonial Burma's modernity, and from opportunities to secure the education, training, and experience to run a modern economy and society.

India and Burma

In August 1917, the Secretary of State for India, Edwin Samuel Montagu, in a statement in the House of Commons, declared that the policy of the British government in India was 'that of the increasing association of Indians in every branch of the administration and the gradual development of self-governing institutions with a view to the progressive realization of responsible government in India'.[43] The Montagu-Chelmsford reforms – Lord Chelmsford was the then Viceroy of

---

[43] Quoted in John Leroy Christian, *Modern Burma: a Survey of Political and Economic Development*. Berkeley, CA: University of California Press, 1942, p. 60. This section draws on ibid., ch. 5, and Cady, *A History of Modern Burma*, Pt. 3, *passim*.

India – were incorporated in the Government of India Act of 1919. The Act provided for a dual structure of government (a so-called 'dyarchy') in the principal Indian provinces, in which specified responsibilities, for example for agriculture, health, and education, would be transferred to Indian ministers, answerable to the provincial legislative council. Burma was of course a major Indian province, but it was excluded from the provisions of the Government of India Act on the grounds that, in the words of the Montagu-Chelmsford proposals, 'Burma is not India. Its people belong to another race in another stage of political development, and its problems are altogether different.'[44]

That exclusion provoked strong protest in Burma. Students at the newly opened University of Rangoon and pupils at government and missionary schools went on strike, the newly formed General Council of Burmese Associations advocated non-cooperation with the government, political monks toured up-country districts demanding home rule and preaching violent revolution, and Burmese political delegations were despatched to Calcutta and London. Thus began the political retreat of the British from Burma that would end with Burma's independence on 4 January 1948 and, the interest here, the serious re-examination of Burma's position as a province of British India that would end, somewhat earlier, on 1 April 1937, with the separation of Burma from India.

Responding to that Burmese protest, the British government, in the Government of Burma Act of 1921, extended to Burma the dyarchy reforms earlier introduced for the other provinces of India. In Burma's new government structure, which came into effect on 1 January 1923, the transferred departments included education, public health, excise, and forests, and the Burmese ministers of those departments were responsible to a Legislative Council comprising 103 members, of whom eighty were elected. The Government of India Act had provided for a review of the new structures after a decade, and in 1927, earlier than initially anticipated, the Indian Statutory Commission led by Sir John Simon was appointed to undertake that review. After first visiting India, the Simon Commission reached Burma in January 1929. Of course Burmese political opinion urged the establishment of full responsible government in Burma. But – and the interest here – at this point it also urged the separation of Burma from India, principally in

---

[44] Quoted in Christian, *Modern Burma*, p. 61.

order to end unrestricted Indian immigration and to curb the dominant economic position of Indians in the province. And indeed the Simon Commission, reporting in June 1930, recommended immediate separation. 'As the Montagu-Chelmsford Report pointed out, "Burma is not India." Its inclusion in India is an historical accident . . . the opportunity should be taken to break a union which does not rest on common interests.'[45]

Burmese political opinion now swung against separation from India. An Anti-Separation League was established in July 1932, and at elections for the Legislative Council the following November, anti-separation candidates secured a clear majority. The fact that the British administration and British business in Burma now strongly supported separation had, it would seem, aroused Burmese suspicion that it was a colonial manoeuvre to prevent Burma's political advance: local British support, that alone, had been sufficient to arouse Burmese opposition.[46] But Burmese anti-separation opinion was also calculating that were Burma to remain a province of British India, it would be included in the more rapid political advances the British, it was assumed, were planning for India. In other words, the anti-separationists certainly did not seek permanent inclusion in India, but inclusion until Burma, having secured all the political advances, decided to secede. However the London government would not agree to Burma's right to withdraw from India at will and therefore pushed ahead – although the discussions leading to the final decision continued for almost three further years – with separation. The Government of Burma Act 1935, which came into effect on 1 April 1937, separated Burma from India. It also abolished Burma's dyarchy structure, replacing it with a cabinet of nine Burmese ministers responsible to an elected House of Representatives. Separated Burma was required to repay to India, in 45 annual instalments, an interest-bearing debt of over 500 million rupees, principally the value of the India-owned Burma Railways and the cost to the Indian government of the

[45] Quoted in ibid., p. 330.
[46] In fact British official and commercial opinion in Burma favoured separation principally because it was felt that in the existing structure, India was taking too large a share of Burma's revenues – a point to be considered shortly below – and therefore that separation would substantially improve Burma's public finances.

annexation of Burma in the nineteenth century.[47] Thus Burma was to pay for its own conquest. Moreover, for a minimum of three years after separation, that is until at least April 1940, Burma was not permitted to alter the tariff on its trade with India or to impose new restrictions on the migration of Indians to Burma. These separation provisions, clearly to the benefit of Indian but also British interests, caused considerable Burmese resentment.

The prominence and persistence in the nationalist politics of Burma during the 1920s and 1930s of the arguments for and against separation from India, undoubtedly reinforced Burmese hostility towards not simply India and the Indians in Burma but, more broadly, towards any external engagement and any foreign presence. The controversy drove home the undoubted fact that in important respects, India was exploiting Burma. For example, as was noted in the previous chapter, a substantial part of the revenue raised in Burma was remitted to the central government, the government of India, which then took responsibility for some areas of public expenditure in the province. From the late 1870s, these financial transfers were governed by a series of five-year Provincial Contracts (or Provincial Settlements). But the financial contract was such that, during the decades in which Burma was a province of British India, it paid over to the central government substantially more than it received in return. There was an imperial surplus, a provincial drain. Indeed, over time, the surplus – the drain – increased very considerably. In the mid-1890s, the imperial share of Burma's revenues was, on average, 34.3 million rupees each year, while each year, imperial expenditure in Burma was on average 18.8 million rupees, producing an annual average imperial revenue surplus of 15.5 million.[48] In the early 1930s, the imperial share of the Burma revenues was 105.4 million rupees, on average each year, imperial expenditure just 15.5 million rupees, producing an average annual imperial revenue surplus of no less than 89.9 million rupees. A former Burma official, G. E. Harvey, later explained the Indian perspective on this financial settlement: 'The unfortunate government of India, never knowing when it might not be faced with a famine or

---

[47] Cady, *A History of Modern Burma*, pp. 354–5.
[48] Maung Shein, Myint Myint Thant, and Tin Tin Sein, '"Provincial Contract System" of British Indian Empire, in relation to Burma – a case of fiscal exploitation', *Journal of the Burma Research Society*, 52, 2 (December 1969), p. 10.

a frontier outbreak, had to keep the provinces down to maintenance level and use their revenues for the central pool.'[49] Moreover, India could point out, Burma had 'never even covered the cost of one of [its] successive annexations before the next was upon us [that is upon the government of India]'. But Harvey also reported Burma's perspective: the province 'was being used [by India] as a milch cow'.

At the same time, those Burmese politicians urging separation from India, principally on the grounds that it would end unrestricted Indian immigration, often played strongly on popular hostility towards the Indian presence, notably during the 1932 election for the Legislative Council.[50] In the extremely difficult economic circumstances of those years, as Burmese and Indian labourers competed desperately for work and as the Chettiars foreclosed on tens of thousands of Burmese cultivators and took their land, the Indians were indeed vulnerable to such attacks. But it is possible that in different, less intense economic and political circumstances, a more nuanced understanding of the Indian presence in Burma might have been achieved. That alternative understanding would have recognized, for example, the crucial contribution long made by Indian labour and capital to Burma's rice economy, an economy that had provided many Burmese with substantial material opportunities, at least during the decades of expansion. But the fierce public arguments for and against separation, and indeed the sudden swings in nationalist opinion, left no room for that alternative perception. Rather, Burmese hostility towards the Indian presence, and by extension perhaps any foreign presence, was strongly reinforced.

The 1930s saw the beginning of the Indian retreat from Burma. During the previous half century, the number of Indians landing at Burma's ports had commonly far exceeded the numbers returning to India in all but two years.[51] But in the 1930s, departures exceeded arrivals in no less than four years – in 1930, 1931, 1933, and 1938. For example, in 1931, 252,000 landed at Rangoon from Indian ports

[49] G. E. Harvey, *British Rule in Burma 1824–1942*. London: Faber and Faber, 1946, pp. 57–8.

[50] Cady, *A History of Modern Burma*, p. 338.

[51] Cheng, *The Rice Industry of Burma*, pp. 262–3. Cheng's figures are for the total numbers landing at and embarking from Burma's ports, not specifically the Indian arrivals and departures. But as she notes, Indians, or rather working class Indians, constituted 'the great majority of passengers'.

but 285,000 embarked from Rangoon for India.[52] Undoubtedly the hostile speeches of Burmese politicians pressing for separation encouraged the Indians to leave in larger numbers. But that was just one of many factors behind the Indian retreat. Thus, for the first time under British rule, there were now serious violent clashes between Burmese and Indians. As was described earlier, the breaking of the Rangoon dock strike by casual Burmese labour in May 1930 and then the dismissal of the Burmese strike-breakers when the Indian dock-labourers returned to work, created a confrontation in which Burmese mobs, reinforced by roughs from the districts, hunted down terrified Indians across Rangoon, leaving hundreds dead and injured. Then the Hsaya San rising, which broke out at the end of that year, provoked numerous attacks by Burmese on Chettiars and on Indian landlords and labourers, notably in the lower delta.[53] An unknown number of Indians were killed and Indian shops, dwellings, and crops were destroyed. Tens of thousands fled to the relative safety of the delta towns, or headed for the ports and a passage back to India.

There was further serious Burmese-Indian violence in mid-1938.[54] The ostensible cause was the republication of a book by a Burmese Muslim critical of Buddhism. The book had attracted little attention when it had first been published in 1931. But when republished, it was seized upon by elements in the Burmese-language press eager to inflame public anger – by exploiting Burmese hostility towards the Indian presence – and thus cause trouble for their political opponents. On 26 July 1938, a protest meeting was held close to the Shwedagon pagoda, in the northern part of Rangoon. As the meeting broke up, the protesters, inflamed by fiery speeches from politically minded monks, moved towards the centre of the city and the main Indian commercial quarter. When the police attempted to halt the procession, violence erupted. Burmese rioters hunted down Indians, wounding and murdering substantial numbers, and attacked, looted, and set ablaze Indian properties. Reports of Indian police assaulting saffron-robed protesters, and rumours that monks, silently carrying their begging-bowls, had been attacked by Muslim Indians enraged the Burmese still

[52] Nalini Ranjan Chakravarti, *The Indian Minority in Burma: the Rise and Decline of an Immigrant Community*. London: Oxford University Press, 1971, p. 190.
[53] Adas, *Prophets of Rebellion*, p. 40.
[54] The following draws on Cady, *A History of Modern Burma*, pp. 393–8.

further. It was not until 1 August that some measure of order was restored in Rangoon, although violence again erupted in the city in early September, and it was not until the middle of the month that order there was fully restored. The violence also spread far beyond the capital, as far as Mandalay and Shwebo in the north. The official count of casualties included 192 Indians killed and 878 injured.

Not only had Burma become politically and physically hostile towards the Indians in the 1930s but it was now failing to offer the economic opportunities that had repeatedly brought them across the Bay of Bengal in their tens of thousands in earlier decades. Indian labourers may well have continued to dominate many unskilled occupations, notably in the rice mills and sawmills, and on the docks at Rangoon. But as is clear from the increasing employment of Burmese in the oil refineries, the breaking of the Rangoon dock strike by Burmese labourers in May 1930, and the increase in the number of Burmese cultivators, former tenants and landowners, looking for seasonal labouring work in the rice districts and beyond, the Indian labourer now faced competition. Indian officials, from the most menial ranks to the most senior, and Indian professionals were in the same position. As noted earlier, at the beginning of the 1930s, well over 70 per cent of the lawyers in Burma were Burmese; and Burmese also accounted for around one-quarter of the doctors in the province practising Western medicine, and over three-quarters of the teachers. In 1940 there were twenty-two Burmese in the Public Works Department at executive or assistant engineer grade, out of a total of 105. And as Burma advanced politically, from dyarchy in 1923 to separation in 1937, with Burmese increasingly taking on responsible political and administrative positions, the opportunities for Indians, at all levels, were certain to contract still further.

But among the Indians in Burma, it was perhaps the Chettiars who experienced the most marked change of fortune in the 1930s.[55] As outlined earlier, when the price of rice collapsed from late 1930, the real burden of agricultural debt soared and large numbers of landowners defaulted and lost their land. Consequently, between 1930 and 1937, almost 1.9 million acres in lower Burma passed into Chettiar hands. But the Chettiars never wished to own agricultural land, and certainly

---

[55] The following two paragraphs draw on Brown, *A Colonial Economy in Crisis*, ch. 3, particularly pp. 67–70.

not in Burma. Their business was to lend money. In earlier, prosperous times, the Chettiar who foreclosed on a failed loan would normally have found, with relatively little difficulty, some other cultivator or owner willing to purchase the tract from him. But with the depression in the rice trade, the market in land had collapsed, and now the Chettiar might find a buyer for a tract acquired through foreclosure only at a sharply reduced price. In other words, the sale value of the agricultural land reluctantly held by the Chettiars – over 2.4 million acres in lower Burma in 1937 – had fallen greatly, and was probably well below the total value of the loans, now failed, for which the land had acted as security.[56]

This was not the end of the Chettiars' difficulties. First, if at all possible, the Chettiar preferred to keep the landowner who threatened to default working his land rather than to foreclose. This was partly because, as just noted, the sale value of the land would be extremely low, almost certainly below the value of the loan. But in addition, were rice prices to recover, there was a possibility that the owner-debtor might in time settle at least part of the loan. If the Chettiar foreclosed, all prospect of settlement was lost. But then if the Chettiar decided not to foreclose but, in hope, kept the owner on the land, he was in effect committing himself to provide further loans to his client to continue cultivation. And thus, in attempting to salvage something from his debtor's impending failure, the Chettiar might be left with even greater losses.

Second, with land prices, and therefore the value of the security being offered, sharply depressed, presumably the level of lending was much reduced. In other words, the Chettiars had less business. And finally, during the depression years the Chettiars came under pressure from *their* creditors, notably the Imperial Bank of India and Lloyds, to reduce, reschedule, or even clear their advances and overdrafts. But faced with large-scale default by Burma's landowners, the Chettiars in turn struggled to clear their position with the banks. Even at the end of the 1930s, there remained a core of unsettled Chettiar accounts, at least with Lloyds. As a Lloyds manager noted in 1936, most Chettiar firms were eager to get out of Burma, and were held there only because 'all

---

[56] The 1937 figure is from Furnivall, *Colonial Policy and Practice*, p. 111. As noted immediately above, almost 1.9 million acres had been added since 1930.

their wealth [much reduced] is locked up in paddy lands'.[57] The 1930s crisis broke the Chettiars' interest in the rice delta, and in Burma.

Finally, the Indian retreat from Burma in the 1930s, perhaps as much a psychological as a physical retreat at that point, was further encouraged by the frequently hostile policies adopted by the Burmese-led administrations established after separation in April 1937. For example, the administration of Dr Ba Maw appointed a Land and Agriculture Committee, which included senior British and Burmese officials, to conduct a series of inquiries into certain key failings in Burma's rice economy, failings long discussed by earlier administrations but rarely, if ever, confronted.[58] These were tenancy conditions, the alienation of land, agricultural finance, and the regulation of moneylending. Legislation followed. The Tenancy Act 1939 sought to end the common landlord practice of granting leases of just a single year, and thus aimed to provide tenants with greater security of tenure. The Act also gave priority, when claims against the tenant's harvest were being settled, to the payment of labourer wages and the clearing of crop loans, ahead of payment of rent to the landlord. And it required a landlord to compensate a departing tenant for any improvements he had made to the holding during his tenancy. The Land Alienation Act 1941 provided that land owned by an agriculturalist could not, with very minor exceptions, be transferred to the possession of a non-agriculturalist, by sale, foreclosure, or in any other way. Neither Act was effective. The war broke out before the provisions of the Land Alienation Act could be brought into force. In any event, the Act did not extend to existing mortgages on agricultural land. Similarly, the implementation of a Land Purchase Act, under which the state would purchase land owned by non-agriculturalists, notably the Chettiars, for allocation to Burmese cultivators as tenants or owners, was interrupted by the outbreak of war. And the 1939 Tenancy Act was unworkable, principally because it was physically impossible for over-stretched district officers to carry out the many thousands of detailed investigations of tenant appeals the legislation required. But the threat to landlord and moneylending interests in these three measures – the thrust of the Burmese administration's thinking on the reform of the rice economy – would

---

[57] Brown, *A Colonial Economy in Crisis*, p. 70.
[58] The following draws on Cady, *A History of Modern Burma*, pp. 390–1, 404–7; Andrus, *Burmese Economic Life*, pp. 80–3.

have been perfectly clear to Indian lenders and owners of agricultural land.

At the same time, Indians working in the Burma administration would have been disturbed to hear calls from senior Burmese politicians for the complete Burmese-ization of the civil service.[59] In 1940, an official report recommended that, except for a number of technical positions for which no Burmese were then qualified, recruitment to government service should in future be restricted to individuals domiciled in Burma. And finally, in 1940, at the first opportunity provided under the terms of the 1937 separation, Burma's administration gave notice to the government of India of its wish to regulate Indian immigration.[60] A tentative agreement between the two governments was reached in mid-1941, but the outbreak of war intervened before it was fully ratified. The prospect of ratification 'aroused a storm of protest in India'.

It is important to emphasize that, despite the separation of Burma from India, despite too the worsening economic and social position of the Indians in Burma during the 1930s, India and the Indians remained a major presence. At the beginning of the 1940s, the Indian population of Burma was still above 900,000, indeed towards one million.[61] And Indians still accounted for just under half the population of Rangoon.[62] Thus Indian labourers, moneylenders, mill owners, merchants, traders, doctors, police, officials and administrators remained hugely important in the running of colonial Burma's modern economy, society, and administration. In addition, after separation, a number of the major institutions of British India continued to function in Burma. For example, British India's central bank, the Reserve Bank of India, established in 1935, continued as Burma's central bank after 1937.[63] It can be argued that this structure – one central bank, two countries – did not always serve Burma's interests well. Most importantly, the Reserve

---

[59] Cady, *A History of Modern Burma*, pp. 423–4.
[60] Nalini Ranjan Chakravarti, *The Indian Minority in Burma: the Rise and Decline of an Immigrant Community*. London: Oxford University Press, 1971, pp. 52–5; Cady, *A History of Modern Burma*, p. 423.
[61] Chakravarti, *The Indian Minority in Burma*, p. 15.
[62] Andrus, *Burmese Economic Life*, p. 34.
[63] The following draws on Sean Turnell, *Fiery Dragons: Banks, Moneylenders and Microfinance in Burma*. Copenhagen: NIAS Press, 2009, ch. 4; U Tun Wai, *Burma's Currency and Credit*. Calcutta: Orient Longmans, revd edn, 1962, ch. 9.

Bank of India, responsible for, in effect, a common currency circulating in two territories, was unable to control the supply of currency specifically in Burma. Moreover, both the reserves maintained by Burma's scheduled banks (the Reserve Bank of India, responsible for supervision of the banks, required them to hold minimum reserves) and the Burma government's accumulating reserves of Indian rupees (Burma ran consistent trade surpluses with India in this period) were held largely in India, the latter entirely in Government of India Treasury Bills and other Indian securities. This reflected in part the failure of the Reserve Bank of India to encourage the development of a local financial market in Burma. And of course, as these reserves were invested in India, the potential for investment in Burma was denied.

A second major British India institution that continued to function in Burma after separation was the army.[64] It is true that a British Burma Army was created on 1 April 1937, by transferring units of the Indian army to the command of the Governor of Burma. But the Indian army was still held in reserve for deployment in Burma during times of severe disorder, and throughout this period, regular British and Indian troops were always stationed in the country. Moreover, in the final years before the war, the military police, deployed in central Burma, remained an almost exclusively Indian force, under the command of British and Indian officers seconded from the Indian army. In addition, Indians accounted for almost three-quarters of the strength of the Burma Frontier Force, the remaining quarter being recruited from the frontier populations themselves.

India remained Burma's principal trading partner by far, taking some 60 per cent of the total value of Burma exports in the years immediately before the war.[65] The importance of India (and Ceylon) as a market for Burma rice had increased substantially through the first four decades of the twentieth century, to account for 59 per cent of the total volume of Burma's rice and paddy exports in the 1930s.[66] For comparison, in the same decade, just under 10 per cent was exported to South East

---

[64] The following draws on Robert H. Taylor, *The State in Myanmar*. London: Hurst, 2009, pp. 99–103; Mary P. Callahan, *Making Enemies: War and State Building in Burma*. Ithaca, NY: Cornell University Press, 2003, pp. 40–2.

[65] John Leroy Christian, *Modern Burma: a Survey of Political and Economic Development*. Berkeley: University of California Press, 1942, p. 126.

[66] Cheng Siok-Hwa, *The Rice Industry of Burma 1852–1940*. Kuala Lumpur: University of Malaya Press, 1968, p. 201.

Asia and a little under 6 per cent to China and Japan. In the last full year before the war, 1940–41, Burma exported over a million and a quarter tons of rice to India.[67] In addition, virtually all Burma's exports of kerosene and oil, and some three-quarters of its exports of teak were shipped to India. In the return direction, India's principal export to Burma in the years immediately before the war was cotton piece-goods and cotton yarn. But also important were jute gunny bags, wheat flour, cigarettes, coal, and iron and steel. As noted earlier, the balance of trade was strongly in Burma's favour. The trade had a powerful economic logic. As a contemporary observer noted, it was built on 'the remarkable capacity of each to supply what the other lacks'; and of course it was encouraged by geographical proximity, and therefore lower transportation costs.[68] But from a Burmese perspective, it also had two disadvantages. First, trade with India, and notably the trade in rice and textiles, was in Indian hands. In other words, it sustained the powerful presence of Indian merchants, traders, and shippers in Burma. And second, for Burma, India was by far its most important trading partner, taking 60 per cent of the total value of Burma exports in the years immediately before the war, as noted above. For India, however, Burma was of only modest significance, accounting for just 7 per cent of India's total trade.[69] Seen in those terms, India was clearly the more powerful partner.

India remained a major presence for one final reason. India was of course Britain's most valuable imperial possession, and consequently its defence was a critical imperial strategic concern. Burma, located on the eastern border of India, was inevitably drawn into that concern, indeed to the extent that the need to defend British India could, without exaggeration, change the course of Burma's history. In the recent past it had in fact done just that, for as noted in the previous chapter, Britain had annexed Burma in the nineteenth century – Burma had become a British possession – principally in order to secure the defence of India from the east.[70] British India first declared war on Burma, in 1824, in

---

[67] Andrus, *Burmese Economic Life*, pp. 188–89.
[68] Christian, *Modern Burma*, p. 126.
[69] Andrus, *Burmese Economic Life*, p. 187.
[70] The following provides the briefest summary of these complex events. For Burma in the nineteenth century see, for example, Thant Myint-U, *The Making of Modern Burma*. Cambridge University Press, 2001; and Cady, *A History of Modern Burma*.

response to Burmese advances into Assam and Manipur and threats to the security of eastern Bengal. And Britain declared war for a third and final time, in 1885, principally in response to fears of French influence in the remaining territory of independent Burma in the north, and the prospect that raised of a French presence on India's eastern border. In later decades, Burma may well have become a notably valuable British possession, 'one of the brightest jewels in the Imperial diadem of India'. But in the decisions to annex Burma, British eyes were not on that potential, certainly not in the 1820s, and in the 1880s only as a subsidiary ambition.[71] In broad terms, Burma was seized not because of what it was but because of where it was.

At the beginning of the 1940s, foreign conquest was again to change the course of Burma's history. And again, Burma was seized not because of what it was but because of where it was. In early 1942, Japanese forces entered Burma and within just a few months, destroyed the British presence. The Japanese had little interest in Burma itself. It did not possess in quantity or quality the resources critical to Japan's war-effort or, in the longer-term, to Japan's economic progress, notably high-grade petroleum, rubber, and tin. These were richly found in British Malaya and in the Netherlands East Indies, which, therefore, were the focus of Japan's territorial ambitions in South East Asia. In fact early Japanese planning for the war did not envisage the taking of Burma.[72] Burma was important to Japan only in that British forces deployed in the south and strongly reinforced from India would be able to attack the Japanese in the Malay Peninsula as they moved toward Singapore. In addition, the Nationalist Chinese were being supplied through Rangoon and then northwards on the Burma Road. But that supply route could be cut and the Japanese attack on British Malaya protected from the British to the west by just a limited campaign in Burma, simply the seizure of Tenasserim and its airfields and the port at Rangoon. This was Japan's initial objective. But subsequently, Japan became far more ambitious. Having destroyed the British in Burma in a matter of months, in time the Japanese turned to the invasion of India. The seizure of Assam, and specifically the destruction of the British base at Imphal, would launch a rising against the British in Bengal, led

---

[71] British commercial interests, notably in Rangoon, also pressed for the final annexation.

[72] Louis Allen, *Burma: the Longest War 1941–45*. London: J. M. Dent, 1984, pp. 6–7, 153–5.

by Subhas Chandra Bose. From there, rebellion would spread across India, and Britain would be taken out of the war. In attempting to realize this greater ambition, Burma was now critical to Japan. But, to re-emphasize the central argument, it was critical not because of what it was, but because of where it was. The course of Burma's history was being changed, once again, by foreign circumstances and ambitions that were of little or no concern to Burma itself.

It is important to add that the Japanese occupation of Burma between 1942 and 1945 changed the course of Burma's history not because it secured the end of British rule – the constitutional changes introduced in the 1920s and 1930s had made Burmese self-determination inevitable – although almost certainly it hastened the final British departure. Rather, the Japanese occupation was critical in that it determined Burma's political, economic, and social condition as the British finally left at the beginning of 1948. Put bluntly, at the end of the war and then as the British gathered to leave, Burma barely functioned.

3 | War and independence

War and the end of British rule

From the outbreak of war in South East Asia in early December 1941, it took the Japanese just six months to drive the British from Burma, although in truth, the British fate was settled long before the final end.[1] On 15 December, a week or so after the attack on Pearl Harbor, Japanese troops crossed the border from Siam and seized Burma's most southern town, Victoria Point, and, crucially, its airfield. From there, the Japanese put out of action the airfields to the north at Mergui and Tavoy, opening the way for the further advance of Japanese forces from the south-east and towards Rangoon. On 23 December, Rangoon was bombed from the air, causing considerable casualties – some 2,000 were killed in the attack and many injured – and extensive physical destruction. Thousands of Indians, the labourers, menials, traders, and shopkeepers without whom Rangoon could not function, fled the city. Two days later, on Christmas Day 1941, Rangoon was again bombed. Then, in mid-January 1942, the main Japanese force, accompanied by units of the newly formed Burma Independence Army, crossed the border from Siam from the south-east. The first major objective of the Japanese force, the port of Moulmein at the mouth of the Salween, fell on 31 January. And then in late February, the British Seventeenth Indian Division, falling back to a position to hold the advancing Japanese, was caught at the Sittang Bridge. When the order was given to destroy the bridge, to deny the crossing to the Japanese, ten of the division's twelve battalions were left on the wrong side of the river.

There was now little between the Japanese and Rangoon, or indeed little left in Rangoon itself. After the panic created by the bombing of

[1] This section draws principally on Maurice Collis, *Last and First in Burma (1941–1948)*. London: Faber and Faber, 1956. But see also the Burma sections of Christopher Bayly and Tim Harper, *Forgotten Armies: the Fall of British Asia, 1941–1945*. London: Allen Lane, 2004; and, for the military campaigns, Louis Allen, *Burma: the Longest War 1941–45*. London: J.M. Dent, 1984.

the city in late December, Rangoon had briefly returned to a measure of normality. But with the rapid advance of Japanese forces from the south-east from mid-January 1942, the departure of vast numbers of Rangoon's inhabitants, Burmese and European as well as Indian, resumed: 'day by day, as Rangoon emptied, there were less shops, less transport, less food brought in, less public services in general. The city was dying'.[2] With the destruction of the Sittang crossing on 23 February, the final, ordered, evacuation of Rangoon took place. The Governor of Burma, Sir Reginald Dorman-Smith, left on 1 March, the final personnel on 7 March. The last to leave were the demolition squads, some 600 British, Indian, and Anglo-Indian volunteers, who, as a final act, dynamited Rangoon's electricity-generating station, the port's loading cranes and warehouses, and the oil refineries at Syriam.

The colonial administration and the army, but also the vast numbers of civilians now made refugees, retreated northwards. The senior administration – Dorman-Smith, his ministers and ranking officials – was re-established at Maymyo, the hill-station north-east of Mandalay. But the Japanese forces too moved northwards, up the main road and railway towards colonial Burma's second city. In mid-April 1942, senior Burmah Oil field staff, acting on military orders, destroyed the installations at Yenangyaung and Chauk in central Burma to deny Burma's oil to the rapidly advancing Japanese. Earlier, on 3 April, Mandalay had been attacked from the air, for with the British eliminated from the skies, the Japanese could bomb almost at will. 'The railway station was destroyed, the hospital gutted and the fire brigade wiped out by a direct hit . . . fierce flames . . . devoured two-thirds of the town in a few hours.'[3] Mandalay's inhabitants fled. At the end of that month, Dorman-Smith and his senior officials left Maymyo for Myitkyina in the far north. And then, on 4 May, on a direct order from Churchill, Dorman-Smith left Myitkyina and Burma by air for Calcutta. In exile, the Governor, his counsellors, ministers, and officials, would establish an administration at Simla, the summer capital

---

[2] Collis, *Last and First in Burma*, p. 85. The population of Rangoon fell from roughly half a million to some 150,000 between late December 1941 and the end of February 1942: Robert H. Taylor, 'The legacies of World War II for Myanmar', in David Koh Wee Hock (ed.), *Legacies of World War II in South and East Asia*. Singapore: Institute of Southeast Asian Studies, 2007, p. 71, fn. 7.

[3] Collis, *Last and First in Burma*, p. 143.

of British India, to plan the reconstruction of Burma after the war. The planning at Simla required two assumptions: that the Japanese would lose the war and be expelled from Burma; and, perhaps a less secure assumption, that the Burmese would then accept a restoration of British colonial authority.

The rapid Japanese advance up through Burma after the fall of Rangoon at the beginning of March 1942 came to an end in the hills of the north-west. This was not because the advance met success-ful British resistance – 'out-manœuvred, outfought, and outgeneralled [*sic*]', the broken British forces were then making their way across the border to the relative security of Assam – but because the Japanese, having advanced so far so fast, were now over-stretched.[4] Moreover, the north-west hills and mountain forests formed a formidable barrier, virtually impassable during the monsoon, which had now broken. For the following two years, the British forces, having retreated to north-east India, reassembled, re-equipped, and now hugely reinforced, pre-pared to resist the anticipated further advance by the Japanese and, in time, to expel them from Burma. There were unsuccessful British offensives into Arakan in 1943 – at that time the military wisdom was that Burma would be retaken from the south, across the Bay of Bengal, for which air cover from Arakan was essential – but the deci-sive engagements began only in early 1944. Between March and July that year, at Imphal [Manipur] and at Kohima [Assam], the Japanese made a final attempt to break through into north-east India, or at least to destroy the ability of the British to retake Burma from that direc-tion. The Japanese failed and were broken. The British Fourteenth Army's re-invasion of Burma began in December 1944 and, although ferociously fought, was rapidly completed. The most severe fighting took place at Meiktila, south of Mandalay, in early March 1945, but then the road to Rangoon was effectively open. Rangoon was retaken by British seaborne forces at the beginning of May, although it took several more months to clear out the remaining Japanese resistance.

Burma's population suffered considerable material hardship, and of course on occasion faced lethal danger, during the war years.[5] With

---

[4] The damning characterization of the British military defeat is by Field Marshal the Viscount Slim, *Defeat into Victory*. London: Cassell, abridged edn, 1962, p. 92.
[5] The following draws on Paul H. Kratoska, 'The impact of the Second World War on commercial rice production in mainland South-East Asia'; and Aiko

respect to the most important sector in the modern economy, rice, the area under cultivation fell sharply, from almost 5 million hectares in 1941 to a little over 2.6 million in 1945.[6] This reduction in planted area, and therefore production, reflected in part the loss of Indian capital and labour, which had returned to India – a crucial departure, to be considered below – and the large-scale destruction of rice mills and port facilities. But in addition, the export of rice, which had accounted for well over half of Burma's production before the war, was also lost during these years. By far the most important pre-war market, India, was obviously closed to Japanese-occupied Burma, while the export of Burma's rice to other territories in South East Asia now also under Japanese control, notably Malaya and Singapore, was severely hindered by wartime disruption to shipping. Thus from the final months of 1943, steamer traffic between Burma and Malaya was completely eliminated by Allied bombing and submarine attacks, so that rice could now be transported on that coastal route only in sailing craft and small wooden boats. In short, little rice was exported from Burma during the war.

The loss of exports might suggest that during the war years there was more than sufficient rice for domestic requirements across the country. But this was not the case, partly because, as noted above, production fell sharply, to below the pre-war level of domestic consumption in the later years of the war, but also because severe disruption to rail and river transportation made it difficult to distribute rice within Burma to deficit areas. Thus the destruction of the Irrawaddy Flotilla Company fleet as the British retreated during the first half of 1942 made

---

Kurasawa, 'Transportation and rice distribution in South-East Asia during the Second World War': both in Paul H. Kratoska (ed.), *Food Supplies and the Japanese Occupation in South-East Asia*. Basingstoke: Macmillan, 1998. But it is interesting to note that in his account of these years, Burma's wartime leader, Ba Maw, claimed that 'On the whole . . . the peasant was not too badly hit by the war'. His core argument was that the departure of the Chettiars, who had 'fled to India along with the British', freed the cultivator from his two basic problems – not owning the land he worked, and 'never-ending indebtedness'. Ba Maw, *Breakthrough in Burma: Memoirs of a Revolution, 1939–1946*. New Haven, CT: Yale University Press, 1968, pp. 298–9. In other words, exploitation by foreign interests explained the dire circumstances of the cultivator – landless and indebted – and therefore the removal of those interests by the war had created 'the beginning of a new future for the Burmese peasant'.

[6] Kratoska, 'The impact of the Second World War on commercial rice production in mainland South-East Asia', p. 23.

it impossible to transport large consignments of rice north from the delta, leading to serious rice shortages in northern Burma. Finally, the disappearance of export markets during the war meant for Burma's rice cultivators a loss of cash income, and many, no longer able to earn a living from the land, moved into the towns to find work as labourers on military projects, or turned to banditry. And it might be added that in pre-war days, much of the cultivator's cash income had been spent on imports such as textiles, lamps, pots, pans, corrugated-iron, and soap. But those imports too were lost during the war, and that created still further material hardship.

The war left three major economic legacies. The first was vast physical destruction.[7] As noted earlier, in the final evacuation of Rangoon in early March 1942, the British put out of action the city's electricity-generating station, reduced the port's warehouses to ruins, dynamited the loading cranes on the docks, and blew up the oil refineries across the river at Syriam. Then in mid-April, Burmah Oil field staff, acting on military orders, destroyed the producing wells at Yenangyaung and Chauk to deny Burma's oil to the advancing Japanese. Three years later, the now-retreating Japanese carried out their own scorched earth operations but in addition, extensive damage was caused, particularly to Burma's transport structures, by Allied aerial bombing. By the end of the war, Burma's industrial facilities and economic infrastructure were shattered. Its oil producing and refining capacity was destroyed. The Burma railways lost 320 of its 354 locomotives, 7,000 of its 9,000 goods wagons, and almost all its 1,000 passenger coaches. Two hundred major bridges were damaged and over 300 miles of track and one million sleepers were torn up: the rest of the rail network received no maintenance during these years and was in an extremely poor condition by the end of the war. The Irrawaddy Flotilla Company's pre-war fleet, over 600 vessels, was almost completely lost. The Rangoon docks were in ruins.

The second major economic legacy of the war was the return to India of the majority of the Indians then in Burma – the labourers, traders, lenders, guards, police, doctors, orderlies, clerks, administrators, officials – in other words, the Indian capital, initiative, and labour that had been essential in the running of colonial Burma's modern economy and administration. As noted earlier, after Rangoon

---

[7] This paragraph is taken from Ian Brown, 'British firms and the end of empire in Burma', *Asian Affairs*, 40, 1 (March 2009), pp. 18–19.

Figure 3.1 An Indian woman on the Prome Road, early 1942
Source: Photograph Archive, Imperial War Museum © JAR 1249

was bombed on 23 December 1941, thousands of Indians, the labourers, menials, traders, and shopkeepers without whom the city could not function, fled. And in the weeks that followed, as the Japanese advanced, the Indians retreated in still greater numbers. Many left by sea, crammed onto all too few ships. But far more sought to escape

Figure 3.2 Indian refugees on the Rangoon-Prome road, early 1942
Source: Photograph Archive, Imperial War Museum © JAR 1231

over land, either through Arakan into Bengal or, in the north, along the Chindwin into Manipur or through the Hukawng valley into Assam. They walked. Conditions on the tracks through the forest-covered border ranges were appalling, particularly when the monsoon rains arrived from April, and it has been estimated that as many as 80,000 of those fleeing Burma for India may have died of disease, exhaustion, or malnutrition.[8] The Indian population of Burma in 1941 was put at 918,000.[9] By late 1942, some 600,000 had fled from Burma for India. And finally, by causing the colonial administration to collapse, the war hugely weakened the ability of the government to assess and collect the highly important land revenue, to tax the cultivator directly.[10] It was never subsequently revived.

---

[8] For a striking account of these tragic events, 'at the time the largest mass migration in history', see Bayly and Harper, *Forgotten Armies*, pp. 167–70, 181–90. The two estimates, of the number who fled from Burma to India and the number who perished, are from p. 167.

[9] Nalini Ranjan Chakravarti, *The Indian Minority in Burma: the Rise and Decline of an Immigrant Community*. London: Oxford University Press, 1971, p. 15.

[10] Robert H. Taylor, 'The legacies of World War II for Myanmar', in Hock (ed.), *Legacies of World War II in South and East Asia*, p. 64.

Figure 3.3 The Rangoon Docks in ruins, mid-1945

Source: Photograph Archive, Imperial War Museum © IWM C5356

The war in Burma also left major political legacies, which in turn had substantial economic implications. In essence, the war created circumstances in which Burmese nationalism became a far more powerful political and armed force.[11] Thus, on 1 August 1943, the Japanese military administration was formally dissolved and Burma was declared an independent state. Dr Ba Maw was both head of state (*Adipadi*) and prime minister, while Aung San was Minister of Defence, and U Nu, Minister for Foreign Affairs. That independence was hollow, in that effective, final authority clearly remained with the Japanese military. Nevertheless, those Burmese who served in that administration came to possess the symbolic prestige of power, and carried out duties and exercised responsibilities that, even if restricted, undoubtedly enhanced their experience and standing. In addition, under the Japanese, the Burmese built a substantial armed force, first the Burma Independence Army (BIA), an 'unwieldy, disorganized, decentralized collection of thousands of thugs, patriots, peasants, and politicians', and then, after the BIA was dissolved by the Japanese in July 1942, the Burma Defence Army (BDA), smaller, tightly organized, trained, professional, renamed the Burma National Army (BNA) in August 1943.[12]

There are two further points to be made with respect to Burma's wartime politics. First, those Burmese who worked with the Japanese did so with considerable calculation and increasing reservation, particularly when the independence allowed by the Japanese in 1943 turned out to be a sham. To varying degrees at various times, almost all Burma's wartime political leaders had contacts with the departed, but returning, British, and this included those working closely with the Japanese. In fact the ministers in the government of Ba Maw from 1943 were themselves prominent in the anti-Japanese resistance: and in late March 1945, with the Fourteenth Army on the road south

---

[11] For an account of Burma's politics in these extraordinary years, see John F. Cady, *A History of Modern Burma*. Ithaca, NY: Cornell University Press, 1958, chs 13 and 14: see also Collis, *Last and First in Burma*, in particular chs 21 and 22. And for an excellent analysis of Burma's wartime politics, see Robert H. Taylor, 'Burma in the Anti-Fascist War', in Alfred W. McCoy (ed.), *Southeast Asia under Japanese Occupation*. New Haven, CT: Yale University Southeast Asia Studies, 1980.

[12] The description of the Burma Independence Army is from Mary P. Callahan, *Making Enemies: War and State Building in Burma*. Ithaca, NY: Cornell University Press, 2003, p. 58.

towards Rangoon, Aung San led his forces, the Burma National Army, north out of the capital and turned them on the Japanese. Second, the war created or exacerbated divisions within Burmese politics and society, principally between those, notably the communists and many of the frontier peoples, who from the first fiercely opposed the Japanese and sought to work with the British and allied forces, and those who collaborated with the Japanese, although with the reservations and calculations noted immediately above. Those divisions ran deep.

On 17 May 1945, two weeks or so after Rangoon was retaken, the British government announced its policy on Burma's future.[13] A key passage ran:

Inevitably Burma's progress towards full self-government has been interrupted and set back by the Japanese invasion and the long interval of enemy occupation and active warfare in her territories, during which she has suffered grave damage not only in the form of material destruction but in a shattering of the foundations of her economic and social life. It is, of course, upon these foundations that a political structure rests, and until the foundations are once again firm the political institutions which were in operation before the Japanese invasion cannot be restored.[14]

In other words, the priority for the restored British colonial administration would be economic and social reconstruction, to be carried out not alongside a restoration of Burma's pre-war political institutions – Burmese ministers responsible to an elected legislature – but under the direct rule of the Governor, acting under article 139 of the 1935 Government of Burma Act. Moreover, only when that reconstruction was nearing completion would the restored British administration turn its attention to Burma's advance to self-government. The focus on economic reconstruction had a strong logic, for as the Secretary of State for Burma, L. S. Amery, had argued in 1943, 'it would be a mockery

---

[13] For an account of the circumstances that brought British rule in Burma to a close – covering the period May 1945 to January 1948 – see Cady, *A History of Modern Burma*, chs 15 and 16; Collis, *Last and First in Burma*, chs 28–31; and Hugh Tinker, 'Burma's struggle for independence: the transfer of power thesis re-examined', *Modern Asian Studies*, 20, 3 (1986). Note too, Hugh Tinker (ed.), *Burma: the Struggle for Independence 1944–1948*. London: HMSO, 1983, 1984, an invaluable, two-volume collection of documents from British official and private sources on the end of British rule.

[14] 'Statement by the Secretary of State for Burma in the House of Commons, 17 May 1945', in Tinker (ed.), *Burma: the Struggle for Independence*, vol. 1, p. 262.

to hand over the country in a ruined condition to Burmans for self-government . . . as soon as we have re-occupied it'.[15] There was also a moral consideration, stated by Sir Reginald Dorman-Smith as early as 1942: Britain had a 'responsibility to rehabilitate the life of [a] country which has been destroyed owing to our inability to defend her'.[16] In other words, in 1941–2, the government of Burma, his administration, had failed in its most basic function, that is to protect the territory and its people against external attack. It must now make amends.

But the Burmese would accept neither direct rule by the Governor, certainly not for the several years it would take to complete Burma's economic reconstruction, nor the postponement of self-government to an unspecified but distant future. Rather they sought a rapid end to British rule. Moreover they were suspicious of the reconstruction being envisaged by the British, not least because planning and implementation would closely involve the British firms that had been so prominent in Burma's economy before the war. British and Indian interests would return to Burma: the pre-war colonial economy would be re-established. This the Burmese would not accept.

Burmese opposition to the British plans for post-war Burma was mobilized through the Anti-Fascist People's Freedom League, initially formed in the early 1940s in the resistance to the Japanese. By the time Dorman-Smith returned to Rangoon, as Governor in a restored civilian administration, in mid-October 1945, the AFPFL coalition included representatives of almost every political group in Burma and, in its fierce opposition to the British, possessed a substantial measure of internal cohesion. And crucially, it had the capacity to use its mass following to create disorder on a devastating scale. Thus when a new Governor, Sir Hubert Rance, reached Rangoon in August 1946 – Dorman-Smith had been withdrawn by London the previous May – he was almost immediately faced with a strike by the police, followed by postal workers, then all government employees, workers in the oil-fields, and railway staff. He faced, in effect, a general strike. Moreover,

---

[15] '"Policy in Burma": Memorandum by the Secretary of State for Burma, 29 March 1943', in Tinker (ed.), *Burma: the Struggle for Independence*, vol. 1, p. 15.

[16] 'Memorandum by the Governor of Burma, enclosed with "Policy in regard to reconstruction in Burma after re-occupation": Memorandum by the Secretary of State for Burma, 7 August 1942', in Tinker (ed.), *Burma: the Struggle for Independence*, vol. 1, p. 3.

it was clear beyond doubt that the AFPFL, if thwarted, had the political and armed strength to unleash a national rising. Perhaps more
tellingly, it was also evident that the British did not have the military
force to suppress a Burma-wide rebellion. Post-war demobilization in
Britain and the substantial commitments of the British army elsewhere
in the world meant that there could be few additional British troops
for Burma.[17] More importantly, the tense state of Indian politics on
the eve of independence made the use of Indian troops to put down a
nationalist rising in Burma simply inconceivable. The colonial administration – Britain – no longer commanded events in Burma.

In January 1947, Aung San led a Burmese delegation to London
to negotiate terms for Burma's independence. Agreement was swiftly
reached, and on 4 January 1948, Burma became an independent state,
several years earlier than the British had planned and without the
reconstruction of the economy they had first intended. Aung San did
not see Burma's freedom. On 19 July 1947, almost five months earlier,
Aung San and a number of his ministerial colleagues had been assassinated at the instigation of a political rival, U Saw.[18] Aung San was
32 when he died.

Independence: the dismantling of the colonial economy

Burma's new government, an AFPFL administration led by U Nu,
faced horrendous difficulties. Within a matter of weeks, its very survival was being threatened by a communist insurrection – and later
by an ethnic insurrection too – its position made more critical still

---

[17] Hugh Tinker, 'The contraction of empire in Asia, 1945–48: the military
dimension', *Journal of Imperial and Commonwealth History*, 16, 2 (January
1988). For a very different and highly detailed assessment of British military
strength, see John H. McEnery, *Epilogue in Burma 1945–1948: the Military
Dimensions of British Withdrawal*. Bangkok: White Lotus, 2000. I have
argued elsewhere that a further important influence on the British decision to
end its rule was the fact that, principally because of Indian independence,
Britain no longer had significant strategic economic interests in Burma: Ian
Brown, 'The economics of decolonization in Burma', in Toyin Falola and
Emily Brownell (eds), *Africa, Empire and Globalization: Essays in Honor of
A.G. Hopkins*. Durham, NC: Carolina Academic Press, 2011.

[18] It has been argued that there may well have been British involvement, by rogue
individuals, in planning the assassination: see Kin Oung, *Who Killed Aung
San?* Bangkok: White Lotus, 1993.

by desertions from the armed forces to the rebels.[19] The communists had been expelled from the AFPFL in October 1946, and had then incessantly opposed the terms being negotiated by Aung San and the League with the departing British. Thus when independence came in January 1948, the communists had no place in government, despite the fact that, mobilizing rural support and sustaining nationalist fervour, they had been perhaps the most visible political force in Burma in the three years since the end of the war and the return of British rule. Excluded from power, from early 1948 the communists therefore sought to bring down the new government. In late March, the authorities responded by moving to arrest the communist leaders. But the party leadership was tipped-off by sympathizers in the administration, and went underground. By mid-April, the threatened communist insurrection had begun, with attacks on police stations and the sabotaging of railway bridges and telegraph communications across the delta. In facing this severe threat, the government could not trust its own forces. The police were unreliable, while substantial sections of the volunteer units, the People's Volunteer Organization (PVO), and indeed the army itself, actively sided with the communists. In August 1948, a unit of the Burma Rifles, ordered into action against the communists in Hwambi, deserted and sought, with local communist rebels and militia, to establish a popular-front administration in that district.

This same period, the first year of independence, also saw growing hostility towards the government in Rangoon on the part of the Karen. The hostility was long-standing but had been exacerbated during the war, and was now being fuelled in part by concern that Karen units in the army were bearing the brunt of the fighting against the communists. In November 1948, the Karen National Union presented Rangoon with a formal demand for the creation of an independent Karen state that would include in part the Tenasserim and Irrawaddy divisions. For Rangoon, it was an impossible demand. The Karen rebellion began in late January 1949, with risings first at Bassein and then at Toungoo and Insein, just north of the capital. Most of the Karen regiments in Burma's army defected to the rebels.

The insurrections and desertions of 1948 and 1949 came very close to destroying the U Nu government, and perhaps the Union of Burma

---

[19] For an account of the causes and course of the insurrections, see Cady, *A History of Modern Burma*, ch. 17; and Christopher Bayly and Tim Harper, *Forgotten Wars: the End of Britain's Asian Empire*. London: Allen Lane, 2007, chs 9 and 11 *passim*.

itself. Perhaps most striking, during these years, Burma's government was left with little territory under its control outside the cities of Rangoon and Mandalay. The delta rice districts, the oilfields to the north, and the mining and forest areas were in rebel hands: and crucially, river, road, and rail communications were constantly vulnerable to rebel attack. That the U Nu government nevertheless survived was due in part to the failure of its various opponents to work together to bring it down, and the fact that, in holding Rangoon, it had access to external military and diplomatic support and control over the income from the export of rice, although this was much reduced.

The insurrections had substantial economic consequences. First they hit the government's finances, presumably in requiring increased expenditure on the army and the police, but certainly in causing a collapse in major revenues, for clearly Rangoon could not collect taxes in districts it no longer controlled. In 1948, the land revenue almost completely disappeared.[20] The result was a substantial budget deficit that was covered by transferring funds accumulated for development to the revenue side. Second, the insurrections hit hard Burma's export industries, which were already struggling to recover from the severe disruption of the war years. The oilfields of Burmah Oil at Yenangyaung and Chauk were occupied by units of the PVO, the People's Volunteer Organization.[21] The company found it possible to continue production only at Chauk, and even there only on a much reduced scale. In each year immediately before the war, Burma had produced around seven million barrels of crude oil.[22] In 1948, it produced just 317,000 barrels, and in 1949, even less. The mining districts in Karenni and Tenasserim were also occupied by rebel forces, and the European staff was hastily withdrawn. From 1949 to 1951, the 'industry was all but dead'.[23] Forest operations – girdling, felling, and the hauling out of the timber – were also brought to a halt, while the floating of logs down to Rangoon and Moulmein ceased completely because of rebel attacks.[24] In 1938–9, 453,000 cubic tons of teak had been extracted

[20] Hugh Tinker, *The Union of Burma: a Study of the First Years of Independence*, 4th edn. London: Oxford University Press, 1967, p. 96.
[21] Ibid., pp. 289–90.
[22] T. A. B. Corley, *A History of the Burmah Oil Company, Volume II: 1924–1966*. London: Heinemann, 1988, pp. 396–97.
[23] Tinker, *The Union of Burma*, p. 290.   [24] Ibid., pp. 247–8, 257.

from Burma's forests but in 1949–50, just 38,000 cubic tons.[25] And finally, the insurrections further disrupted the cultivation and internal movement of Burma's principal crop and export, rice, at a time when the cultivated area and exports were already far short of pre-war levels. Frequently forced to pay tribute to rebel forces or to the more lawless elements on the government side, farmers simply abandoned their fields, while it was reported in 1948 that 300,000 tons of rice had been left lying in up-country warehouses because transport to the ports was either unsafe or non-existent.[26] In the years immediately before the war, just over five million hectares had been planted with rice. In the late 1940s, that figure fell to well under four million hectares.[27] Before the war, Burma had exported close to three million tons of rice each year. In 1950, it exported 1.184 million tons.

Burma's new government faced two further major difficulties on the economy. The first was that, three years after the end of the war, reconstruction of the country's transport infrastructure and industrial capacity was far from complete. Some progress had been made. High priority had understandably been given to the Rangoon docks, in ruins at the end of the war.[28] The river approaches had been swept clear of mines, military pontoons towed into place, and some two and a half miles of Nissen huts erected to replace, temporarily, the warehouses destroyed by wartime bombing. Even so, by 1947, the port was handling just 40 per cent of its pre-war tonnage. Burma's railways, similarly in ruins at the end of the war, made a fuller recovery in the final two years of British rule. By 1947, 1,800 miles had been reopened to traffic (there had been 2,060 miles of track before the war) and most of the locomotives, carriages, and goods wagons destroyed during the war had been replaced from the Indian railways. Much of the fleet of the Irrawaddy Flotilla Company had also been replaced, or wrecks salvaged, and pre-war services had been restored. But in contrast, the oil refinery at Syriam remained a charred wreck: reconstruction of the site would not begin until 1954. Moreover, in 1948, just 510

---

[25] Louis J. Walinsky, *Economic Development in Burma 1951–1960*. New York: The Twentieth Century Fund, 1962, pp. 660–1. [A cubic ton was a standard volume measurement used for timber in the British Empire and was the rough equivalent of 1.8 cubic metres.]

[26] Tinker, *The Union of Burma*, pp. 229, 257.

[27] Teruko Saito and Lee Kin Kiong (comp.), *Statistics on the Burmese Economy: the 19th and 20th Centuries*. Singapore: Institute of Southeast Asian Studies, 1999, p. 81.

[28] Tinker, *The Union of Burma*, pp. 286–7, 290, 301.

establishments were registered under the Factories Act, half the pre-war figure, reflecting in large part the reluctance of foreign capital, particularly Indian capital, to return to Burma. But whatever had been achieved in the reconstruction of Burma's transport infrastructure in the final two years of British rule was then brought to a halt, and even lost, during the insurrections:

For over two years no trains ran farther than ten miles outside Rangoon; about twelve miles of track north of Pyinmana were taken up, and here the main line from Rangoon to Mandalay and Myitkyina completely ceased to exist. Between Rangoon and Mandalay every station except that at Pegu was burned down, almost every bridge was dynamited, [and] the signalling system was wrecked beyond repair.[29]

The final major difficulty faced by Burma's new government with respect to the economy was perhaps less immediately visible but still highly potent. On independence in 1948, there were far too few Burmese with the training, skills, and experience necessary to run effectively a modern economy, society, and government administration. There were far too few Burmese commercial managers, engineers, doctors, higher-grade civil servants, senior police, traders, merchants, statisticians, accountants, contractors, a far too thin cadre of Burmese specialist professionals.[30] This acute manpower crisis was a colonial legacy, for, as emphasized in earlier chapters, in the decades of British rule, Burma's modern economy, society, and administration had been run principally by the British themselves together with the Indians, the Burmese being largely excluded from those responsible positions and thus denied sufficient opportunity to acquire specialist training and experience. But the crisis at independence was perhaps made worse by the understandable Burmese hostility to the return of foreign commercial interests and the continued employment of senior British and Indian officials, for their temporary retention could have provided a belated opportunity to bring on their Burmese successors. It is interesting to note that both India and Pakistan, independent from 1947, retained British officials 'if there were no suitable nationals to

---

[29] Ibid., p. 287.
[30] This observation was strongly emphasized by J. S. Furnivall, when Adviser on National Planning in the 1950s: J. S. Furnivall, *An Introduction to the Political Economy of Burma*, 3rd edn. Rangoon: Peoples' Literature Committee and House, 1957, Preface.

fill specific appointments'.[31] In contrast, independent Burma dismissed immediately all its British and Indian officials.

In view of the huge difficulties confronting Burma's new government with respect to the economy – a still-damaged transport infrastructure, an industrial sector still largely in ruins, far too few trained and experienced Burmese to run a modern economy, society and administration, and then the insurrections – it is striking that, from the new government's very first months, it sought nothing less than to dismantle the colonial economy. That the U Nu administration was so highly ambitious in such difficult circumstances can be seen as a measure of the ferocity with which the Burmese rejected the colonial economic legacy. But in that case, the new government's ambition is perhaps less surprising. For were the beleaguered U Nu administration to overturn the colonial economic legacy, or indeed simply attempt to do so, it would outflank its political rivals, the communists, and secure its position.

The attempt by the U Nu government to dismantle the colonial economy had two broad components. The first involved removing foreign interests from important economic and commercial positions. One major measure here was the Land Nationalization Act, introduced in October 1948, under which the government resumed ownership of all agricultural land then owned by non-agriculturalists, all land owned by agriculturalists in excess of 50 acres, and land then being worked by tenant cultivators in excess of a certain area.[32] The first category – land owned by non-agriculturalists – of course included the holdings owned, or at least claimed, by the Chettiars. As described in the previous chapter, during the 1930s depression there had been a huge increase in Chettiar holdings of rice land, as cultivators had defaulted on their loans and forced foreclosure. Between 1930 and 1937, almost 1.9 million acres in lower Burma had passed into Chettiar hands. But then most Chettiars fled Burma for India in late 1941 and early 1942. Many attempted to return after the war. But with former tenants having by now occupied their holdings for a number of years, ferociously supported by the AFPFL, initially in its struggle with the British and

---

[31] Tinker, *The Union of Burma*, pp. 152–3.
[32] The following draws on Maung Myint, 'Agriculture in Burmese economic development'. PhD, University of California, Berkeley, 1966, pp. 166–74; Tinker, *The Union of Burma*, pp. 95–6, 228–9, 238–45; David I. Steinberg, *Burma's Road toward Development: Growth and Ideology under Military Rule*. Boulder, CO: Westview Press, 1981, pp. 125–6.

then in government, many Chettiar landlords now cut their losses, took whatever little they could, and returned finally to India. Those who remained, much diminished in number, 'were left holding . . . now worthless title-deeds'. In brief, the once mighty Chettiar position in the Burma delta was now clearly lost, indeed had been effectively lost from the moment the Chettiars had fled Burma in the early 1940s. In that case, the Land Nationalization Act 1948 simply put the expulsion of the Chettiars beyond any possible doubt.[33]

The agricultural land being returned to government ownership – not only the land previously owned by non-agriculturalists, notably the Chettiars, but also the land owned by Burmese agriculturalists in excess of 50 acres and the land being worked by tenant cultivators above a certain area – was then to be distributed to deserving cultivators, that is the owners of small plots, tenants on holdings seen as being too small to be worked efficiently, and, lastly, landless labourers. Those receiving land were required to form mutual aid teams, to cooperate in cultivation, borrowing, and marketing. In time, according to the government, the mutual aid teams would evolve into producers' cooperatives, which in turn would evolve into collective farms: 'a complete revolution in Burmese agriculture would [thus] be accomplished'.[34]

The implementation of the U Nu administration's land redistribution programme was highly troubled. The Land Nationalization Act 1948 had been hastily constructed in order to outflank the communists and secure rural support for the government. In fact it was put into operation only in Syriam township, and even there only on a limited scale. A subsequent Land Nationalization Act, in 1953, was much more carefully drafted and considerably more detailed in its provisions. But implementation was severely disrupted by the communist insurrection and the continuing lack of security across much of rural Burma well into the 1950s, and also by the fact that there were far too few officials on the ground with the training, experience, political judgement, and indeed the honesty that were undoubtedly required.

---

[33] There remains the question of compensation. The 1948 Act included no basis for calculating compensation for land forcibly expropriated. A subsequent Land Nationalization Act, in 1953, established a schedule of compensation. But it would appear that the government made no provision in its accounts for the payment of compensation. 'A silent decision seems to have been taken . . . to expropriate the land without payment': Tinker, *The Union of Burma*, p. 245.

[34] Tinker, *The Union of Burma*, p. 241.

The government's aim was to redistribute ten million acres by the end of 1955. In fact as late as 1958, a total of just 1.4 million acres had been redistributed.[35] But even where land redistribution did take place, the gains were not always clear. For example, the redistribution did not involve, as apparently had been originally intended, a fresh survey of the land itself. It was merely an office transaction, involving the redrawing of lines on probably out-of-date maps, and thus in terms of new rights, the cultivator acquired little more than a piece of paper, a certificate. More importantly, the redistribution appears to have done little to encourage Burma's agriculture to become more productive and progressive. By expropriating land where the agriculturalist held in excess of 50 acres, the reform discouraged the growth of large-scale, potentially more efficient, farming; the holdings created by redistribution were commonly too small or too fragmented; and the hoped-for mutual aid teams and cooperatives remained only on paper. In short, there was no revolution in Burmese agriculture. In the words of a near-contemporary observer, the land nationalization programme appears to have been directed less 'at establishing a sound agrarian base for a prosperous agriculture' than 'at correcting alleged injustices arising out of the colonial pattern of development', that is, putting an end to landlordism and in particular to the Chettiar landlord.[36]

The removal of foreign interests from other important positions in Burma's economy can be considered more briefly. At the end of the war in mid-1945, the export trade in rice was not restored to the British and Indian firms, Steel Brothers, the Anglo-Burma Rice Company, Bulloch Brothers, that had dominated it before the war. This was a period of rice shortages. Therefore the British Military Administration, Burma's government from the end of the war through to the restoration of civilian rule in October 1945, established an Agricultural Projects Board, responsible for the procurement, assembling, and export of rice.[37] In this period, Burma's entire rice for export was sold to Britain's Ministry of Food, which then resold it to the various deficit countries

[35] Ibid., pp. 240–1; Maung Myint, 'Agriculture in Burmese economic development', p. 171.
[36] Maung Myint, 'Agriculture in Burmese economic development', p. 171.
[37] This section draws principally on Maung Myint, 'Agriculture in Burmese economic development', pp. 125–59; and Myat Thein, *Economic Development of Myanmar*. Singapore: Institute of Southeast Asian Studies, 2004, pp. 28, 33, 36.

in line with allocations made by the International Emergency Food Council. In 1947, the Agricultural Projects Board was superseded by the State Agricultural Marketing Board, the SAMB. The SAMB had a statutory monopoly in the export of rice. It bought paddy from the cultivators, either directly or through middlemen, and rice from the millers, in both cases at prices fixed by official decree. Export sales were secured either through inter-government agreements or through private traders, Burmese of course, under a tender system in which each sale was subject to the Board's approval. In 1955, just under one-third of rice exports was through private traders, and in the late 1950s, around one-tenth.[38]

But the State Agricultural Marketing Board was intended to achieve more than just the elimination of foreign interests from the rice export trade. From the late 1940s through to the beginning of the 1960s, the price at which the State Agricultural Marketing Board bought paddy from the cultivator was kept unchanged. Moreover, it was held at substantially below the export price. This achieved two important objectives. Low and stable domestic rice prices clearly benefited the Burmese consumer, and in particular the urban populations. And second, the considerable difference between the purchase price and export price secured for the SAMB, in effect the government, a very substantial income. Indeed, in the nine years from 1947/48 to 1955/56, SAMB transfers to the government accounted for, on average, 41 per cent of total government revenue receipts.[39] This proportion had fallen to 14 per cent in 1959/60, reflecting in part a decline in the international rice price in the second half of the decade. In other words, the State Agricultural Marketing Board was the instrument by which the cultivation of rice was taxed – the government extracted a surplus from the rice economy – and in this it replaced the land revenue, a major revenue line in the pre-war colonial budget but which, with the lack of security in the rice districts, had dwindled into insignificance in the 1950s. However, the fact that under the SAMB regime the cultivator received a low, undifferentiated, and unchanged price for his crop clearly discouraged growth and improvement in the rice economy in the 1950s. This important point will be taken up later in the chapter.

---

[38] Maung Myint, 'Agriculture in Burmese economic development', p. 131.
[39] Ibid., pp. 158–9.

The State Agricultural Marketing Board showed little business acumen. This was partly because it possessed limited autonomy, for even routine operational decisions had to be referred to its ministry. Moreover, responsible positions in the SAMB were filled by civil servants who, understandably, had little or no practical experience of business. According to one near-contemporary observer, that lack of business experience forced the SAMB to adopt pricing and grading practices that were simply the easiest to administer, although they might also be commercially and economically damaging.[40] Thus until the mid-1950s, the SAMB bought paddy at a fixed price, irrespective of the quality of the grain or the time of the year. Consequently, the Burmese cultivator had no incentive to produce the higher grades, and therefore the quality of Burma's rice rapidly deteriorated. In addition, the cultivator faced a financial disincentive – storage costs – were he to hold back his crop for later sale. In other words, the rigid pricing practice of the SAMB produced a rush by cultivators to sell immediately after the harvest, and this caused domestic shortages in later months. Furthermore, the SAMB's mismanagement of actual storage and milling led to yet further declines in quality. And finally, while Burma had exported over a dozen markedly different grades of rice before the war, until well into the 1950s, the SAMB chose to export just a single grade, of low quality. It was administratively easier. The reputation of Burma's rice was much diminished in the 1950s.

The first months of the new government also saw the elimination of foreign interests from Burma's teak industry. On 1 June 1948, the forest concessions of the foreign timber firms, Steel Brothers, Macgregor, Foucar, T.D. Findlay, the Bombay Burmah Trading Corporation, together with certain of their sawmills and timber-yards, were taken over by the State Timber Board which now became responsible for the extraction, milling, and export of teak.[41] On that very same day, the Irrawaddy Flotilla Company was nationalized. However, Burma's new government hesitated to nationalize the foreign companies which dominated the oil and mining sectors, apparently because it lacked the funds that would be required for reconstruction and future expansion, as well as the essential technical and managerial expertise.[42] Instead

[40] Ibid., pp. 136–7.   [41] Tinker, *The Union of Burma*, pp. 95, 247.
[42] Tin Maung Maung Than, *State Dominance in Myanmar: the Political Economy of Industrialization*. Singapore: Institute of Southeast Asian Studies, 2007, pp. 90–1.

it established joint ventures, notably with Burmah Oil and with the Burma Corporation, which controlled the Bawdwin-Namtu mines. In the joint venture with Burmah Oil, established in 1954, Burma's government provided one-third of the capital.[43]

To expel or at least to curb foreign interests was, as noted earlier, one component in the U Nu government's strategy to dismantle the colonial economy. The second was to end Burma's excessive specialization in the production and export of primary commodities, overwhelmingly of course the cultivation and export of rice. Or rather, it was to diminish the corollary of primary export specialization, that is Burma's excessive dependence upon imports to meet the needs of its population for even basic consumer goods. In other words, Burma would industrialize. The government's perspective was well caught by a contemporary American observer.

To industrialize . . . would somehow remove Burma from the toils of what is called the 'colonial economy'. The economic rationalization for any industrial program, whatever its wisdom, was based on this prior political decision: that Burma must emerge from the colonial past both economically (by development of industry) and politically . . . Industrialization is the presumed mark of a modern nation. The Burmese leadership chose to be modern.[44]

In its *Two-Year Plan of Economic Development for Burma*, published in April 1948, the government listed the new industrial concerns to be established immediately.[45] They included factories to produce tiles, paper, sugar, steel, soap, rubber goods, textiles, and household pots. At the same time, serious consideration would be given to the establishment in the near future of the domestic production of, for example, chemicals, paints, varnish, industrial alcohol, insecticides, pharmaceutical products, plastics, and glass. This was the wish-list. In refining its thinking in 1949, the government made references to a restricted role for foreign capital in the planned industrialization.[46] And it also indicated a role for private Burmese capital, although again restricted.

[43] For the negotiations leading to the establishment of the joint venture, the Burma Oil Company (1954) Ltd, see T. A. B. Corley, *A History of the Burmah Oil Company, Volume II: 1924–1966*. London: Heinemann, 1988, ch. 6.

[44] Frank N. Trager, *Building a Welfare State in Burma 1948–1956*. New York: Institute of Pacific Relations, 1958, pp. 22, 102.

[45] Myat Thein, *Economic Development of Myanmar*. Singapore: Institute of Southeast Asian Studies, 2004, p. 40.

[46] Tin Maung Maung Than, *State Dominance in Myanmar*, pp. 70–1.

But in reality the government saw that each of the planned industries, including those engaged in the production of basic consumer goods, would be state-owned.[47] This was both an ideological issue – a commitment to socialism – but also a practical one, in that there was then little prospect that private capital, either foreign or domestic, would show an interest. Foreign capital would clearly be discouraged from investing in Burma's planned industries by the new government's evident hostility towards foreign economic interests, despite its occasional lukewarm encouragement, and by continuing security concerns. And Burmese private capital was unlikely to respond, partly because, emerging from colonial rule, there were too few experienced Burmese entrepreneurs but also because, apparently, Burmese with wealth strongly preferred then to invest in agriculture. This last point was made in a report on Burma's new industries by a Burmese senior official, U Kyaw Min, published in 1947. U Kyaw Min argued forcefully for the establishment of industries, and for private Burmese participation. But he noted that the returns on lending to agriculture had been far higher than the dividends paid by industrial concerns. And while that remained the case, he concluded, 'no Burman is going to indulge in industrial undertakings'.[48] A comparable point was later made by Hugh Tinker, based in part on his observations as a visiting Professor of History at the University of Rangoon in the mid-1950s:

[W]ealthy Burmans have not yet become accustomed to investing capital in long-term economic development. Houses erected for letting to wealthy foreigners, new cinemas, garages, and motor firms: these are among the investments most favoured by present-day Burmans with surplus capital.[49]

Nevertheless, when the government's Industrial Development Corporation was established in November 1952, it was responsible not only for developing and operating the state's industrial enterprises but also

[47] U Thet Tun, *Burma's Experience in Economic Planning*. Rangoon: Government Printing and Stationery, 1960, pp. 8–9.

[48] U Kyaw Min, *Preliminary Report on New Industries for Burma*. Rangoon: Government Printing and Stationery, 1947, p. 24. U Kyaw Min took an extremely dark view of the prospects for private Burmese, or indeed state, participation in Burma's industrialization. The final paragraph of his report is extraordinary: 'And so we come to the end of the perfect day, when the Director of Industries, having failed to interest the Burman in industries or to induce the Government . . . to participate in industry commits suicide' (p. 68).

[49] Tinker, *The Union of Burma*, p. 303.

for providing finance and other assistance for a private industrial sector, presumably Burmese.[50]

The faltering economy

Between the late 1940s and the beginning of the 1960s, Burma's gross domestic product (GDP) increased in real terms at an average annual rate of just over 5 per cent.[51] However, that rather impressive figure is misleading, in that, as a result of the destruction and disruption of the war years, it was an increase from a notably low base. If the economy's output in the 1950s is set against its pre-war output, the performance looks far less impressive. Thus Burma's GDP in 1949/50 was barely 60 per cent, in real terms, of its 1938/39 figure, and in fact it was not until 1958/59 that it recovered that pre-war level.[52] Indeed Burma's GDP per capita – to take into account the increase in population – failed by some margin to recover its 1938/39 level even by the end of the 1950s.

One major reason for Burma's faltering economic recovery in the 1950s was the failure to restore rice cultivation and export to their pre-war levels, or even to come close. As noted earlier, in the years immediately before the war, just over five million hectares had been planted with rice.[53] In the late 1940s, that figure was well under four million hectares but even in the late 1950s, it was only just over four million, still well short of the pre-war hectarage. And with respect to the trade in rice, before the war, Burma had exported close to three million tons each year. In 1950, it exported 1.184 million tons, and then under a million tons in 1953. But even in 1960, Burma exported just 1.722 million tons of rice, a little more than half the immediate pre-war volume. A number of factors explain the failure to restore rice cultivation and export to their pre-war levels.[54] First, cultivation and

[50] Tin Maung Maung Than, *State Dominance in Myanmar*, pp. 88–9.
[51] Myat Thein, *Economic Development of Myanmar*, p. 17.
[52] Louis J. Walinsky, *Economic Development in Burma 1951–1960*. New York: The Twentieth Century Fund, 1962, pp. 660–1.
[53] Teruko Saito and Lee Kin Kiong (comp.), *Statistics on the Burmese Economy: the 19th and 20th Centuries*. Singapore: Institute of Southeast Asian Studies, 1999, p. 81.
[54] The following draws mainly on Myat Thein, *Economic Development of Myanmar*, pp. 32–6.

the movement of rice to the ports were severely disrupted by the insurrections, particularly in the first two years of Burma's independence.
Second, the increase in Burma's population, from under 17 million in
1941 to about 20 million in the early 1960s, inevitably resulted in a
considerable increase in the domestic consumption of rice, and therefore a reduction in the surplus for export, even were total production
to have been restored to its pre-war level. The fact that production in
the 1950s fell some way short of the pre-war figure resulted in a still
greater reduction in the export surplus.

The third factor was the state's apparent neglect of agriculture,
particularly in the early 1950s. For example, having seen off the
Chettiars, the government established a number of rural credit institutions, notably the State Agricultural Bank in 1953, to provide loans to
cultivators.[55] But the volume of rural credit provided by the government in these years, through the new agricultural bank, the re-created
cooperatives, and through direct loans, fell far short of the cultivators' needs. And as further examples of the government's apparent
neglect: the irrigated acreage in the early 1960s was roughly the same
as in the late 1930s; fertilizer use remained extremely low; there were
few tractors; and there were less work-animals even by the mid-1950s
than there had been before the war. The final, and probably the most
important factor in the failure of rice cultivation and export to recover
their pre-war levels was that, as noted earlier, from the late 1940s
right through to the beginning of the 1960s, the State Agricultural
Marketing Board, which had a statutory monopoly in the export of
rice, bought its paddy from the Burmese cultivator at an unchanged
price, and moreover, a price substantially below the export price. In
other words, through these years, the fixed and low unit return to
the rice cultivator provided little encouragement for him to increase
acreage, or indeed to invest in more productive inputs or cultivation
methods.

Teak and oil also failed by some distance to recover their pre-war
production in the 1950s. As noted earlier, annual crude oil production
in Burma in the late 1930s had been around seven million barrels.[56]

---

[55] For full details and an assessment of the government's provision, see Sean
Turnell, *Fiery Dragons: Banks, Moneylenders and Microfinance in Burma.*
Copenhagen: NIAS Press, 2009, pp. 174–202.
[56] T. A. B. Corley, *A History of the Burmah Oil Company, Vol. II: 1924–1966.*
London: Heinemann, 1988, pp. 396–7.

Following the destruction of the industry during the war, annual production recovered to a little under 1.5 million barrels in the mid-1950s. But even by the early 1960s, it had reached only 3.5 million barrels, half the immediate pre-war figure. The recovery in crude oil production was seriously disrupted by rebel activities, threats of sabotage, labour strikes, and transport difficulties, but also slowed by the approaching exhaustion of the oilfields at Yenangyaung and the reluctance of foreign interests – the majority partners in the Burma Oil Company (1954) – to meet the high cost of investing in new field exploration while the threat of nationalization was still present, despite government assurances.[57] Substantially reduced local production coupled with a considerable increase in domestic demand meant that in the mid-1950s, Burma was an importer of kerosene, although this had been a significant export in the colonial era, as well as of petroleum.[58] As for teak, annual production in the late 1930s had been roughly 450,000 cubic tons.[59] Devastated during the war, in the late 1950s production had recovered to around 250,000 cubic tons, only a little over half the pre-war figure. Teak exports in the second half of the 1930s had averaged 274,000 tons a year.[60] In the early 1950s they were below 50,000 a year and falling sharply. Each operation in the extraction of teak, from girdling and felling to floating the teak-log rafts down to the sawmills at the ports, was severely disrupted by the insurrection. At times it brought the industry to a halt.

But of course the production and export of rice, oil, and teak had defined the colonial economy, and Burma's new government was possessed with the prospect of creating a quite different economic structure, one defined by industrial production serving the domestic market. In 1951 the government engaged an American firm, the Knappen-Tippetts-Abbett Engineering Company of New York (KTA), to prepare a comprehensive economic and engineering survey and report on Burma. The economics work, to provide broad economic analysis and to develop the economic framework for a comprehensive development programme for Burma, was undertaken by a firm of

[57] Tinker, *The Union of Burma*, pp. 300–2; Corley, *A History of the Burmah Oil Company, Vol. II*, ch. 7.
[58] Myat Thein, *Economic Development of Myanmar*, p. 39.
[59] *Economic Survey of Burma 1962*. Rangoon: Government Printing and Stationery, 1962, p. 21.
[60] Tinker, *The Union of Burma*, pp. 247–8.

consulting economists, Robert R. Nathan Associates of Washington DC. In a preliminary report, the American economists understandably placed strong emphasis on industrialization, to correct Burma's 'excessive dependence' on the cultivation and export of rice, to raise per capita output, 'to conserve foreign exchange', and 'to make larger quantities and more varied supplies of goods available' to the Burmese consumer.[61] The report became the basis for the Eight-Year Plan, also called the *Pyidawtha* Plan, which was launched in August 1952.

The programme of state industrial enterprises included a steel mill, a factory to produce jute sacks (gunnies), a pharmaceuticals plant, two sugar mills, a tea-packing plant, and a brick and tile factory, on which work had in fact started in 1951.[62] The initial financing of this programme was made secure by the high export price of rice in the early 1950s – the outbreak of the Korean War in June 1950 led to the stockpiling of primary commodities and thus soaring prices – in that it greatly increased the profits made by the State Agricultural Marketing Board on the procurement and sale of rice, and therefore the government's revenues. The soaring price of rice on world markets – it doubled between mid-1950 and 1952 – also helped Burma to achieve a substantial trade surplus in these years, and added considerably to its foreign exchange reserves.[63] But the primary commodity boom then came to an end, and as the export price of rice fell, the government's financial position deteriorated, the trade surplus disappeared, and Burma's foreign exchange reserves began to drain away. The Eight-Year Plan, constructed and confirmed when the rice price was high, implicitly projected substantial comprehensive budget surpluses through the 1950s.[64] But in reality, there was a deficit in each year, and notably large ones in 1953/54 and 1954/55. The need to restrain government expenditure and to conserve foreign exchange – the construction of factories commonly required heavy imports of plant and equipment – meant that no new significant manufacturing projects were added to the initial list. In 1957, the U Nu administration decided

---

[61] Quoted in Tin Maung Maung Than, *State Dominance in Myanmar*, p. 71.
[62] The following draws principally on Louis J. Walinsky, *Economic Development in Burma 1951–1960*. New York: The Twentieth Century Fund, 1962, ch. 17; and Tin Maung Maung Than, *State Dominance in Myanmar*, ch. 4.
[63] Tinker, *The Union of Burma*, p. 101.
[64] U Thet Tun, *Burma's Experience in Economic Planning*. Rangoon: Government Printing and Stationery, 1960, pp. 26–7.

Figure 3.4 Prime Minister U Nu in 1955
Source: C. Maxwell-Lefroy photographs, Centre for South Asian Studies, University of Cambridge

that no new state industrial enterprises would be undertaken, a position later confirmed by the Ne Win caretaker administration.

But the state industrialization programme of the 1950s disintegrated not simply because, once the export price of rice fell, there were not the financial resources to sustain it. Also important were serious concerns that often the management of the manufacturing projects that were being undertaken and completed was, frankly, incompetent. Interesting here are the views of Louis J. Walinsky, general manager and chief economist for the Burma office of Robert R. Nathan Associates between 1953 and 1959, with respect to the pharmaceuticals plant, the first of the new state manufacturing concerns to come into production. Of course Walinsky was not a disinterested observer.

From the outset [the pharmaceuticals plant] was beset with serious problems. The Ministry of Health should have been the largest customer, since it
procured drugs and medicines not only for its hospitals and clinics but also
for subsidized distribution to people who could not afford to buy commercially the medicines they needed. But the Ministry failed to seek adequate
budgets for these purposes. The army, another large buyer, was reluctant to
purchase from the new Government factory at higher prices than it was able
to obtain from its traditional suppliers abroad . . . The volume of operation
was, therefore, pitifully low.[65]

He continued.

Almost ludicrous difficulties were encountered in the distribution of yeast
tablets. It transpired that an individual consumption of ten or more tablets
per day would be required to correct the vitamin deficiencies. There were
complaints from those who attempted to participate in the initial distribution
that the consumption of so many tablets led to flatulence and other undesir-
able results. This problem was solved by fortifying the tablets so that a daily
intake of only one would suffice. The production cost of the fortified tablet,
however, was almost equal to the cost of imported and much-preferred vita-
mins (and [the production cost of the fortified tablet was] mostly in foreign
exchange).[66]

But worse was yet to come. The plant turned out a million tablets a day and
shipped them out to a list of Government agencies which were supposed to
distribute them free – especially in the schools. The distribution 'scheme',
however, failed to move the tablets beyond their initial distribution points.
Tablets soon backed up at the pharmaceuticals plant until they numbered
120 to 150 million – and still no satisfactory distribution plan had been
introduced.[67]

The state industrialization programme of the 1950s failed for other
reasons too. Louis Walinsky identified no less than twelve major problems in implementation, although as a present-day Burmese writer
has tartly commented, and with some justification, his list 'apparently
absolved the KTA consultants [including of course Robert R. Nathan

---

[65] Walinsky, *Economic Development in Burma*, p. 303.
[66] Ibid., pp. 303–4. According to Walinsky, the pharmaceuticals plant was a pet
project of U Nu. And the prime minister was impressed 'with what he
understood to be the efficacy of yeast as a remedy for prevailing dietary
deficiencies, [and] he was determined that the factory should be capable of
producing as much yeast as was needed for diet supplements' (p. 302).
[67] Walinsky, *Economic Development in Burma*, p. 304.

Associates] of any major responsibility for the failure' of the industrialization programme.[68] But there were undoubtedly serious failings in planning. One was noted earlier, the mistaken assumption that the export price of rice would remain relatively firm throughout the period of the plan, and this despite the fact that a prominent Burmese economist, Dr U Tun Wai, then of the UN Economic Commission for Asia and the Far East, had 'warned as early as mid-1952 of an impending break in the world price of rice'.[69] A further failing was noted by a World Bank mission to Burma in 1953. It reported in planning 'a preoccupation with engineering and financial aspects of individual projects [the expertise, respectively, of Knappen-Tippetts-Abbett and of Robert R. Nathan Associates] without adequate consideration for Burma's limited administrative, managerial, and technical capacities'.[70] Two further factors fatally undermined the state industrialization programme. As Frank Trager, a senior official in the US aid mission in Burma in the early 1950s, argued:

The difficulty of training, or otherwise acquiring, within the years of the KTA [Eight-Year] plan, the more than 13,000 persons, highly qualified in scientific, engineering, managerial, and other skills, necessary for only the public sector part of the total program – to say nothing of the skills necessary for the remainder – was and is vastly under-estimated.[71]

In other words, there were far too few Burmese with the training, skills, and experience necessary to run effectively a modern industrial sector, and too little time to produce them.[72] And finally, the state industrialization programme of the 1950s was undermined by the government's neglect of the rice economy, indeed its deliberate exploitation of the

---

[68] Tin Maung Maung Than, *State Dominance in Myanmar*, p. 74. The implementation problems identified by Walinsky – he devoted a full chapter to each of the twelve – included those of cultural adaptation, internal security, annual budgeting, and supervision and coordination: Walinsky, *Economic Development in Burma*, chs 21–32.

[69] U Thet Tun, 'A critique of Louis J. Walinsky's "Economic Development in Burma 1951–1960"', *Journal of the Burma Research Society*, 47, 1 (June 1964), p. 176.

[70] Quoted in Tin Maung Maung Than, *State Dominance in Myanmar*, p. 74.

[71] Trager, *Building a Welfare State in Burma*, p. 98.

[72] On an earlier page, Trager had put the point more broadly and perhaps more brutally: 'Burma does not yet possess the technical, administrative and financial resources necessary for building a modern economic society': Trager, *Building a Welfare State in Burma*, pp. 6–7.

rice cultivator through the procurement pricing of the SAMB. The implications were explained by a lecturer in economics at the University of Rangoon in the early 1960s, K. S. Mali.

The most serious defect in the total planning was the heavy emphasis on industrialization which overshaded the development of the basic economic activity of Burma – agriculture and other primary industries . . . Rising income for the rural population would in turn create demands which would develop internal markets for the planned new industries.[73]

Here was a paradox. In order to finance its industrialization programme, the government sought to extract a major surplus from Burma's rice economy. But in doing so, it depressed domestic demand, and thus undermined the commercial prospects for the new industrial concerns that were being established to supply the local market. Of course it would have been possible to balance those conflicting circumstances, to raise sufficient revenue from the rice economy to finance a measure of state industrialization without depressing too sharply domestic demand. But in its determination to dismantle the colonial economy, Burma's government in the 1950s – heavily emphasizing industrialization and severely depressing rural incomes – made little attempt at such a reconciliation, and thereby undermined its own strategy.

As the failings of the state industrialization programme became ever more clear – the Eight-Year Plan was abandoned in 1955 – the government repeated its encouragement to private capital, both domestic and foreign, to invest in Burma's industrial sector. In a statement in December 1953, U Nu ruled that '[u]ltimately all trade and industry must be organized into public corporations and co-operatives': but he also promised to 'help' the private sector to fulfil the role the government was allocating to it.[74] A government statement on investment policy, issued in June 1955, included not only measures intended to protect and support private investment – a guaranteed allocation of foreign exchange to cover imports of machinery and raw materials,

[73] K. S. Mali, *Fiscal Aspects of Development Planning in Burma 1950–1960.* Rangoon: Department of Economics, University of Rangoon, 1962, p. 85.

[74] Tin Maung Maung Than, *State Dominance in Myanmar*, p. 72. The Eight-Year Plan calculated that a little under half of the projected net capital formation, in the economy as a whole, would be undertaken by the private sector: U Thet Tun, *Burma's Experience in Economic Planning.* Rangoon: Government Printing and Stationery, 1960, pp. 16, 19.

and the imposition of tariffs on competing finished imports, were both apparently promised – but also a list of industrial fields for which private capital, foreign and domestic, would be sought.[75] Addressing Burma's parliament in September 1957, U Nu repeated that the government sought to encourage domestic and foreign investment in the industrial sector.

But as noted earlier, foreign capital was never likely to be tempted by the encouragement and inducements being offered, not least because it was clear that state ownership remained the government's central economic ambition. Indeed, even in encouragement the government could appear threatening, to both foreign and domestic capital. For example, in 1957 U Nu sought to encourage private enterprise with a guarantee of ten years without nationalization, thereby confirming for wary investors the near-certain prospect of nationalization once the ten years had passed.[76] Thus the only significant new industrial investment by foreign capital in this period was made by Unilever, a joint venture with the government for the manufacture of soap.[77] That there was almost no new foreign investment in Burma's industry in the 1950s – and commonly only cautious reinvestment by the established foreign concerns – is therefore clear. In contrast, it is difficult to determine the scale of new investment in industry being made by local private capital. The issue this raises – whether local private capital was vigorous, or fragile and near-inconsequential, in the first full decade of independence – is a crucial one. Indeed it can be seen as a defining issue, no less, in Burma's modern economic history.

It could not be anticipated that a significant Burmese entrepreneurial class would have emerged in the 1950s. As earlier chapters made clear, the structures of the colonial economy had largely excluded the Burmese from modern industry and commerce. And subsequently, in the first decade or so of independence, the insurrections, the repeated

---

[75] Tin Maung Maung Than, *State Dominance in Myanmar*, pp. 72–73.

[76] Myat Thein, *Economic Development of Myanmar*. Singapore: Institute of Southeast Asian Studies, 2004, p. 43. The 1957 guarantee should be read alongside earlier, 1952, remarks by U Nu on the establishment of joint ventures to rehabilitate Burma's oil and mining industries: 'as soon as we have rehabilitated these enterprises and acquired all necessary knowledge and ability to manage and operate them, we shall nationalize these enterprises': cited in Hugh Tinker, *The Union of Burma: a Study of the First Years of Independence*, 4th edn. London: Oxford University Press, 1967, p. 116.

[77] Tin Maung Maung Than, *State Dominance in Myanmar*, p. 89.

commitment of the government to state ownership, and, too often, poor government economic management and administration, had surely discouraged private Burmese initiative. Contemporary observers confirmed the weak performance of local capital in the 1950s. For example, writing in 1957, Frank Trager, then Director of the Burma Research Project, New York University, reported that 'domestic capital has not as yet indicated either the financial or entrepreneurial capacity' to fill the role assigned to it in the government's economic plans.[78] Or again, as noted earlier, Hugh Tinker, a visiting Professor of History at the University of Rangoon in the mid-1950s, argued that Burmese with surplus capital had 'not yet become accustomed to investing [it] in long-term economic development'.[79] Addressing the Annual General Meeting of the Burma Chamber of Commerce in early 1960, the Chairman reported that although the past year had seen 'a little industrial development in the private sector . . . the rate of such development [is] still disappointingly low'.[80]

Recent writers, however, have taken a decidedly more optimistic view. For example, in a book published in 2000, a group of Burmese economists argued that:

The performance of private sector manufacturing production was . . . very impressive during the period of the democratic regime [1948–62]. This was in spite of the fact that the main priority of the government in the industrial field was for large state enterprises. On the other hand, the government leaders had learnt the serious limitations of the state being a dominant player in industrial development . . . The government by the early 1960s was clearly moving towards accepting private participation in [industrial] development.[81]

A few years later, Tin Maung Maung Than, the principal authority on the political economy of industrialization in Myanmar, argued that in the 1950s

the private industrial sector made substantial progress despite numerous obstacles such as inadequate financial resources, restrictions on foreign exchange, state control on imports of capital and intermediate goods,

---

[78] Trager, *Building a Welfare State in Burma*, p. 103.
[79] Tinker, *The Union of Burma*, p. 303.
[80] Burma Chamber of Commerce, *Annual Reports for 1959–1960*, pp. 48–9.
[81] Khin Maung Kyi, Ronald Findlay, R. M. Sundrum, Mya Maung, Myo Nyunt, Zaw Oo, et al., *Economic Development of Burma: a Vision and a Strategy*. Stockholm: Olof Palme International Center, 2000, pp. 9–10.

technical backwardness, and lack of managerial expertise. In fact, [a] World Bank Mission's Report...[in June 1958] stated that it was 'surprised to find...the manufacturing sector...larger than and considerably more diversified than it had expected.' Moreover, [according to the Report] 'there has been a growing movement of capital and people into manufacturing'.[82]

The importance of these observations lies in the fact that the military government that would seize power in Burma in March 1962 moved rapidly to nationalize all industrial concerns. In effect, it took an approach that had evidently failed in the 1950s – the state industrialization programme – and now, in the 1960s, worked it harder. Thus if a sturdy local manufacturing sector had indeed begun to emerge during the 1950s, it can be argued that the subsequent nationalization by the military did not simply destroy that Burmese entrepreneurial initiative but closed off an alternative approach – an alternative to state ownership – that had apparently begun to offer a truly viable path to economic development. But on the other hand, if the argument advanced by the Burmese economists above is misjudged – that in truth the expansion of domestic private manufacturing in Burma in the 1950s was fragile and insubstantial – then two inferences can be drawn. First, that the colonial legacy in excluding the Burmese from modern industry and commerce remained powerful. And second, in the face of the evident failure of state industrialization by the mid- or late-1950s, there were now few options open to the managers of Burma's economy. This is indeed a defining issue in Burma's modern economic history.

The strength and substance of Burma's private industrial sector in the 1950s should be assessed not only by its size and rate of expansion but also by the nature of its production and processes, and the economic standing of the businessmen involved. It is difficult to provide a precise assessment of size. The share of industrial production in gross national product (GNP) rose from 6.5 per cent in 1950/51 to 15.1 per cent in 1960/61.[83] Of course that figure includes production by the state enterprises: and sadly it appears that state production and private production were not recorded separately.[84] However, as noted earlier, no new significant projects were added to the initial list of

[82] Tin Maung Maung Than, *State Dominance in Myanmar*, pp. 89–90.
[83] Myat Thein, *Economic Development of Myanmar*, p. 42.
[84] Certainly 'the contribution of private capital formation to industrial investment cannot be ascertained', as 'disaggregated data are not available': Tin Maung Maung Than, *State Dominance in Myanmar*, p. 82.

state industrial concerns included in the Eight-Year Plan when it was launched in 1952, while the performance of those concerns that were included and completed was relatively poor, and this suggests that Burma's private sector may well have accounted for the major part of the impressive increase in the share of industrial production in GNP in the 1950s. This view might then find support in figures which show an increase in the number of private manufacturing establishments employing ten or more persons, from 2,465 in 1953 to 3,930 in 1957, a rise of 60 per cent in just four years, with total employment in those concerns increasing from 102,000 to 154,000 in the same period, a rise of 51 per cent.[85]

On the other hand in, for example, 1957, the average number employed in private manufacturing establishments in Burma, according to these figures, was a rather modest 39. Moreover, total employment in private manufacturing in 1957 – 154,000 – fell far short of the nearly 250,000 civil servants employed by government departments, boards, and corporations at the end of the 1950s.[86] In other words, private manufacturing, although growing, remained on a relatively modest scale in this period. The principal articles manufactured included textiles, metal and plastic utensils, food (biscuits, noodles, confectionery), soft drinks (notably aerated water), cigarettes, umbrellas, leather goods, furniture, paper, candles and safety matches, soap, and footwear.[87] The sharp increase in production in these lines in these years was clearly encouraged by the high tariffs imposed on competing imports and the low tariffs imposed on imports of raw materials and industrial machinery.

With respect to each of the manufactures listed above, production took place in a large number of establishments. For example, in 1961/62, no less than 38 firms were registered as producing aerated water, 28 firms in biscuits, 117 in textile printing and dyeing, 49 firms manufactured boots and shoes, 139 produced soap, and 46 concerns

---

[85] Louis J. Walinsky, *Economic Development in Burma 1951–1960*. New York: The Twentieth Century Fund, 1962, pp. 346–8. It should be noted that Walinsky warns that 'many of the additional manufacturing establishments were "new" only by definition. They had previously been classified as cottage industries and were now re-classified because they now had ten or more employees'.

[86] Robert H. Taylor, *The State in Myanmar*. London: Hurst, 2009, pp. 284–5.

[87] Khin Maung Kyi et al., *Economic Development of Burma*, p. 9; personal communication from Tin Maung Maung Than, 20 March 2012.

were involved in the manufacture of umbrellas.[88] In other words, these were small-scale manufacturing concerns.[89] Each employed, as noted above, a relatively modest number of workers and, presumably, was owned and run by a businessman with relatively limited commercial interests and resources. In sharp contrast, in other economies of South East Asia in the 1950s, recently emerged or emerging from colonial rule, there could be found powerful local capitalists, commonly of Chinese origin. To give just three from many possible examples, in Indonesia, William Soeryadjaya founded Astra in 1957 to export primary commodities: in the mid-1960s the company began importing cars and trucks, later creating joint ventures with Toyota and General Motors to import components and assemble locally.[90] In Malaya in the late 1950s, Robert Kuok was building a powerful position in the sugar trade and sugar refining: eventually his interests would embrace property development, palm oil, flour milling, and hotels across Asia. And in Thailand in the 1950s, Charoen Pokphand, a company which had its origins before the war as an importer of seeds and then fertilizers, created a substantial integrated business in the production of animal feed and the breeding of poultry and pigs in the north-east of the country: later the company, owned by the Chearavanont family, diversified into food retailing and fast-food restaurants, and, dramatically, established itself in other parts of South East Asia, in China, the United States, and in Turkey. In brief, Robert Kuok, the Chearavanont family, William Soeryadjaya, and many other local capitalists were well-established by the 1950s and, in the following decades, expanding and diversifying, played key roles in the economic transformation of Malaysia, Thailand, and Indonesia. In Burma in the late 1950s, there was no local capitalist of equivalent standing.

Economists in Burma

Prominent in the economic administration of Burma in the 1950s were a number of notably fine economists. Indeed in subsequent decades, one would achieve a world reputation in his discipline. The final section

[88] *Economic Survey of Burma 1963*. Rangoon: Central Press, 1964, pp. 33–41.
[89] In fact this point is made by Khin Maung Kyi et al., *Economic Development of Burma*, p. 9.
[90] Rajeswary Ampalavanar Brown, *Chinese Big Business and the Wealth of Asian Nations*. Basingstoke: Palgrave, 2000, pp. 52, 86–7, 91–101.

of this chapter will briefly examine three of these men, J. S. Furnivall, Louis Walinsky, and Hla Myint. Each had a distinctive understanding of the Burmese economy at that time, its problems, prospects, and the options open to it.

John Sydenham Furnivall had first arrived in Burma at the end of 1902, aged 24, as an official in the Indian Civil Service (ICS).[91] During the following two decades he rose through the ranks of the Burma administration, to become Commissioner of Settlements and Land Records at the beginning of the 1920s. But from early in his ICS career, Furnivall's Burma sympathies were clear – he mastered the Burmese language, married a Burmese woman in 1906, and in 1910, with others, founded the Burma Research Society – and in June 1923, unsettled by the direction long taken by colonial administration in Burma, he retired from government service. Apart from an early brief return to England, he then remained in Burma until 1931. During this time he founded the Burma Book Club, a magazine, *World of Books*, and the Burma Education Extension Association. In addition he was invited to give lectures at the newly established University of Rangoon on 'the economic conditions of Burma', and these formed the basis for his first major book, *An Introduction to the Political Economy of Burma*, published by the Burma Book Club in 1931.

Furnivall then returned to England. In the early 1930s, he undertook research at Leiden University and in Java on Dutch administration in the East Indies, and then between 1935 and 1941, he was the ICS Lecturer in Burmese Language, History, and Law at Cambridge. In late 1942 he was asked by the government of Burma in exile at Simla for his views on post-war reconstruction, 'with particular reference to features of colonial rule in Netherlands India that might suitably be adopted in Burma', and this work became the basis for his most

[91] Furnivall's life, publications, ideas, and influence are considered in: R. H. Taylor, 'Disaster or release? J. S. Furnivall and the bankruptcy of Burma', *Modern Asian Studies*, 29, 1 (1995); U Thet Tun, 'The writings of John Sydenham Furnivall (on Myanmar)', in *Selected Writings of Retired Ambassador U Thet Tun*. Yangon: Myanmar Historical Commission, 2004; Julie Pham, 'Ghost hunting in colonial Burma: nostalgia, paternalism and the thoughts of J. S. Furnivall', *South East Asia Research*, 12, 2 (2004); Julie Pham, 'J. S. Furnivall and Fabianism: reinterpreting the "Plural Society" in Burma', *Modern Asian Studies*, 39, 2 (2005); and Neil A. Englehart, 'Liberal Leviathan or imperial outpost? J. S. Furnivall on colonial rule in Burma', *Modern Asian Studies*, 45, 4 (2011).

Figure 3.5 J. S. Furnivall at his home in Cambridge, 1948
Source: The collection of John Ady

important book, *Colonial Policy and Practice: a Comparative Study of Burma and Netherlands India*, published by Cambridge University Press in 1948. In that same year, the year of Burma's restored independence, Furnivall returned to Burma as the new government's Adviser on National Planning. He held that position for ten years, although he had been aged 70 when appointed, until he and many other foreign advisers were dismissed by the caretaker administration of

Ne Win in 1958. Furnivall left Burma for the final time in April 1960, for although U Nu, on his return to power, offered him a position as Professor of Economics at the University of Rangoon, he died before he could take up that post.

Furnivall's central criticism of British rule in Burma, first established in *An Introduction to the Political Economy of Burma* at the beginning of the 1930s, was that it had thrown open an unsuspecting and defenceless society to unrestrained capitalism. Focused solely on commercial gain, the British colonial administration imposed no restriction on the entry, economic role, or material advance of foreign interests in Burma, or in other words, it offered no protection to the Burmese who, in the absence of that intervention, could rarely find a place in the modern economy and society that was being created around them. A plural society evolved under British rule, or was allowed by the British to evolve, whose structure denied the Burmese access not simply to secure material advance, but to modernity. This crucial last point was strikingly made by Furnivall in his preface, 'for European readers', to the first, 1931 edition of *An Introduction to the Political Economy of Burma*.

England opened up Burma to the world but did not open up the world to Burma, and the [Burmese] in a larger world was condemned to live a smaller life. His religion and culture were degraded and he could no longer exercise the social, commercial and industrial functions that had formerly been open to him, limited as those had been... The narrowing of his life may be measured by the impoverishment of his language. Formerly... a lad who could read and write Burmese was fully equipped to become a citizen of Burma with the whole of Burmese civilisation at his command. Now it is merely a language of the domestic circle and the cultivator, and [those] who only know Burmese know less of their own world than their fathers and no more of the modern world.[92]

In 1957 the Peoples' Literature Committee and House in Rangoon republished *An Introduction to the Political Economy of Burma*, Furnivall contributing a lengthy new preface. On the opening page he restated his long-held conclusion as to the destructive character of British rule:

[92] J. S. Furnivall, *An Introduction to the Political Economy of Burma*. Rangoon: Burma Book Club, 1931, p. xiv.

under foreign rule all social relations were dominated by the economic motive, the desire for material gain, continually pitting the individual against society, and ... consequently the social order ... disintegrated and Burma [was] transformed from a human society into a business concern.[93]

A major part of the 1957 preface was devoted to Burma's current economic circumstances. Here Furnivall was not concerned 'to examine what the [new] government has done or has not done, or to show what it could or should have done', but rather 'to clarify some of the major problems inherent in the situation of Burma at the dawn of independence'.[94] Furnivall's analysis, it is crucial to note, evolved directly from his understanding of the destructive impact of British rule. In other words, Burma's major economic problems at independence were a colonial inheritance. From a rich analysis here, just two of his central arguments are noted. Both arise from the observation that colonial Burma's modern economy and administration had been dominated by British and Indian interests; in other words, that under British rule, the Burmese had been excluded from the modern world. The first observation was a practical one. 'The fundamental obstacle to industrial expansion [since independence in 1948] was not the lack of capital but the lack of human resources – of manpower.'[95] At independence there were far too few Burmese with the education, training, and experience to run a modern economy and society. The second observation concerned ideology, and perhaps the psychology of the Burmese. Since independence, Burma's government had removed almost all the principal foreign interests from the economy. The Burmese had decisively rejected the plural society. Furnivall continued: 'In repudiating the capitalist society into which the social order had been transformed, [the Burmese] were impelled also to repudiate the capitalist economy with which it was associated.'[96] This was clearly a reference to the strong statist ambitions of the U Nu administration. But in fact Furnivall's observation could also be read in a quite different way. The plural society – the exclusion of the Burmese from all that was distinctively modern in the economic life of their country – had been created when Burma under British rule had been thrown open to the world.

---

[93] J. S. Furnivall, *An Introduction to the Political Economy of Burma*, 3rd edn. Rangoon: Peoples' Literature Committee and House, 1957, p. e.
[94] Ibid., p. ax.   [95] Ibid., p. z.   [96] Ibid., p. an.

Furnivall certainly did not now advocate withdrawal: '[Burmese] cannot lead a healthy national life in isolation from the outside world.'[97] But it would not have been surprising if many Burmese, working from the Furnivall argument that their economic problems at independence had their origins in the unrestricted integration of Burma into the world economy from the mid-nineteenth century, now, in the mid-twentieth century, saw the solution to those problems in withdrawal and isolation.

Louis J. Walinsky, as noted earlier, was general manager and chief economist in the Burma office of Robert R. Nathan Associates, the American consulting economists. The office had been established in 1951. For the first two years, the dollar cost of the firm's services was met from a US government aid programme.[98] But in mid-1953, the Burmese government abruptly terminated the programme – from early 1949 remnants of the Kuomintang army had been occupying parts of north-east Burma, with American encouragement and clandestine supplies – and from that point, Robert R. Nathan Associates was engaged at the Burma government's own expense.[99] It is perhaps surprising that the U Nu administration, with its strong socialist ambitions, would have chosen and then continued to fund for five years an American firm of economic consultants. Louis Walinsky later provided some context for the relationship, noting the earlier work of Robert Nathan, the head of the firm, in economic planning for the new state of Israel and with Jean Monnet in France, and his 'reputation as a liberal New Dealer and his support for the economic positions and policies of organized labor in the United States'.[100] But as will be demonstrated below, that context does not fully settle the issue of the appropriateness of the appointment.

From 1953 the contractual responsibilities of Robert R. Nathan Associates in Burma were very substantial. The office was required to assist in the preparation of each year's development programme, to advise on the economic aspects of plans, programmes, projects, and policies in the fields of manufacturing, power, transport, and construction, to assist in the preparation of the annual budget by commenting

[97] Ibid., p. g.   [98] Walinsky, *Economic Development in Burma*, p. 555.

[99] For the Kuomintang crisis and the termination of American aid, see Matthew Foley, *The Cold War and National Assertion in Southeast Asia: Britain, the United States and Burma, 1948–1962*. London: Routledge, 2010, ch. 5.

[100] Walinsky, *Economic Development in Burma*, p. 84.

on the relationship of the development programme to the government's budget prospects, and much else.[101] Increasingly, as problems in the practical implementation of the government's economic plans became more acute, the American consultants also commented, critically, on the structure, procedures, and attitudes of the administration itself. The general manager and chief economist, Walinsky, was formally required to report to the government through the Economic and Social Board, a supra-cabinet committee, established in 1952 and responsible for the supervision and coordination of the development programme. But in practice, individual staff from the American firm were in almost constant contact with senior officials, and Louis Walinsky himself had a close relationship with the prime minister, U Nu. At more than one cabinet meeting, the prime minister sat Louis Walinsky and Robert Nathan on his immediate left and right, at the head of the table.[102] To all appearances, the American chief economist was a powerful influence, a perception that caused considerable resentment on the part of many in the administration and indeed beyond.

On 1 December 1958, the caretaker government of Ne Win terminated the American consultants' contract at three months' notice. The official reason given was a need to reduce government expenditure, with Ne Win apparently thinking that the consultants were working mainly on the creation of new costly projects which the country could not in fact afford.[103] Several months earlier, thinking along similar lines, a Rangoon newspaper had offered a distinctly sinister interpretation of the consultants' work: 'a firm of formulators of schemes – the K.T.A. [in effect, Robert R. Nathan Associates] – was sent to Burma to destroy [the] Burmese economy'.[104] That interpretation was restated in the press when the termination of the Americans' contract was announced.

Could it be because these American Economic Experts, whose advice made Burma this much penurious, were really [so] inefficient that they gave poor advice, or could it be because, for the American Government, it was only

---

[101] Ibid., pp. 555–9.

[102] Joan Marie Nelson, 'Central planning for national development and the role of foreign advisors: the case of Burma'. PhD, Radcliffe College, 1960, p. 340.

[103] Louis Walinsky, 'Meeting with the Hon'ble Prime Minister [Ne Win]', 17 December 1958, Louis Walinsky Papers, Box 5, Folder 4.

[104] Naing Htun Win, 'An American firm engaged on spy espionage', *The People Journal*, 7 June 1958 (translation), Louis Walinsky Papers, Box 5, Folder 4.

when Burma crumbled to ashes that loans would be taken from [America] so that it would come to the stage of depending on them that [the advisors] gave advice purposely detrimental to Burma?[105]

But more measured Burmese opinion could also be hostile to the departing American economists. In 1962, Louis Walinsky published his *Economic Development in Burma 1951–1960*, a 680-page, highly detailed insider-account of economic planning and implementation in Burma in the 1950s. The book was critically reviewed by U Thet Tun, then Director of the Central Statistical and Economics Department (CSED), in the *Journal of the Burma Research Society* in June 1964. In the mid-1950s, relations between the American consultants and U Thet Tun and the CSED had frequently been strained, and now the Director was devastating in his criticism.[106] Much of his long review focused on the serious misjudgements allegedly made by the economic consultants on specific issues, for example, their mistaken prediction that the international price of rice would hold relatively firm through to the end of the 1950s. This had been a major error, with serious consequences. But U Thet Tun also had two broader criticisms. The first was that when, in the final part of his book, Louis Walinsky drew on his several years of experience of development planning and implementation in Burma to produce a series of guidelines for other similarly placed countries, he offered no more than the blindingly obvious.

The moral for other developing nations Mr. Walinsky draws from the Burmese experience is that if they want to develop, they should have good government, good leadership, good political system, good implementation, good public administration, good economic policies and good faith in private enterprise. A corollary is that by that time these developing countries may not even need good economic advisers like Mr. Walinsky.[107]

In a similar way, U Thet Tun concluded, 'many things [Louis Walinsky] told the Burmese Government to do [were] the right things to do, but

[105] *Mirror*, 2 December 1958, quoted in Nelson, 'Central planning for national development', p. 371.

[106] For relations in the 1950s, see Nelson, 'Central planning for national development', pp. 360–65.

[107] U Thet Tun, 'A critique of Louis J. Walinsky's "Economic Development in Burma 1951–1960"', *Journal of the Burma Research Society*, 47, 1 (June 1964), p. 181.

he did not tell them how and when which is after all the task of an adviser'.[108] In brief the American's 'high cost advice' had failed to guide at precisely those points where guidance was really needed – or his 'how and when' were no more than vague generalities.[109]

U Thet Tun's second broad criticism was more devastating still. Moreover it ventured into that defining issue in Burma's modern economic history noted earlier in this chapter. It is clear that Walinsky opposed the three central economic ambitions of the Burmese government he served: Burmanization, nationalization, and state-led industrialization. Writing to U Kyaw Nyein, the Minister for Industry, in 1956, Walinsky argued that:

Despite increasing participation by the State in recent years, the major contribution to industrial activity in [Burma] is still made by the private sector ... I believe a great potential for increased industrial activity and output is to be found in the modernization and expansion of these existing [private sector] industries, as well as in the initiation of new industrial activities within the private sector by native capital.[110]

And to give a further example, at a meeting with Ne Win in December 1958, shortly after the decision to terminate the consultants' contract, Walinsky challenged the caretaker prime minister on Burmanization. As Walinsky recorded shortly after the meeting:

I stated that I thought the [economic] minority groups [specifically the Indian community] had a great contribution to make to the development of his country – that indeed, development seemed always to be fostered more by minority groups than by majority groups, and that I hoped Burma would utilize the contribution they could make to her future.[111]

---

[108] Ibid., p. 181.
[109] This angry review certainly exposed Burmese sensitivities. At one point (p. 174) U Thet Tun dismissed a particular Walinsky assertion as 'both preposterous and insulting to the [Burmese] parties concerned'.
[110] Louis Walinsky to U Kyaw Nyein, 3 May 1956, Louis Walinsky Papers, Box 11, Folder 22.
[111] Louis Walinsky, 'Meeting with the Hon'ble Prime Minister [Ne Win]', 17 December 1958, Louis Walinsky Papers, Box 5, Folder 4. That Walinsky was thinking specifically of the Indian community is clear from earlier papers: Louis Walinsky, 'Comments on the petition (undated) of the All-Burma Indian Congress to the Hon'ble Prime Minister', 18 June 1958, and a note by Walinsky of 10 August 1957 [1958?], Louis Walinsky Papers, Box 11, Folder 22.

In his 1962 book, Louis Walinsky then made plain his opposition on all fronts.

[U]ndoubtedly the most difficult and important problems the consultants [Robert R. Nathan Associates] faced were those which arose out of the Government's impractical socialization and Burmanization policies and, once the program was well under way, out of its inept performance in public administration and implementation.[112]

In his review, U Thet Tun correctly noted that the central economic ambitions of the government, nationalization, Burmanization, and industrialization, were 'the very roots on which the state of Burma was founded', and he commented: 'what one [therefore] cannot get over is why advisers with an ideology so divergent from the client's were hired at all'.[113] This is fair comment but it misses a far more important point.

The core economic strategies pursued by Burma's government in the 1950s, once again, nationalization, Burmanization, and industrialization, had clearly failed to secure the structural changes and material advance that had been anticipated on independence in 1948. In other words, judging by economic performance and progress alone, Walinsky had sound reasons for his misgivings. But this then suggests a brutal paradox: the core ambitions which defined Burma as it emerged from the colonial economic experience – 'the very roots on which the state of Burma was founded' – had also failed Burma. Indeed, in the future, pushed further still, they would lead Burma to bankruptcy.

The first decade of Burma's restored independence saw the rise to prominence of a remarkable generation of Burmese economists. A major factor in the creation of that generation was undoubtedly the teaching of the discipline at the University of Rangoon in the decades before the war. The Department of Economics had been established in 1923 – the University itself had been founded in 1920 – with the appointment of H. Stanley Jevons, the son of the prominent nineteenth-century economist, William Stanley Jevons, to the Chair of Economics.[114] Later in the 1920s, as noted above, Furnivall was invited to give lectures at the University on 'the economic conditions

---

[112] Walinsky, *Economic Development in Burma*, p. 560.
[113] U Thet Tun, 'A critique of Louis J. Walinsky's', pp. 181, 179.
[114] *The Straits Times*, 12 September 1923, p. 8.

of Burma'. These formed the basis for his *An Introduction to the Political Economy of Burma*, published in 1931, which became 'a widely read text used for many years at Rangoon University'.[115] Another influential figure in these years was Harro Bernardelli, an Austrian refugee to Britain from Nazi Germany and a student of Friedrich Hayek. Bernardelli was appointed to Rangoon from a post at the London School of Economics in 1935.[116]

Among the 1950s generation were two economists who have already appeared in this chapter, one at some length: U Tun Wai, whose Yale doctoral thesis was published as *Burma's Currency and Credit* in 1953, was at various times a lecturer in economics at the University of Rangoon and, as noted earlier, a member of the UN Economic Commission for Asia and the Far East (ECAFE) before he joined the International Monetary Fund (IMF); and U Thet Tun, educated at the University of Rangoon, in wartime Japan, and in post-war London, was, again as noted earlier, Director of the Central Statistical and Economics Department, although he was also appointed for short periods to ECAFE in Bangkok and to the IMF in Washington DC.[117] The 1950s generation also included Maung Shein, a lecturer in economics at Rangoon University in the early 1960s, whose Cambridge doctoral thesis was published in 1964 as *Burma's Transport and Foreign Trade (1885–1914)*; Aye Hlaing, who was writing on economic growth and income distribution in Burma under British rule and who, in the early 1960s, was Professor of Economics at the University of Rangoon; U Ba Nyein, a student of Bernardelli at Rangoon before the war and, in the late 1940s, a member of the Economic Council; and Ronald Findlay, a graduate of Rangoon University in the mid-1950s who, on completing his doctorate at the Massachusetts Institute of Technology (MIT) in 1960, returned to Burma first as lecturer and then research professor at the Institute of Economics in Rangoon. But the outstanding economist of that remarkable 1950s generation was undoubtedly Hla Myint.

Born in March 1920, Hla Myint became a student at the University of Rangoon in the mid-1930s, reading economics, his teachers

---

[115] R. H. Taylor, 'Disaster or release? J. S. Furnivall and the bankruptcy of Burma', *Modern Asian Studies*, 29, 1 (1995), p. 50.

[116] Interview with Professor Hla Myint, Bangkok, 29 January 2012; personal communication from Professor Ronald Findlay, 21 February 2012.

[117] For the latter's recollections of an extremely interesting life, see U Thet Tun, *Waves of Influence*. Yangon: Thin Sapay, 2011.

Figure 3.6 Hla Myint at Mingaladon Airport in the mid-1950s
Source: The collection of Professor Hla Myint

including the recently appointed Harro Bernardelli.[118] After he graduated from Rangoon, in 1940 he was sent as a state scholar to the
London School of Economics to study for a doctorate in the field of
welfare economics. During the war, the LSE was evacuated to Cambridge, and Hla Myint took this opportunity to make friends with
John Furnivall who, as noted earlier, had been living and working in
Cambridge for several years. Hla Myint returned to Burma in 1947,

---

[118] The following draws in part on an interview with Professor Hla Myint in
Bangkok on 29 January 2012. According to U Thet Tun (*Waves of Influence*,
p. 16), the university's regulations then stated that a student taking the
first-year exams 'must be at least 15 years old'.

as Professor of Economics at Rangoon University and then in addition as Economic Adviser to the new government under U Nu. In 1948 he was sent briefly back to Cambridge to persuade Furnivall to return to Rangoon as the Adviser on National Planning, although Furnivall required little persuading.

But Hla Myint did not remain long in Rangoon. He returned to Britain in 1950, to an appointment as a lecturer in colonial economics at Oxford. As he later explained to Louis Walinsky, in Rangoon he had struggled and failed to maintain academic standards at the university – and subsequently undergraduate teaching 'had gone to the dogs beyond recall' – and he had been sceptical about and frustrated by the economic direction then being taken by Burma.[119] He returned to Burma in 1954 under United Nations auspices, to serve for a year as an economic adviser to the government.[120] And then in 1958, Hla Myint was persuaded – in part by Ne Win who 'personally wired' him in Oxford – to become Rector of Rangoon University and, once again, an economic adviser.[121] But this second return to a major position at the university and as an economic adviser to the government proved to be at least as frustrating as the first, and, deeply despondent, he returned to Oxford in 1960, never to work in Burma again.[122] A short time later he left Oxford for the LSE, to an appointment as Professor of Economics, and he remained there until his retirement in the mid-1980s.

Hla Myint was a highly influential pioneer in the field of development economics.[123] Much of the early thinking in that field as it emerged as a distinct sub-discipline after the Second World War was strongly critical of the nineteenth-century colonial pattern of international trade, in which, crudely, the colonies shipped primary exports to

---

[119] Hla Myint to Louis Walinsky, 26 February 1956, Louis Walinsky Papers, Box 5, Folder 1; Hla Myint to Louis Walinsky, 4 February 1960, Louis Walinsky Papers, Box 3, Folder 20.

[120] Walinsky, *Economic Development in Burma*, p. 166, fn. 2.

[121] 'American advisors to quit within 4 months', *The Vanguard* [*Botataung*], 1 December 1958, Louis Walinsky Papers, Box 5, Folder 3.

[122] Interview with Professor Hla Myint, Bangkok, 29 January 2012. He was also shocked by Ne Win's expulsion of Furnivall, for he felt 'morally responsible' for persuading the latter to return to Burma in 1948.

[123] For a brief consideration of Hla Myint's position in and contribution to the field, see Amitava K. Dutt, 'International trade in early development economics', in K. S. Jomo and Erik S. Reinert (eds), *The Origins of Development Economics: How Schools of Economic Thought have Addressed Development*. London: Zed Books, 2005, pp. 100, 121–2.

the industrial metropole in exchange for manufactures. That exchange, it was argued, had created in the former colonies, now regaining independence, a pronounced primary export bias that left them highly vulnerable to fluctuations in the international economy. The development strategy which flowed from that analysis required the former colonies, the 'less developed countries', to become inward-looking, to play down the importance of primary commodity exports and instead to focus on state-led industrialization supplying the domestic market. Of course this was the orthodoxy being pursued by Burma in the 1950s.

But in two major theoretical essays, in 1954 and in 1958, that orthodoxy was challenged from Oxford by Hla Myint.[124] His challenge was rich and nuanced, but his core practical conclusion was that the most effective strategy for the less developed economies – and he drew particular attention to those, such as Burma, which under colonial rule had achieved an extraordinary expansion in primary exports by bringing into production previously unutilized land and labour – would be to maintain the strong commitment to exports, even primary commodity exports. The nationalist hostility towards the nineteenth-century colonial pattern of international trade, he urged, should be resisted, for only exports, and in practice this meant the export of raw materials, would fund adequately the development plans of the less developed.

This position underpinned Hla Myint's more empirical published work in the 1960s and 1970s. In a brief survey of the experience of five South East Asian economies since 1945, published in 1967, Hla Myint distinguished between, on the one hand, Malaya, Thailand, and the Philippines, and on the other, Indonesia and Burma. The former had been outward-looking.

They...seemed to have realised that...the key to expanding their total national product was to be found in expanding the volume of their exports. Since a large share of these exports was produced by the foreign-owned mines and plantations, the governments of these countries took care to guarantee the security of foreign property and freedom to remit profits, and generally created a favourable economic environment which encouraged the foreign

---

[124] Hla Myint, 'The gains from international trade and the backward countries', *Review of Economic Studies*, 22, 2 (1954–1955); Hla Myint, 'The "Classical Theory" of international trade and the underdeveloped countries', *Economic Journal*, 68, 270 (June 1958).

enterprises not only to continue their existing production but also...to strike out into new lines of exports.[125]

In contrast, Indonesia and Burma had been inward-looking. They had been

> obsessed by the fear that once the foreign enterprises were allowed to re-establish themselves in the export industries, they would regain their old 'stranglehold' on the economy...[Moreover the governments of Indonesia and Burma seem to have taken the view that] it was not important to carry on with [the] 'colonial economic pattern' and [had] diverted their attention and resources to [an] industrialization programme in the form of building...state-owned factories.[126]

And crucially, as Hla Myint pointed out, since 1945 the rate of economic growth in Malaya, Thailand, and the Philippines had been substantially above that in Indonesia and Burma.

In 1969, the Asian Development Bank was asked by the Fourth Ministerial Conference for the Economic Development of Southeast Asia, held in Bangkok, to undertake a study of the region's economic prospects, problems, and potential for the 1970s. The study produced six sectoral reports and an overall report. The latter, which was later published separately to make it accessible to the wider public, was written by Hla Myint alone, and is a vigorous statement of his outward-looking, export-driven, development strategy. It urged that the economies of the region exploit to the full their potential as exporters of primary commodities, not least by encouraging private foreign investment in that sector: and most strikingly, it urged the abandonment of the existing import-substitution industrialization policies and the pursuit of 'a new industrialization strategy based on the expansion of manufactured exports'.[127] Following precisely that strategy, a number of South East Asian countries – Thailand, Malaysia, Indonesia but not Burma – were to achieve remarkable economic growth and structural change in the final three decades of the twentieth century.

---

[125] Hla Myint, 'The inward and outward looking countries of Southeast Asia', *Malayan Economic Review*, 12, 1 (1967), p. 3.

[126] Ibid., p. 3.

[127] Hla Myint, *Southeast Asia's Economy: Development Policies in the 1970's: a Study Sponsored by the Asian Development Bank*. New York: Praeger, 1972, p. 160.

In his 1967 article, Hla Myint had argued that the inward-looking economic policies that had been pursued by Burma (and Indonesia) 'spring ultimately from deep-seated political and psychological attitudes'. He then added, perhaps poignantly: 'it is not the function of a mere economist to urge [the Burmese] to relax some of their prevailing attitudes for the sake of expanding their exports . . . they must make their own decision about the correct balance between political and economic objectives'.[128] In other words, as the clash between U Thet Tun and Louis Walinsky at the beginning of that decade had made clear, the Burmese had to decide between continued nationalist hostility towards the colonial economic legacy – 'the very roots on which the state of Burma was founded' – and the prospect of sustained development.

[128] Hla Myint, 'The inward and outward looking countries of Southeast Asia', p. 9.

4 | *In pursuit of socialism*

Military rule and the establishment of the Burmese Way to Socialism

In April 1958, the AFPFL government of U Nu, in power since Burma had regained its independence in January 1948, split into a 'Clean' faction, led by U Nu and the Minister of Agriculture and Forests, Thakin Tin, and a 'Stable' faction led by the socialists U Ba Swe and U Kyaw Nyein. U Nu's parliamentary position was now precarious – he scraped through a vote of confidence in June, but in August was forced to use a presidential decree to pass the annual budget – and in late September the prime minister was convinced by two senior Rangoon-based staff officers to transfer power to an army caretaker government under the army commander, General Ne Win, pending the holding of elections.[1] It was a coup with pressured consent. The formal transfer of power took place in late October 1958.

The caretaker government set itself three main objectives, in its own words, 'to bring about law and order; secondly, to combat economic insurgents; and thirdly, to hold a fair and free election'.[2] And it was broadly successful in meeting those objectives. Serious crime fell by one-third, and economic crimes, notably 'black-marketeering rackets', were more rigorously investigated and brought to the courts; over 150,000 squatters were removed from Rangoon's slums and settled in new satellite towns; and a national election was held, even if not

---

[1] For a detailed account of these events and of the subsequent period of caretaker government, see Mary P. Callahan, *Making Enemies: War and State Building in Burma*. Ithaca, NY: Cornell University Press, 2003, pp. 184–97.

[2] *Is Trust Vindicated? A Chronicle of the Various Accomplishments of the Government Headed by General Ne Win during the Period of Tenure from November, 1958 to February 6, 1960*. Rangoon: Director of Information, Government of the Union of Burma, 1960, p. 1.

131

altogether fair and free and somewhat later than first intended, in February 1960.[3]

However, the brief period of caretaker government between October 1958 and February 1960 had an arguably more important impact on the army itself. Most notably, it saw a considerable expansion in the army's economic interests, as the Defence Services Institute (DSI), established in 1951 to run the canteens, now 'opened or bought banks, an international shipping line, an import-export business, the single coal import license, a hotel company, fisheries and poultry distribution businesses, a construction firm, a [Rangoon] bus line . . . and the biggest department store chain in Burma'.[4] In other words, the army built an important position in Burma's modern economy, indeed a monopoly position in a number of lines of business. Moreover, the period of caretaker rule provided experience of civil government administration for a considerable number of senior army officers, for while the ministers remained civilian politicians, under General Ne Win as prime minister, brigadiers, colonels, majors, lieutenants, and captains were seconded to each major ministry and department. Thus Brigadier Aung Gyi, earlier a senior figure in the Burma Socialist Party and now close to Ne Win, became chairman of the Budget Allocation Supervision Committee in the Ministry of National Planning, while, to take a more mundane example, a Colonel Kyi Win was attached to the Income Tax Department.[5] This experience of civil administration was an encouraging one, for with military directness, practical solutions were found to immediate problems. Squatters were removed from Rangoon, black market racketeers were brought to book, and, again in the capital, 'sweat brigades' of civil servants, students, teachers, and other residents cleared the streets of thousands of tons of accumulated rubbish. The evident vigour of the caretaker administration and its visible achievements not only gave the military a belief in its ability to govern, but also created or confirmed its contemptuous view of Burma's civilian politicians, its parliamentary democracy, and its bureaucracy as ineffective, indeed corrupt and destructive.

---

[3] David I. Steinberg, *Burma's Road toward Development: Growth and Ideology under Military Rule.* Boulder, CO: Westview Press, 1981, pp. 16–18.

[4] Callahan, *Making Enemies*, p. 191.

[5] A list of military officers attached to civil departments, almost 150 names in 19 ministries, is found in *Is Trust Vindicated?*, Appendix 9.

The February 1960 election produced a decisive parliamentary majority for U Nu and the Clean AFPFL, renamed the Union (*Pyidaungsu*) Party, and the army returned to the barracks.[6] However the new civilian government was soon seen as incompetent or, worse, blundering. A constitutional amendment passed by parliament in August 1961 made Buddhism the state religion. This fulfilled a campaign promise by U Nu, but it angered the Kachin and the Karen, a substantial proportion of whom were Christian. U Nu had also promised state status to both the Arakanese and the Mon, and this, together with his allegedly sympathetic response to increasing pressure from the Shan for greater autonomy, appeared to threaten the territorial integrity of the union. Meanwhile, there was little growth in the economy, and the politicians endlessly bickered. In the early hours of 2 March 1962, the military led by General Ne Win took power in an almost bloodless coup, ruthlessly removing the political opposition. Leading ministers and officials, including the prime minister, U Nu, Burma's first president, and the Chief Justice, were arrested: most of those detained spent the following five years in detention. Parliament was dissolved and the constitution suspended. Student protest was crushed. On 7 July, troops opened fire on a demonstration at Rangoon University: and early the following morning, the Rangoon University Student Union building, a major site of nationalist organization and agitation since the 1930s, was blown up on the orders of General Ne Win.[7]

In the year following the coup, the Revolutionary Council, Burma's new military rulers, published three slim documents that articulated its social and economic objectives, the political means by which those objectives were to be achieved, and the philosophical basis upon which they rested.[8] The first document, published on 30 April 1962, was (in its English translation) *The Burmese Way to Socialism*. It began:

[6] Subsequently General Ne Win was awarded the Ramon Magsaysay Award for 'his conscientious custodianship of constitutional government and democratic principles in Burma through a period of national peril', although he declined the award, and the $10,000 prize, on the grounds of Magsaysay's CIA connections: Callahan, *Making Enemies*, p. 197.

[7] For description and analysis of the 1962 coup, see for example: Steinberg, *Burma's Road toward Development*, pp. 21–6; Callahan, *Making Enemies*, pp. 198–204; Bertil Lintner, *Burma in Revolt: Opium and Insurgency since 1948*, 2nd edn. Chiang Mai: Silkworm Books, 1999, pp. 210–15.

[8] The following, including the quotations, draws on Steinberg, *Burma's Road toward Development*, pp. 27–31.

Figure 4.1 General Ne Win at a peasants' seminar in 1964
Source: Burma Socialist Programme Party, *Amyú-tei pa-ti-hmá pyei-thú pa-ti-thó* [Illustrated history of the BSPP]. Rangoon, 1974?

[The Revolutionary Council] does not believe that man will be set free from social evils as long as pernicious economic systems exist in which man exploits man and lives on the fat of such appropriation. The Council believes it to be possible only when exploitation of man by man is brought to an end and a socialist economy based on justice is established . . . Thus affirmed in this belief the Revolutionary Council is resolved to march unswervingly and arm-in-arm with the people of the Union of Burma towards the goal of socialism.

Thus *The Burmese Way to Socialism* declared that all forms of agricultural and industrial production but also distribution, transportation, and external trade must be owned by the state or by cooperatives.

Private ownership, a pernicious economic system in which man exploited man, must be eliminated. But then the document contradicted itself: 'national [Burmese] private enterprises which contribute to national [Burma's] productive forces will be allowed with fair and reasonable restrictions.' It continued:

On the full realization of socialist economy the socialist government, far from neglecting the [Burmese] owners of national private enterprises which have been steadfastly contributing to the general well-being of the people, will even enable them to occupy a worthy place in the new society.

The remaining two Revolutionary Council defining documents need be noted here only briefly. The first, published on 4 July 1962, was *The Constitution of the Burma Socialist Programme Party*. The BSPP (Burma Socialist Programme Party) provided the Revolutionary Council with a political structure. At first it was a cadre party, indeed its membership was mainly restricted to the Revolutionary Council itself, but in the early 1970s it would become a mass organization. And the final document, published in January 1963, was *The System of Correlation of Man and his Environment: the Philosophy of the Burma Socialist Programme Party*. Drawing implicitly on Marxist ideas and Buddhist thought, it established that 'The socialist society based on justice, upon which we have set our hearts, is a prosperous and affluent society, free from exploitation or oppression of man by man.'

In its pursuit of socialism, the Revolutionary Council moved rapidly to nationalize the remaining British commercial interests in Burma. In January 1963, Burma's government bought out the British majority stake in Burma Oil, the joint venture that had been created in 1954.[9] The following month, all of Burma's private commercial banks, including the fourteen foreign banks, among them the Chartered, the Mercantile, and the Hongkong and Shanghai, were nationalized and reconstituted as serially numbered People's Banks.[10] In this same period, the Burma Corporation, the Bombay Burmah Trading Corporation, and the local subsidiaries of Unilever, British Oxygen, the British Match Corporation, and of Imperial Chemical Industries

[9] T. A. B. Corley, *A History of the Burmah Oil Company, Vol. II: 1924–1966*. London: Heinemann, 1988, pp. 254–71.
[10] Sean Turnell, *Fiery Dragons: Banks, Moneylenders and Microfinance in Burma*. Copenhagen: NIAS Press, 2009, pp. 224–8. The Chartered Bank became the People's Bank No. 2, and the Hongkong and Shanghai became the People's Bank No. 9.

were also nationalized. The British commercial presence, dominant in the colonial economy, was brought to a final end. Indian commercial interests too were forced out. One half of the foreign banks nationalized in early 1963 were Indian concerns, but the decisive blow against Indian interests came with the nationalization of private trade and private manufacturing, to be noted below. An estimated 300,000 Indians left Burma in 1963–4, leaving behind just the stateless and the poor.[11] What had been another hugely important presence in Burma's colonial economy was thereby finally brought to an end.

Burmese private commercial interests welcomed these expulsions. Earlier they had also been encouraged by the appointment of the reputedly business-minded Brigadier Aung Gyi, formerly chairman of the Budget Allocation Supervision Committee in the caretaker government, as Minister of Trade.[12] A powerful figure, said to be the second most influential member of the coup group, behind Ne Win, he had persuaded the first policy meeting of the Revolutionary Council that local private capital would have a significant place in the Burmese way to socialism. But in early 1963 Aung Gyi was forced from office, driven out by political-personality rivalries and by opposition within the Revolutionary Council to his stand on private capital. Economic policy was now dominated by two socialist hardliners, Brigadier Tin Pe and U Ba Nyein, the latter an economics graduate of Rangoon University before the war and later a founder of the Burma Workers and Peasants Party.[13]

The Revolutionary Council now pushed on with fierce determination to bring the Burma economy into state ownership. The nationalization of all the private commercial banks in February 1963 has already been noted. That same month, the Revolutionary Council announced that all major industries would be nationalized by 1 June: and Ne

---

[11] John H. Badgley, 'Burma's zealot wungyis: Maoists or St Simonists', *Asian Survey*, 5, 1 (January 1965), p. 55; Nalini Ranjan Chakravarti, *The Indian Minority in Burma: the Rise and Decline of an Immigrant Community*. London: Oxford University Press, 1971, p. 186.

[12] The following draws principally on Kyaw Yin Hlaing, 'Reconsidering the failure of the Burma Socialist Programme Party government to eradicate internal economic impediments', *South East Asia Research*, 11, 1 (2003), pp. 8–10.

[13] For a brief biographical note for U Ba Nyein, and for a number of other prominent Burmese of this period, see David I. Steinberg, *Burma: a Socialist Nation of Southeast Asia*. Boulder, CO: Westview Press, 1982, pp. 127–9.

Figure 4.2 The nationalization of an Indian textile shop shortly after the 1962 military take-over
Source: Burma Socialist Programme Party, *Amyú-tei pa-ti-hmá pyei-thú pa-ti-thó* [Illustrated history of the BSPP]. Rangoon, 1974?

Figure 4.3 The nationalization of the retail and wholesale trade following the
military coup of March 1962
Source: Burma Socialist Programme Party, *Amyú-tei pa-ti-hmá pyei-thú pa-ti-
thó* [Illustrated history of the BSPP]. Rangoon, 1974?

Win himself laid down that the state would take over the production,
distribution, import, and export of all major commodities.[14] In
October 1963, a ban was imposed on private imports: and in April
1964, Burma's entire export trade was nationalized.[15] Foreign trade
was now a state monopoly. That same year also saw the nationalization of all wholesale trade and also retail outlets, not only department
stores and cooperatives, but small shops too. It has been estimated
that more than 15,000 private concerns were nationalized in this

[14] Steinberg, *Burma: a Socialist Nation of Southeast Asia*, p. 77.
[15] Turnell, *Fiery Dragons*, p. 229.

period.[16] It would appear that 'such draconian measures in the name of socialism' disturbed even the Soviet and East European diplomats in Rangoon and visiting officials from those communist states.[17]

There may well have been hesitation too within the government itself. Most notably it would appear that 'Many senior officials believed that Ne Win was not sure about the extent to which nationalization', fiercely advocated by Ba Nyein and Tin Pe, the socialist hardliners noted above, 'should be pursued'.[18] In 1965, Ne Win asked Ba Nyein and Chan Aye, who had graduated in economics from Rangoon and was well-regarded by Hla Myint, each to propose an economic strategy for the government.[19] Chan Aye, a committed communist in the late 1940s – he had gone underground with the rigidly uncompromising Thakin Soe – but who had subsequently become disillusioned with orthodox communist doctrine, sought the help of, among others, U Thet Tun, the earlier critic of Louis Walinsky, Aye Hlaing, Professor of Economics at the University of Rangoon, and a young Dr Ronald Findlay, recently returned from the Massachusetts Institute of Technology and now a lecturer in economics at Rangoon. The economic strategy drawn up by the group was export-oriented, in line with the thinking of Hla Myint, and focused on the expansion of Burma's primary commodity exports. This would be achieved in part by re-establishing price incentives for producers, notably rice cultivators, to secure increased output. Chan Aye and his colleagues were thus highly critical of the government's long-established policy of squeezing the cultivator through the imposition of low procurement prices, on the grounds that it had depressed production and prevented the exploitation of Burma's economic potential. Ne Win was not persuaded. He told Chan Aye that his economic strategy 'would put the country into

[16] Steinberg, *Burma's Road toward Development*, p. 35. In March 1964 a local periodical reported that 13,469 merchandise shops had been nationalized: Tin Maung Maung Than, *State Dominance in Myanmar: the Political Economy of Industrialization*. Singapore: Institute of Southeast Asian Studies, 2007, p. 147, fn. 27.

[17] Khin Maung Kyi, Ronald Findlay, R. M. Sundrum, Mya Maung, Myo Nyunt, Zaw Oo, et al., *Economic Development of Burma: a Vision and a Strategy*. Stockholm: Olof Palme International Center, 2000, pp. 10–11.

[18] Kyaw Yin Hlaing, 'Reconsidering the failure of the Burma Socialist Programme Party government', p. 33.

[19] The following draws on U Thet Tun, *Waves of Influence*. Yangon: Thin Sapay, 2011, pp. 173–5, 185–6; interview with U Thet Tun, Yangon, 25 January 2012; personal communication from Professor Ronald Findlay, 21 February 2012.

the hands of the CIA', perhaps shorthand for allowing the re-entry of foreign economic and then political interests, clearly an anathema to Ne Win and many others. U Ba Nyein and Brigadier Tin Pe therefore remained dominant in economic decision-making.

The Revolutionary Council's economic strategy was, in its essentials, a continuation of the economic strategy that had been pursued by the civilian government of U Nu from 1948 – but now on occasion pushed to the extreme. Thus the final expulsion of British and Indian commercial interests in the first years of military rule was clearly in line with the strategy of Burmanization, a central ambition of Burma's government since independence in 1948, but here driven to the very limit. Continuity occasionally pushed to the extreme was also evident in the Revolutionary Council's strategy for agriculture. Thus, as in the 1950s, the sector received far less support from the government than its very substantial economic importance would have justified. In the first year of military rule, the agricultural sector was allocated just 13 per cent of total state investment: a decade later, in 1970/71, its allocation was down to a mere 8 per cent.[20] Under-investment in agriculture was evident, for example, in the fact that throughout the 1960s, just one-tenth of the net sown area in Burma was irrigated. Moreover the volume of credit provided to the cultivator by the government – private moneylending was officially prohibited and of course the Chettiar had long gone – fell far short of the amount he required, despite the fact that soon after taking power, the Revolutionary Council had substantially increased its provision.[21] In the early 1970s, the credit provided by the government to the rice cultivator covered just 11 per cent of average cultivation costs. And it should be added that the loans provided through the State Agricultural Bank and its network of village banks were short-term loans, seasonal loans at best. No medium- or long-term loans were provided to finance improvements that would increase productivity. And finally, continuing the policy of the previous civilian administration, from 1962 through to the mid-1970s, the military government held the price at which it procured rice little changed and far below the export price.[22] The strategic objectives, as

---

[20] U Khin Win, *A Century of Rice Improvement in Burma*. Manila: International Rice Research Institute, 1991, pp. 79, 113.

[21] This passage draws on Turnell, *Fiery Dragons*, pp. 233–5, 240–8.

[22] Mya Than and Nobuyoshi Nishizawa, 'Agricultural policy reforms and agricultural development in Myanmar', in Mya Than and Joseph L. H. Tan (ed.), *Myanmar Dilemmas and Options: the Challenge of Economic Transition in the 1990s*. Singapore: Institute of Southeast Asian Studies, 1990, pp. 96–8.

in the 1950s, were to hold down the cost of living, important for the urban population and for labourers, and to provide the state with the revenue – created by the difference between the procurement price and the export price – to finance its development ambitions.

Elsewhere the Revolutionary Council pushed the agriculture strategy of the earlier civilian administration to the extreme. As noted in the previous chapter, the State Agricultural Marketing Board (SAMB), formed in 1947, had a statutory monopoly in the export of rice. It bought paddy from the cultivators, either directly or through middlemen, and rice from the millers, in both cases at prices fixed by official decree. Export sales were secured either through inter-government agreements or, to a diminishing extent, through private Burmese traders. The core aims of the SAMB had been to eliminate foreign interests from the rice export trade and to impose a low procurement price on the rice cultivator, for the reasons explained immediately above. It is important to note that under this regime, the domestic trade in rice, the distribution for local consumption, was left to private traders: and also that Burma's farmers were free to decide which crops they would cultivate, on what scale, the methods to be used, and to whom they would sell their output.[23]

The military government was far more interventionist. In July 1963, trade in eleven essential commodities, including rice, wheat, and many vegetables, was nationalized, that is procurement, distribution, and export were now undertaken solely by the Union of Burma Agricultural and Marketing Board (UBAMB), as the SAMB had been renamed.[24] By the following year the rice cultivator could sell only to Trade Corporation No. 1 (a further change in name), private trade in rice in the domestic market, as well as for export, being officially prohibited. The government's procurement system was said to be voluntary. But in reality cultivators were compelled to deliver a compulsory quota, and of course at a price both fixed and low. This was far from the limit of the state's intervention in agriculture. In certain rural districts, classified as 'planned' areas, distant administrators with little agricultural expertise or experience directed cultivators as to which crop to grow, how, and when.

---

[23] Myat Thein, *Economic Development of Myanmar*. Singapore: Institute of Southeast Asian Studies, 2004, p. 90.

[24] Mya Than and Nobuyoshi Nishizawa, 'Agricultural policy reforms and agricultural development in Myanmar', pp. 93, 96; Myat Thein, *Economic Development of Myanmar*, pp. 90–1.

A final Revolutionary Council agrarian measure, and perhaps an omission, should be noted. In 1965 the military government abolished agricultural tenancy, although in practice it may well have continued on some scale into the early 1970s at least.[25] The Indian and indeed Burmese landlord had been among the most damning legacies of colonial rule. But completing a process which had begun with the land legislation of 1948 and 1953, the Revolutionary Council had now finally removed that presence from rural Burma. But perhaps surprisingly, the military government did not then bring agricultural land into state ownership, despite the fact that *The Burmese Way to Socialism* stated that all forms of production must be owned by the state or by cooperatives. It is true that the state was the ultimate owner of the land. But cultivators had the right to work it *as individuals*, although they could not sell or mortgage their holding or purchase a further holding. For this last reason, but also because land redistribution favoured those who had no land, holdings were small. In the early 1970s, almost 64 per cent of cultivating households worked holdings of less than five acres. Almost 87 per cent of households worked less than ten acres.[26] An agricultural holding of ten acres or, for many, far less was too small either to secure economies of scale in cultivation, or to produce for the household a surplus income to invest in higher-yield inputs and methods. In other words, the size distribution of holdings – almost nine out of ten farming households worked less than ten acres, more than six out of ten households less than five – sacrificed increasing productivity to equity.

In the decade or so of Revolutionary Council government, Burma's agriculture stagnated and even regressed. This was almost certainly inevitable, given the circumstances outlined above – the low procurement prices, left virtually unchanged year after year; the extension of state monopoly to all trade in essential agricultural commodities; the inadequate provision of credit to the cultivator; reduced state investment in agriculture; micro-management and indeed mismanagement of cultivation through official directives; and the perpetuation of an uneconomic distribution of land holdings. Production of rice, wheat, maize, groundnut, pulses, and cotton was actually lower, in volume

[25] Mya Than and Nobuyoshi Nishizawa, 'Agricultural policy reforms and agricultural development in Myanmar', pp. 90–1.

[26] Myat Thein, *Economic Development of Myanmar*, p. 89.

terms, in 1972/73 than it had been a decade earlier.[27] Only sugar cane, jute, and tea saw a substantial increase in production in this period.

Rice was still by far the most important crop, of course, accounting for almost two-thirds of total sown acreage in the early 1960s. The area under rice increased slightly in the middle of the decade but by the early 1970s had partly fallen back. Production of paddy, 7.55 million tons in 1962/63, also rose slightly in the mid-1960s but, as indicated above, had fallen more sharply, to 7.24 million tons in 1972/73. And at the same time, Burma's growing population consumed a much increased share of that falling production, leaving a smaller and smaller surplus for export. In 1962, Burma still exported 1.718 million tons of rice.[28] In 1973, rice exports were down to a mere 146,000 tons. The once mighty shipments, feeding millions across Asia, had shrunk to a bare trickle.

The focus of the military government's economic strategy in this first decade was, however, on state-led industrialization, with the aim to secure for Burma self-sufficiency in a range of manufactures. By the mid-1970s, no less than a quarter of state investment was being allocated to manufacturing and processing.[29] Of course the earlier civilian government had also given priority to state-led import-substitution industrialization. But the military now drove that strategy to the extreme. In the previous decade there had been joint ventures with foreign capital – Burma Oil in 1954 – and, it is said, substantial progress in local private sector manufacturing. But, as noted earlier, shortly after taking power, the Revolutionary Council nationalized all the joint ventures – Burma Oil, the Burma Corporation, the Bombay Burmah Trading Corporation, and the local subsidiaries of Unilever, British Oxygen, the British Match Corporation, and Imperial Chemical Industries – and indeed all private industrial concerns of any significant size, both foreign and Burmese.[30] In addition, no new private industrial concerns were permitted. And where an existing manufacturing concern was regarded as too small to be brought into state ownership, it was brought under state direction through a hierarchy of supervision and coordination committees. These exercised control over each concern by, for example, determining the supply of raw materials,

---

[27] Ibid., pp. 95–6.
[28] U Khin Win, *A Century of Rice Improvement in Burma*, p. 125.
[29] Myat Thein, *Economic Development of Myanmar*, p. 61.   [30] Ibid., p. 104.

plant, and spares; fixing the prices of the finished manufacture; and deciding operational and management matters.[31] Faced with this most intrusive bureaucratic meddling, the small-scale Burmese manufacturer was driven from existence – or rather, it appears, was driven into the illegal economy, a point to be taken up below.

The performance of manufacturing in the decade or so after the 1962 coup was 'dismal', to quote one authority.[32] In almost every year, production either barely increased or actually fell, so that the real value of processing and manufacturing output in 1971/72 was barely 7 per cent above the sector's output a decade earlier, and this despite substantial state investment.[33] Moreover, the composition of manufacturing remained virtually unchanged between the early 1960s and the early 1970s, with food and beverages accounting for just over 60 per cent of the total value of manufacturing production in both periods.[34] More pertinently, the relative importance in manufacturing of construction materials, household goods, agricultural equipment, industrial equipment, transport vehicles, and electrical goods, that might have been expected to increase substantially, given the government's industrialization strategy, also remained unchanged – and dismally low. Finally, in one crucial respect, the sector regressed: its share of GDP actually fell between the early 1960s and the mid-1970s, and this despite the fact that in this period, agricultural production was stagnating.[35]

The dismal performance of manufacturing in the 1960s is explained by a number of circumstances.[36] Shortages of foreign exchange, a reflection of the poor performance of Burma's exports in this period, severely restricted the import of machinery, spare parts, and raw materials essential to the industrialization drive. Thus intermittent and inadequate access to imported machinery and spares led to the continued use of less productive, now obsolete plant, and to low rates of maintenance and repair. There were also restrictions in the supply of

---

[31] Tin Maung Maung Than, *State Dominance in Myanmar: the Political Economy of Industrialization.* Singapore: Institute of Southeast Asian Studies, 2007, pp. 123–4.

[32] Myat Thein, *Economic Development of Myanmar*, p. 105.

[33] Calculated from Tin Maung Maung Than, *State Dominance in Myanmar*, Table 5.3, p. 127.

[34] Myat Thein, *Economic Development of Myanmar*, p. 107.

[35] Ibid., pp. 87, 105.

[36] The following draws principally on Myat Thein, *Economic Development of Myanmar*, pp. 106–9; and Tin Maung Maung Than, *State Dominance in Myanmar*, pp. 128–9.

some local raw materials, for example, of raw cotton for the textile mills and of wood products for the paper factories, but here because of failures in local production. In addition, it would clearly be a huge challenge for any desk-bound bureaucracy to run a command-control economy with a measure of efficiency and effectiveness, to align successively industrial inputs, plant capacity, manpower allocations, and consumer demands. But for the Burmese bureaucracy of this period, with limited practical experience of commercial principles and allowing no room for individual initiative or judgement, that challenge was near-impossible to meet. These two circumstances – the insecure, inadequate access to raw materials and to imported machinery and spares; and the near-insuperable bureaucratic task of aligning each and every process – meant that in the 1960s, Burma's state industrial concerns were left working far below capacity. And finally, in the running of the state industries, abandoning the market meant that there was no commercial discipline, no commercial pressure to improve performance or incentive to do so, but only bureaucratic directive and exhortation. The result was inertia, slackness, and waste.

Two further aspects of the Revolutionary Council economic strategy should be noted. The first was the nationalization of private internal trade. In the civilian period, some 12,000 wholesalers, more than 100,000 retail shops, and around 4,000 cooperatives had been involved in the distribution of goods to the Burmese consumer.[37] By 1964, only some 3,000 wholesale and retail shops remained. The private sector had accounted for just under 70 per cent of total trade, foreign and domestic, at the end of the civilian period, but just 15 per cent in the mid-1960s.[38] Internal trade in consumer goods and commodities was now largely in the hands of the People's Store Corporation and its network of public and cooperative stores. The state stores struggled. Tight restriction on the import of consumer goods – a consequence of the poor performance of Burma's exports and the fact that priority was given in imports to industrial raw materials, machinery, and spares – together with the dismal performance of local manufacturing, meant that there were far too few goods to distribute.

---

[37] Kyaw Yin Hlaing, 'Reconsidering the failure of the Burma Socialist Programme Party government to eradicate internal economic impediments', *South East Asia Research*, 11, 1 (2003), p. 19. This section draws principally on Kyaw Yin Hlaing, pp. 14–20.

[38] Lawrence D. Stifel, 'Economics of the Burmese Way to Socialism', *Asian Survey*, 11, 8 (August 1971), p. 805.

In addition, the administrators in the People's Store Corporation and its outlets faced a near-insuperable task when attempting to align supplies with consumers' needs and preferences across Burma. Moreover, there were almost certainly too few administrators. In the civilian period, the distribution of goods to Burmese consumers had involved perhaps two million people: in the 1960s, the entire system of public stores employed just 50,000. In brief, the state distribution network failed to meet the needs of Burma's population. Shelves were often bare – or piled high with goods for which there was no demand. The sudden availability of a small consignment of a much sought-after item would quickly produce crowds and queues. Rice, and indeed many other basic items, was regularly rationed. In 1967 there were riots in Insein in part over the unavailability of essential commodities.[39] In fact people survived by turning to the now greatly expanding illegal economy.

The final aspect of the Revolutionary Council economic strategy to be noted was a retreat from the international economy, towards autarky. The fall in rice exports in the 1960s, down to a bare trickle in the mid-1970s, was noted earlier. Total export value fell by roughly a half between the early 1960s and the early 1970s.[40] The sharp fall in foreign earnings forced the authorities to restrict imports, achieved by imposing quantitative allocations rather than by raising tariff rates. But the fall in total import value, although considerable, was not as severe as the contraction in export earnings – the industrialization drive required heavy imports of machinery, raw materials, and spares – and consequently, from the mid-1960s, each year Burma ran a substantial balance of trade deficit.

Foreign trade, as officially recorded, was now clearly of considerably less importance. In the early 1960s, total export value was equivalent to a little under 20 per cent of GDP, total import value, towards

---

[39] David I. Steinberg, *Burma's Road toward Development: Growth and Ideology under Military Rule*. Boulder, CO: Westview Press, 1981, p. 36. According to a further observer, in that year 'there were serious rice shortages and the government permitted consumers to purchase directly from the farmers in order to reduce the spreading panic in the cities': Stifel, 'Economics of the Burmese Way to Socialism', p. 805.

[40] Mya Than, *Myanmar's External Trade: an Overview in the Southeast Asian Context*. Singapore: Institute of Southeast Asian Studies, 1992, Table 3.3, p. 16, provides the figures that underpin the observations in this paragraph, unless otherwise noted.

15 per cent.[41] In the early 1970s, both the export and import figures were down to about 6 per cent of GDP. The authorities appear
to have welcomed that contraction as demonstrating that Burma had
become more self-reliant.[42] At the same time, the Revolutionary Council banned foreign private investment – although it is difficult to imagine that a foreign commercial concern would think of venturing into
Burma in the wake of the recent expulsion of British and Indian business interests – and did not seek large aid provision from either foreign
governments or international financial agencies. Interestingly, however, the small volume of official development assistance (ODA) that
Burma *did* accept during these years was crucial in partially offsetting
the balance of trade deficits that occurred from the mid-1960s and in
meeting the high foreign exchange costs of the government's industrial
projects.[43] In other words, the pursuit of self-reliance rested on an
external dependence.

Adjusting the route to socialism

The evident failure of the Revolutionary Council economic strategy –
the stagnation in rice production and the 1967 riots noted above would
have particularly disturbed the authorities – demanded change.[44] In the
early 1970s, the architects and enforcers of that strategy, Brigadier Tin
Pe and U Ba Nyein, were forced out. The BSPP then produced a substantial document, *Long-Term and Short-Term Economic Policies of
the Burma Socialist Programme Party*, which was first considered at
the BSPP Congress in mid-1971 and then formally adopted at a meeting of the BSPP Central Committee in September 1972. With notable
frankness, the document set out the failings of the economy over the
previous decade, and then re-plotted Burma's route to socialism.

The revised economic strategy had four key provisions. The first was
that priority would now be given to the exploitation of Burma's natural endowment, in agriculture, of course, but also forestry, fisheries,

[41] Myat Thein, *Economic Development of Myanmar*, Table 3.6, p. 77.
[42] Ibid., p. 60.
[43] For details of the foreign financial assistance accepted by Burma under the
Revolutionary Council government, see Tin Maung Maung Than, *State
Dominance in Myanmar*, pp. 135–7.
[44] The following draws principally on Steinberg, *Burma's Road toward
Development*, pp. 43–8.

Figure 4.4 A postcard produced for the first Party Congress of the BSPP in 1971, showing productive and ebullient agricultural and industrial workers
Source: Burma Socialist Programme Party, *Amyú-tei pa-ti-hmá pyei-thú pa-ti-thó* [Illustrated history of the BSPP]. Rangoon, 1974?

and mining. State-led import-substituting industrialization, the core development ambition of Burma's governments since independence in 1948, remained: that aim, here restated, was to create an industrial economy within twenty years, in other words by the early 1990s. But now it was agreed that the industrial sector would focus on processing and manufacturing from Burma's own agricultural, forest, fisheries, and mineral resources, to meet domestic demand but also, crucially, for export, as indeed was being advocated at that time by Hla Myint.[45] In summary, Burma's industrialization ambition was being adjusted in two important respects: the sector would now focus on the use of local resources, and thus would be less import-dependent; and it would now have a substantial export potential.

The second key aspect of the revised economic strategy was an implicit recognition that administrative directive and official exhortation alone would not stimulate growth, and therefore that material incentives must be built into Burma's economic structures, for example, in the operation of state industrial enterprises and in the state's procurement of agricultural production. Third was a recognition that state enterprises alone could not provide sufficient employment or sufficient consumer goods – witness a vastly growing illegal economy – and therefore that local private capital had an important place in Burma's socialist economy. And fourth, the revised economic strategy sanctioned a return to foreign borrowing and the receipt of foreign aid and technical assistance on a substantial scale. During the 1970s and 1980s, Burma would receive more than $2 billion from the Asian Development Bank, the IMF, the World Bank, the United Nations Development Programme, and many individual donor countries, including the United States, Australia, France, the Federal Republic of Germany, Japan, the United Kingdom, China, and the Soviet Union.[46] Finally it is important to note that each of these revisions to the BSPP economic strategy agreed in the early 1970s – to pursue local resource-based industrialization, insert material incentives, accept an

---

[45] In his *Southeast Asia's Economy: Development Policies in the 1970's: a Study Sponsored by the Asian Development Bank*. New York: Praeger, 1972, p. 61, Hla Myint argued that 'export-substitution', that is the substitution of the export of raw materials in an unprocessed state by the export of processed or semi-processed materials, 'offers the Southeast Asian countries the most promising way of expanding manufactured exports'.

[46] Kyaw Yin Hlaing, 'Reconsidering the failure of the Burma Socialist Programme Party government', p. 23.

important role for local private capital, and to return to foreign borrowing and foreign aid – saw the doctrinaire beliefs that had under-pinned *The Burmese Way to Socialism* a decade earlier being tempered by a sense of pragmatism. In one important respect, however, there was no revision, no retreat. While Burma returned to official foreign borrowing and foreign aid in the 1970s, there was no return to for-eign direct investment (except in offshore oil exploration by foreign oil companies), no return of foreign commercial interests. In other words, there was no prospect here that Burma would follow a number of its South East Asian neighbours in pursuing export-driven industrializa-tion through heavy inward private investment.

In 1972, the price at which the government procured paddy from the cultivator was increased by just under 20 per cent, the first rise since 1967.[47] The following year, 1973, the procurement price was more than doubled, and there were further, modest, increases in 1978 and 1980. This period also saw a dramatic increase in the use of high-yield variety (HYV) seeds, the arrival in Burma of the 'Green Revolution'. At the beginning of the 1970s, just 4 per cent of Burma's rice area had been planted with modern varieties.[48] In the middle of the decade, that figure was edging towards 10 per cent, but it then rose very sharply indeed. In 1980, 40 per cent of the rice area was planted with modern varieties, and in 1985, over 50 per cent. At the same time there was a great increase in the use of chemical fertilizers and a marked expansion in the irrigated area, both essential to exploit the full potential of the HYV seeds. In 1970, just 36,000 tons of fertilizer had been applied to Burma's rice land.[49] In 1980, that figure had risen to over 200,000 tons, and in 1985, to 328,000 tons. Before 1975, all fertilizer was imported. But then two local factories producing urea – a third was constructed in the mid-1980s – met a major part of Burma's fertilizer requirements. The irrigated rice area increased by just over 140,000 hectares between 1972 and 1980.[50]

The extent of these changes should not be exaggerated. In most years between 1972 and 1985, the government left its rice procurement price

[47] Mya Than and Nobuyoshi Nishizawa, 'Agricultural policy reforms and agricultural development in Myanmar', in Mya Than and Joseph L. H. Tan (eds), *Myanmar Dilemmas and Options: the Challenge of Economic Transition in the 1990s*. Singapore: Institute of Southeast Asian Studies, 1990, p. 97.
[48] U Khin Win, *A Century of Rice Improvement in Burma*. Manila: International Rice Research Institute, 1991, p. 65.
[49] Ibid., pp. 69–71.   [50] Ibid., p. 113.

unchanged on the previous year: and despite the increases which did take place from 1972, the price received by the cultivator remained far below the rice export price, which in fact jumped sharply in the mid-1970s. Or again, despite the great increase in the use of chemical fertilizer, application per hectare in Burma remained substantially below that in, for example, Bangladesh, Indonesia, and the Philippines in the same years. And despite the marked expansion in irrigation, in the mid-1980s, still only 15 per cent of Burma's net sown area was irrigated. Nevertheless, these changes, together with greater use of tractors and work-animals and improvements in cultivation practices, were sufficient to secure a marked increase in rice yields, from 1.8 tons per hectare in 1973 to 3.2 tons in 1982.[51] Consequently, Burma's total rice production, having stagnated in the decade from 1962, now rose sharply, from 8.6 million tons in 1973 to 14.4 million tons in 1982.[52] This increase was achieved, it is important to note, while the area planted with rice remained constant, in fact fell slightly in the early 1980s. In other words, for the first time in the modern era, a substantial and sustained increase in the production of Burma's principal crop, rice, was achieved not through an expansion in the cultivated area but by raising yields, by the application of improved inputs and cultivation methods. Part of the increased production was undoubtedly consumed by Burma's growing population, but that still left a substantially larger surplus for export. A mere 146,000 tons in 1973, a bare trickle, by 1983, rice exports had reached 858,000 tons.[53]

Production of other crops – wheat, maize, groundnut, pulses, cotton, sugar – also increased substantially in the late 1970s and early 1980s, as a result of, again, higher procurement prices, heavier use of fertilizer, increased use of draught animals and tractors, and improvements in cultivation practices.[54] Favourable weather conditions were also important. The increase in sugar production was particularly marked, from 2.0 million tons in 1972/73 to 3.7 million tons in 1982/83. In summary, the total net value of Burma's agricultural output, at constant prices, rose by almost 90 per cent between the mid-1970s and the mid-1980s.[55] Over that decade, the growth rate in each year was

[51] Ibid., p. 61.   [52] Ibid., p. 62.   [53] Ibid., p. 125.
[54] Myat Thein, *Economic Development of Myanmar*. Singapore: Institute of Southeast Asian Studies, 2004, p. 95.
[55] Mya Than, *Growth Pattern of Burmese Agriculture: a Productivity Approach*. Singapore: Institute of Southeast Asian Studies, 1988, p. 10. Mya Than here

commonly above 5 per cent: and in the late 1970s to early 1980s, it averaged above 8 per cent. This was impressive.

Other sectors also showed substantial growth in this period. Natural gas production rose from 5.6 billion cubic feet in 1974/75 to 41.9 billion in 1987/88, an average annual growth of 16.8 per cent.[56] The production of crude oil rose from 6.77 million barrels in 1974 to 11.02 million in 1979, although output then stagnated as onshore extraction faltered and offshore exploration, undertaken with foreign partners from the mid-1970s, failed to produce significant finds.[57] Production of tin, tungsten, lead, zinc, and jade also rose substantially from the mid-1970s through to the early 1980s, although, with the exception of tin, it was still well below the levels that had been achieved at the beginning of the 1960s, so severely had production fallen in the first decade of military rule. Finally, production of both teak and hardwood increased markedly from the mid-1970s into the 1980s. In the mid-1980s, these were Burma's major export-earners.[58]

Between 1974 and 1977, fully one-quarter of public investment was allocated to the processing and manufacturing sector, and between 1978 and 1985, substantially above one-third.[59] As noted earlier, state-led import-substituting industrialization remained the core development ambition – the aim now was to create an industrialized socialist state by the early 1990s – although, with the formal adoption of the *Long-Term and Short-Term Economic Policies of the Burma Socialist Programme Party* in 1972, that industrial sector would in future focus on processing and manufacturing from Burma's own natural resources. However, the performance of the sector from the mid-1970s was falling substantially short, if that core ambition was in fact to be achieved by the early 1990s, and indeed short of the growth stipulated in the economic plans and anticipated, given the heavy public investment. Between 1974 and 1977, processing and manufacturing grew at an average annual rate of 7.1 per cent.[60] The rate then fell, to

provides a detailed analysis of the factors that secured the increases in yields and output in Burma's agriculture from the mid-1970s.

[56] Tin Maung Maung Than, *State Dominance in Myanmar: the Political Economy of Industrialization*. Singapore: Institute of Southeast Asian Studies, 2007, pp. 263–5.

[57] Hal Hill and Sisira Jayasuriya, *An Inward-Looking Economy in Transition: Economic Development in Burma since the 1960s*. Singapore: Institute of Southeast Asian Studies, 1986, pp. 55–7.

[58] Ibid., p. 48; Myat Thein, *Economic Development of Myanmar*, p. 101.

[59] Myat Thein, *Economic Development of Myanmar*, p. 61.

[60] Tin Maung Maung Than, *State Dominance in Myanmar*, p. 258.

5.3 per cent from 1978 to 1981 (the planned rate was 12.2 per cent) and to 4.7 per cent from 1982 to 1985 (against a target of 9.0 per cent). Then, in the two or three years from 1986, growth turned negative (the target was 7.7 per cent): processing and manufacturing value-added output actually contracted.

In addition, although the total number of industrial enterprises increased considerably over this period, the increase was concentrated exclusively in the smallest units, concerns employing less than ten workers, almost all of which were in private hands.[61] The number of small privately owned industrial enterprises rose from over 23,000 in 1974/75 to over 37,000 in 1987/88. Between the same years, the number of medium-sized industrial enterprises, those employing between ten and 100 workers, almost halved, from 4,792 to 2,531. The fall was most severe for those concerns in private ownership. The number of large industrial enterprises, employing more than 100 workers, was exactly the same in 1987/88 (493) as it had been in 1974/75. However, within that stationary total, the number of state enterprises rose markedly (from 411 to 489) while private enterprise was virtually wiped out, falling from twenty-six concerns in 1974/75 to a mere four in 1987/88.

In other words, although the revision of the BSPP economic strategy in the early 1970s had included a recognition that local private enterprise had an important place in Burma's socialist economy, a recognition that state enterprises alone could not provide sufficient employment or sufficient consumer goods, the subsequent decade or more had seen a sharp reduction in the position of private Burmese capital in medium-sized and large-scale processing and manufacturing. In that sector, private capital was now largely confined to the smallest segment. However, to judge by the marked increase in the number of small-scale private concerns over this period noted above, there it flourished. It reportedly flourished too in the illegal economy, an important point to be taken up shortly.

The revision of the BSPP economic strategy in the early 1970s had also established that material incentives and discipline must be built into the operation of Burma's state industrial enterprises. The latter would now be run on commercial principles, to a degree. This was a quite fundamental change in approach and, perhaps not surprisingly,

---

[61] The following draws on data from Tin Maung Maung Than, *State Dominance in Myanmar*, Tables 7.4, 7.5, 7.6, pp. 260–1.

it proved to be impossible to implement.[62] Through the 1970s and into the 1980s, the state's industrial enterprises remained subject to centralized bureaucratic instruction, not least in price-setting; the workforce remained poorly motivated; true financial costs were obscure or unknown; and no external financial discipline was imposed – through the restriction of budget allocations or the refusal of loans by the state banks – provided that the enterprise followed the investment schedule laid down in the state's economic plans. Moreover, as in the previous decade, continuing and then worsening shortages of foreign exchange, despite the substantial increase in foreign loans and aid from the mid-1970s, restricted the import of raw materials, machinery, and spare parts, essential for the state industries. Not least, it led to the continued use of less productive, often obsolete plant, and to poor rates of maintenance and repair. Capacity utilization in Burma's state-owned industries in the mid-1980s was, on average, below 60 per cent, and was to fall much further still.[63] As most of the state manufacturing enterprises held a monopoly of domestic production, under-utilization of capacity on that scale substantially exacerbated the shortages already being faced by Burmese consumers. Once again, the illegal economy, in this case illegal imports coming across the borders with Thailand, China, India, and Bangladesh, flourished.

The disintegration

From the mid-1980s, Burma's economy fell apart. In November 1985, Ne Win, allegedly without consulting his senior officials, ordered the demonetization of the K100, K50, and K20 currency notes.[64] For a limited period (initially 11 November to 31 December, but later shortened), holdings of those notes to a total value of K5,000 could be exchanged immediately at designated banks and offices (on the basis of one person per household) for legal tender of the same value. For

---

[62] The following draws principally on Tin Maung Maung Than, *State Dominance in Myanmar*, pp. 265–72.

[63] Myat Thein, *Economic Development of Myanmar*, p. 108.

[64] The following draws on Kyaw Yin Hlaing, 'Reconsidering the failure of the Burma Socialist Programme Party government to eradicate internal economic impediments', *South East Asia Research*, 11, 1 (2003), pp. 52–4; Turnell, *Fiery Dragons*, pp. 237–40, 252–4.

holdings above K5,000, the authorities would retain one half of the excess, pending investigation. If the holder could then prove that the money had been earned by legal means and that all tax had been paid, the full sum was exchanged for legal tender. But if tax had not been paid on the money deposited, the tax liability, together with a fine, was deducted and the balance then exchanged. And if it was evident that the money had been made through illegal activities – the black market – the total sum was confiscated by the authorities. In brief, the core aim of demonetization was to force into the open – and break – the very substantial number of Burmese who were making their living beyond the control and direction of the state.

This instrument had been deployed on an earlier occasion. In May 1964, the Revolutionary Council had demonetized all K100 and K50 currency notes. For a limited period (initially one week but then extended), total holdings of less than K4,200 were to be exchanged for legal tender in full. But holdings above K4,200 led to 'special scrutiny of the individual concerned' and the imposition of a 'special tax'. The primary target of the 1964 demonetization was, in the Revolutionary Council's own words, 'the indigenous and foreign capitalists who have for many years unfairly accumulated the people's money with which they now oppose the Burmese Way to Socialism'.[65] The target in 1985 was the *hmaung-kho* (illegal) trader, the hugely flourishing private economy that lay beyond the state's control.

But it was relatively simple for the *hmaung-kho* traders to circumvent the 1985 demonetization, by distributing their stock of demonetized notes to friends and subordinates in bundles of K5,000 or less, to be exchanged for legal tender on their behalf. Thus they were left relatively unscathed. In September 1987, Ne Win therefore ordered a further demonetization – of K25, K35, and K75 currency notes – apparently without consulting the BSPP Central Committee. But unlike the demonetizations of 1964 and 1985, on this occasion, no provision was made for exchanging the demonetized notes for legal tender. In other words, at a stroke, between 60 and 80 per cent of all money in circulation in Burma had been made worthless.[66] The impact was devastating. Ordinary Burmese were forced to use their remaining

[65] Quoted in Turnell, *Fiery Dragons*, p. 238.
[66] Bertil Lintner, *Burma in Revolt: Opium and Insurgency since 1948*, 2nd edn. Chiang Mai: Silkworm Books, 1999, p. 338.

notes and coins solely to cover essential food purchases, including rice, cooking oil, and salt, and abandoned or deferred buying consumer articles, even basic clothing. The *hmaung-kho* traders were thus hit extremely hard, as indeed was the government's intention. But of course, this had been achieved by destroying much of the cash holdings of ordinary Burmese, causing great material hardship. Moreover, as the *hmaung-kho* traders had long provided consumer goods and employment, where the state industries had clearly failed, their retreat brought still greater distress to much of Burma's population.

In December 1987, just three months after that final demonetization, the United Nations classified Burma as a 'least developed country' (LDC), a status that would secure for it a reduction in interest rates on existing international loans as well as increased financial assistance from UN agencies. This was a humiliating step, forced on Burma by the rapidly approaching prospect of external default. As noted earlier, from the mid-1970s, Burma had returned on a substantial scale to the Asian Development Bank, the IMF, the World Bank, the United Nations Development Programme, and many individual donor countries. In 1974, the total value of bilateral and multilateral foreign loans and aid received by Burma had been $65.4 million.[67] In 1979 that figure was $518.1 million, and in 1986, $413.8 million. Burma's total external debt in 1985 was approaching four billion US dollars. At no point in the second half of the 1970s had the dollar cost of servicing Burma's external debt exceeded 20 per cent of the dollar value of Burma's exports, and in a number of years it had been substantially less.[68] But after 1980, as amortization and interest charges rose sharply and export earnings stagnated, that figure soared, to an astonishing and clearly unsustainable 80 per cent of export earnings in 1986/87. To make matters even worse, a run of ever more substantial balance of payments deficits from the mid-1980s resulted in a fall in Burma's foreign exchange reserves to dangerously low levels.[69] While the World Bank maintained that reserves should be held at a level equivalent to two months' imports, by 1985 Burma's reserves would cover just 1.2 months, and in March 1987, less than one month. It is interesting

[67] Khin Maung Nyunt, *Foreign Loans and Aid in the Economic Development of Burma 1974/75 to 1985/86*. Bangkok: Institute of Asian Studies, Chulalongkorn University, 1990, pp. 25, 116.

[68] Tin Maung Maung Than, *State Dominance in Myanmar*, Figure 6.27, p. 213.

[69] Ibid., pp. 211–12, 245, fn. 188.

to note that having been granted LDC status in December 1987 in an attempt to avoid external collapse, Burma's government made no announcement until the end of March the following year.

In early September 1987, as news broke of a second demonetization in less than two years, and of a demonetization with no provision for exchange, students at the Rangoon Institute of Technology, required to pay their tuition fees but now holding worthless notes, stormed on to the Insein Road, where they burnt government vehicles.[70] The authorities responded by closing Rangoon's universities and colleges and by bussing students from the provinces back to their own towns and villages. Shortly after the colleges and universities were reopened in late October, there were further violent student demonstrations at Sittwe and at Pyinmana and bomb blasts in Rangoon.

During this period, the government attempted economic reform. In August 1987, Ne Win had called a joint meeting of the Central Committee of the Burmese Socialist Programme Party and the various People's Councils and, acknowledging Burma's economic failure, instructed those core institutions of the state to create plans for economic and political reform within one year. He added that the government could not continue to lie with statistics to disguise the economic failure, a stunning admission. Then on 1 September 1987, the government removed controls on domestic trade in agricultural commodities, including, crucially, rice. Burma's rice cultivators were now free to sell their production to whomever they wished at whatever price they could secure: the state monopoly in the procurement of rice at a low, rigid price was at an end. But although this and other reform measures may have brought benefit to certain groups – cultivators would clearly gain from the subsequent rise in rice prices when they came to sell their crop – other groups suffered markedly. Burma's urban population, often on fixed incomes, faced much higher prices in the market: and almost all families were hit by the demonetization that took place just five days after the liberalization of trade. Senior

---

[70] The following section on the 1988 crisis draws on Lintner, *Burma in Revolt*, pp. 338–53; Bertil Lintner, *Outrage: Burma's Struggle for Democracy*, 2nd edn. London and Bangkok: White Lotus, 1990; Robert H. Taylor, *The State in Myanmar*. London: Hurst, 2009, pp. 375–91; David I. Steinberg, *Burma: the State of Myanmar*. Washington, DC: Georgetown University Press, 2001, pp. 1–12; Dr Maung Maung, *The 1988 Uprising in Burma*. New Haven, CT: Yale University Southeast Asia Studies, 1999.

government officials and higher-ranking military still had privileged access to consumer goods and food. But outside those protected ranks, Burmese faced steep rises in the cost of living, and worsening shortages, indeed frequently the complete collapse of provision. The following year, violent protest erupted in Burma, protest that eventually brought down the BSPP regime. It was driven by many complex causes. But economic failure was a fundamental factor.

On 12 March 1988, a fight broke out at a teashop close to the Rangoon Institute of Technology between three RIT students and some local youths, one of whom, it later emerged, was the son of a senior local official. The fight arose from a trivial dispute over the music to be played on the teashop tape recorder, a love song by a well-known Burmese crooner or something more sharp-edged. One of the students was hit across the head with a chair. The students retreated and reported the incident to the police, who then arrested the alleged culprits at the teashop. But the following day, the accused were released. RIT students reacted with fury, attacking local government offices and clashing with local youths. But the students, growing in number, were then confronted by the riot police, the feared *Lon Htein*, armed with clubs and automatic rifles. They fired. One student was fatally hit – two further students subsequently died in hospital – and many were wounded. Two days later, the riot police and soldiers stormed the RIT campus and arrested scores of students. The student protests immediately spread across the city, notably to the main Rangoon University campus, and into Rangoon's central districts. The authorities met the protests with full force. On 16 March, a large demonstration making its way down Prome Road was blocked and then charged by *Lon Htein* and army units. Tens but possibly several hundred were killed. Forty-one demonstrators suffocated – later the number was officially confirmed – when held, tightly packed, in an airless police van. On 18 March, the authorities closed universities and schools, to establish relative order.

The universities and schools were reopened on 30 May. Students arrested in March but later released now told of torture, beatings, and rape while in prison. In mid-June, the demonstrations in Rangoon resumed but the protests now also spread to Pegu, Moulmein, Prome, and Mandalay. On 23 July, at an extraordinary congress of the Burma Socialist Programme Party, Ne Win announced that he was resigning as party chairman and as a party member. A further five senior figures, the inner core of party and state leaders, were also to step down. In addition Ne Win asked the congress to approve a national referendum for the people to decide whether Burma should return to a multi-party political system. The congress did not approve. On 26 July, the Central Committee of the BSPP elected Sein Lwin as party chairman in succession to Ne Win, and the following day, he was elected president by the *Pyithu Hluttaw* (People's Assembly). Immensely loyal to Ne Win, Sein Lwin had been de facto head of the riot police, the *Lon Htein*, during the violent confrontations of the previous March and June.

The demonstrations continued, together with calls for a nationwide general strike on 8 August. On that day (8.8.88), large-scale demonstrations took place in cities and towns across Burma. In Rangoon itself, hundreds of thousands from the capital's townships streamed into Sule Pagoda Road, towards City Hall and Bandoola Park, calling for the end of the BSPP regime and the socialist economic system. For most of the day, the military held back. But towards midnight, troops rushed out from behind City Hall and fired into demonstrators close to the Sule Pagoda. At almost the same time, troops fired into protesters on Shwegondine Road, in the northern part of the city. There followed three days of the most appalling violence that left several thousand dead. On 12 August, Sein Lwin resigned.

Sein Lwin's successor as president and BSPP chairman, appointed on 19 August, was Dr Maung Maung, a lawyer educated at Rangoon, Lincoln's Inn, Utrecht, and Yale, and the author of numerous books on modern Burma. His administration now sought to defuse the crisis. At various points, martial law was lifted, troops were withdrawn from the streets of Rangoon, public demonstrations were permitted, and prominent opposition figures recently arrested were released. In late August Dr Maung Maung promised a national referendum on a return to multi-party politics, while a second BSPP emergency congress in mid-September proposed, admittedly in the final days of the regime, that multi-party general elections be held.

But the protesters were far too angry to be appeased. Not only the students, monks, protesting civil servants, lawyers, doctors, nurses, film actors, drivers, striking railway and factory workers, but also former senior army officers – Aung Gyi, the second most influential member of the 1962 coup group behind Ne Win but forced from office in early 1963, and nine of the eleven surviving Thirty Comrades – as well as the daughter of Aung San, Aung San Suu Kyi, who had recently returned to Burma from Britain, demanded the end of the BSPP regime and the establishment of an interim government 'acceptable to all the people'. Rangoon was rapidly approaching a complete collapse in social order. On 18 September 1988, the defence forces under the Chief of Staff, General Saw Maung – there had been only a few low-ranking defections from the armed forces to the opposition during the crisis – seized power.

As indicated earlier, while the 1988 crisis undoubtedly had complex dynamics, economic failure was clearly a fundamental factor.[71] Thus while, as seems clear, the demonstrations and strikes were increasingly driven by fury at the regime's savage reaction to earlier protest – the initial shooting of the RIT students, the trapping and then charging of the demonstration on Prome Road, the beatings and torture, the forty-one deaths in the police van – absolutely central from the earliest stages was public anger, turning to rage, at the failure of the Burmese Way to Socialism, after twenty-five years, to provide employment, consumer goods, and even food. That failure was seen each day in Burma in the shortages, queues, rationing, the poverty of choice, quality, and provision – the endless struggle for basic survival for the many, but privileged access for the few – and announced to the world when, in December 1987, the United Nations classified Burma as a 'least developed country'. Why did Burma's economy fall apart from the mid-1980s? Why did Burmese socialism fail?

As an economic strategy, the Burmese Way to Socialism contained fatal flaws. One of the most fundamental arose from the fact that from independence in 1948, Burma's governments had had only a limited and fragile capacity to raise tax revenues. For example, in every year except one between 1980 and the end of the BSPP regime in 1988, tax revenue was equivalent to less than 10 per cent of GDP – for example,

---

[71] Robert Taylor makes the point that although 'there is little dispute among all sources about the events which took place between March and September [1988]...their meaning [is] much disputed': Taylor, *The State in Myanmar*, pp. 383, fn. 14, 386. In his brief analysis David Steinberg emphasises 'economic and political frustration...internal economic problems and dissatisfaction with the government': David I. Steinberg, *Burma/Myanmar: What Everyone Needs to Know*. New York: Oxford University Press, 2010, pp. 77, 80.

just 6.59 per cent in 1987/88.[72] Indeed, since there was also a vast untaxed illegal sector, the government's tax take from the economy would in fact have been even lower than that figure indicates. The low tax revenues were in part a consequence of lax administration and widespread evasion. But there was also a major structural weakness. In the 1980s, around 60 per cent, no less, of the government's tax revenue came from a commodities and services tax.[73] A further 20 per cent and more came from customs duties. In contrast, income tax and profit tax accounted for around 5 per cent of tax revenues, although 10 per cent in the final two years of the BSPP government. And 'tax on the use of state properties', presumably including land revenue, was again around a mere 5 per cent.

The central issue here was the taxation of the major sector of the economy, agriculture, and principally the rice cultivator. Land revenue had been the single most important government revenue under the British, accounting for around 30 per cent of total revenue receipts in the late 1930s.[74] Assessment and collection had required a highly trained and experienced administration.[75] In brief detail, a land revenue assessment – settlement – was undertaken in each of Burma's forty or so districts at intervals of twenty to thirty years. A settlement party of about fifty under a senior civil servant would spend some two years in a detailed survey of all the cultivable land in that district. The survey would record for each holding the owner and others liable for the land revenue, and determine the rate at which it would be paid, reflecting principally the fertility of the soil, water conditions, and location. Then each year, land records officers in each district brought the registers and maps prepared at settlement up to date, and, on the basis of those revised records, produced the land revenue assessment lists for

---

[72] Myat Thein, 'Monetary and fiscal policies for development', in Mya Than and Joseph L. H. Tan (eds), *Myanmar Dilemmas and Options: the Challenge of Economic Transition in the 1990s*. Singapore: Institute of Southeast Asian Studies, 1990, p. 77.

[73] Ibid., p. 78.

[74] J. Russell Andrus, *Burmese Economic Life*. Stanford University Press, 1948, p. 318.

[75] Ibid., pp. 317, 319. For a detailed description of the colonial land revenue administration, see J. S. Furnivall, *An Introduction to the Political Economy of Burma*. Rangoon: Burma Book Club, 1931, pp. 204–22. Furnivall had been Commissioner of Settlements and Land Records, Burma.

that district for that year. Working from the annual assessment lists, officials in the District Office then wrote out the tax tickets, to be sent out to the headmen. The headmen had then collected the land revenue.

British Burma's land revenue administration collapsed in early 1942, as the Japanese advanced, and in the two years or so between the return of the colonial civilian government in October 1945 and the end of British rule in January 1948, a turbulent period, little of that imposing structure was re-established.[76] Perhaps too, in those years of great material hardship and political upheaval, many of Burma's rice cultivators, encouraged by the communists, refused to pay the land revenue. In brief, from 1948, Burma's new government had neither the rural administration nor perhaps the consent of the cultivating population to return to what had been the single most important fiscal instrument in the colonial period. In any event, in the first years of independence, much of rural Burma lay beyond the control of Rangoon – and thus the rice cultivator was beyond the reach of the tax collector. In the mid-1950s, the land revenue provided just 4 per cent of the government's tax revenue and a mere 2 per cent of its total income.[77]

And yet, were Burma's new government to finance development – state-led industrialization – from domestic resources, it was essential to tax effectively Burma's rice cultivators, the most important sector of the economy by far. In the absence of the land revenue, this might be achieved by taxing the export of rice, for given the high elasticity of foreign demand and the structure of domestic production and trade, the burden of an export tax on rice would almost certainly be borne by the cultivator in the form of a major reduction in the domestic price. This was the instrument used in Thailand between the mid-1950s and the mid-1980s.[78] The instrument used by Burma's new government

---

[76] In a fine memoir, one British official recalled that in Pyapon District in late 1946, a new Deputy Commissioner, an Arakanese, found that only about 2½ per cent of the land revenue demand, already much reduced, had been collected. He was taking steps to hasten collection when a strike of civil servants, to include in Pyapon all the land records staff, was called. Robert Mole, *The Temple Bells are Calling: a Personal Record of the Last Years of British Rule in Burma*. Bishop Auckland: Pentland Books, 2001, p. 244.

[77] Taylor, *The State in Myanmar*, p. 258.

[78] It has been calculated that the Rice Premium, as the export tax was called, together with an over-valuation of the currency, 'reduced the [Thai] domestic price of rice by 43 per cent between 1975 and 1979, and by 34 per cent between 1979 and 1984': Chris Dixon, *The Thai Economy: Uneven Development and Internationalisation*. London: Routledge, 1999, p. 141.

was compulsory procurement of paddy from the cultivator – and rice from the millers – at a fixed low price, the state securing a substantial income by exporting rice at the much higher market price. As noted in the previous chapter, in the nine years from 1947/48 to 1955/56, financial transfers from the State Agricultural Marketing Board (SAMB) to the government accounted for, on average, 41 per cent of total government revenue receipts, although this had fallen to 14 per cent in 1959/60, reflecting in part a decline in the international rice price in the second half of the 1950s.

But again as noted in the previous chapter, this instrument, at least as employed here, was seriously flawed. Most importantly, the rice cultivator, faced with a fixed, low, and undifferentiated price for his crop, had little or no incentive to increase the acreage under cultivation or to invest in more productive inputs or cultivation methods.[79] That failure, together with poor state provision of agricultural credit and the relative neglect of agriculture in state investment throughout most of this period, left Burma's rice economy to languish far below its potential. Burma's rice exports, a potentially major source of government income under state procurement, as well as foreign exchange, were down to 1.7 million tons in 1960 and just 0.6 million in 1980 – from in excess of three million tons in 1940.[80] If agriculture were to finance Burma's development – the firm ambition of economic strategy from 1948 – then agriculture must flourish. In reality, its potential was severely stunted, by the government itself.

Thus in the two decades or more of the Burmese way to socialism, tax revenues and the income from state economic enterprises – although in fact the latter ran substantial deficits from the late 1970s – constantly fell far short of the government's expenditure ambitions, which included, it should be noted, a high priority for the military budget.[81] State investment in development projects was therefore

---

[79] For further criticism of rice procurement – 'an unambiguous economic failure' – see Peter John Perry, *Myanmar (Burma) since 1962: the Failure of Development*. Aldershot: Ashgate, 2007, pp. 65–8.

[80] U Khin Win, *A Century of Rice Improvement in Burma*. Manila: International Rice Research Institute, 1991, pp. 32, 51, 125.

[81] Tin Maung Maung Than, *State Dominance in Myanmar: the Political Economy of Industrialization*. Singapore: Institute of Southeast Asian Studies, 2007, pp. 194–200. In the early 1980s, official defence spending accounted for just under a third of total government expenditure, although the proportion then fell: Taylor, *The State in Myanmar*, p. 338.

frequently cut back. Even so, from the late 1970s, the government ran large, indeed unsustainable, budget deficits. As domestic resources failed, the BSPP, following the revision of its economic strategy in the early 1970s, turned to foreign borrowing and foreign aid on a substantial scale. Indeed the expansion of state industrial enterprises from the mid-1970s was financed largely by foreign loans and aid.[82] But within a short time, that external dependence exposed a second fatal flaw in the Burmese way to socialism.

The hostility of the Burma government to foreign private capital had been plain right from the beginning, from the establishment of the State Agricultural Marketing Board in 1947, which removed foreign interests from the rice export trade, and the nationalization of the foreign timber firms and the Irrawaddy Flotilla Company in 1948. The last foreign economic interests had been removed by the Revolutionary Council in the mid-1960s and at no point through to the end of the BSPP regime in 1988 would they be invited back. Of course the exclusion of foreign private capital denied Burma a potentially major resource. And here it must be noted that in this same period a number of Burma's South East Asian neighbours were to use foreign direct investment on a very substantial scale to finance rapid industrialization.[83] But that exclusion was at least consistent with a core principle of Burma's economic strategy from 1948 – economic independence, control of Burma's economy exclusively in the hands of Burmese. In contrast, substantial foreign borrowing and foreign aid from the mid-1970s – by the end of the BSPP regime, Burma had received more than $850 million in grants and nearly $3.5 billion in loans – broke that core principle.[84] Put bluntly, in the 1980s, the Burmese way to socialism was dependent on foreign multilateral and bilateral capital. It covered the persistent substantial deficits in both the budget and the balance of payments, it financed the expansion of state industrial enterprises, paid for imports, and serviced earlier borrowings.

But far more serious than this breach of principle was the fact that the turn to substantial foreign borrowing from the mid-1970s was not tied to a sustained major expansion in exports, to the creation of the

[82] Tin Maung Maung Than, *State Dominance in Myanmar*, p. 265.
[83] For example, net foreign direct investment into Thailand rose very sharply in the late 1980s, to over $2 billion in 1990 alone: Dixon, *The Thai Economy*, p. 124.
[84] Tin Maung Maung Than, *State Dominance in Myanmar*, p. 209.

means by which the debt would be serviced and repaid. The average annual value of Burma's exports in the second half of the 1970s was a little under $250 million.[85] It was substantially higher in the early 1980s but in the last five years of BSPP rule, it had fallen back to $278 million. Without a sustained substantial growth in exports – Burma's South East Asian neighbours tied inward foreign direct investment to a major expansion in the export of manufactures – the strategy was incoherent. As noted earlier, by 1986/87 the dollar cost of servicing Burma's external debt was an astonishing 80 per cent of the dollar value of Burma's exports. The strategy of foreign borrowing was in ruins.

The Burmese way to socialism contained two further strategic flaws that would prove fatal. In the revision of its economic strategy in the early 1970s, the BSPP recognized that state enterprises alone could not provide sufficient employment or sufficient consumer goods for Burma's population. It followed that local private capital must have an important place in Burma's socialist economy. And yet, in the remaining decade or more of BSPP rule, private small and medium-sized industrial concerns, the very enterprises that could most effectively create employment and produce consumer goods, suffered severe restrictions in financing, in securing raw materials, transport, and in gaining access to the market, 'as the state allocated scarce resources to the state and co-operatives sectors and suppressed market-based activities'.[86] In other words, the BSPP government explicitly sought a substantial reduction in the importance of the private manufacturing sector in the 1970s and 1980s. It was not a coherent strategy.

With the state industries working well below capacity, foreign private capital eliminated and local private capital suppressed, and consumer goods imports tightly restricted, the vast illegal economy – private enterprise – flourished. A huge range of consumer goods – textiles, colour televisions, food products, soft drinks, alcohol, household appliances, medicines – came across Burma's borders with Thailand, China, India, and Bangladesh, to be sold quite openly in the major cities, at a price.[87] And back across Burma's borders went precious

---

[85] Calculated from Myat Thein, *Economic Development of Myanmar*. Singapore: Institute of Southeast Asian Studies, 2004, Table 3.4, p. 75.
[86] Tin Maung Maung Than, *State Dominance in Myanmar*, p. 275.
[87] The details here are from Myat Thein, *Economic Development of Myanmar*, p. 81.

stones, timber, rice, minerals, and rubber. No one can know the scale of that trade. Estimates in the mid-1980s ranged from 50 to 85 per cent of the total value of official recorded trade, but it might have been still higher.[88] The attitude of the authorities to the illegal economy was ambivalent.[89] On the one hand, as was all too obvious, the *hmaung-kho* (illegal) traders provided Burma's population with consumer goods, including basic necessities, on a scale and of a range and quality that the state industries simply could not match. For this reason, local party-state officials hesitated to take strong action against *hmaung-kho* traders and their activities, for to close them down or simply to disrupt their trade would cause severe shortages, and this could then lead to serious disturbances. But in addition, the officials themselves were dependent on their local *hmaung-kho* businesses to finance party-state activities – the local celebration of national days, such as Independence Day or Union Day, as well as visits by senior party-state figures – and on occasion to provide funds for new schools or hospitals. In brief, the illegal economy reduced the prospect of social unrest and made it possible for the party-state at the local level to function.

But at the same time, the BSPP government was severely weakened by this vast illegal trade. It deprived the state of huge revenues: and it constituted a surrender of control over the economy by the regime to *hmaung-kho* capital. It could not be tolerated. In the demonetizations of November 1985 and September 1987, the government finally set out to break the *hmaung-kho* traders and reassert its control, and so end its ambivalence towards the illegal economy. But as described earlier, that action, by creating great economic hardship for the Burmese, and thus sharply increasing the prospect of social unrest, and by undermining the party-state at the local level, triggered the events that brought an end to the BSPP regime.

The final fatal flaw in the Burmese way to socialism lay in its pursuit of an economic strategy that Burma's administration, lacking expertise and experience, simply could not make to work. It might well be argued that no state administration, no matter how skilled and experienced, could hope to run a highly complex command-control

---

[88] Myat Thein, *Economic Development of Myanmar*, p. 80. See also Mya Maung, *The Burma Road to Poverty*. New York: Praeger, 1991, pp. 214–15.

[89] The following draws on Kyaw Yin Hlaing, 'Reconsidering the failure of the Burma Socialist Programme Party government to eradicate internal economic impediments', *South East Asia Research*, 11, 1 (2003), pp. 45–54, 57–8.

economy efficiently and effectively. Any corps of desk-bound officials and state-appointed managers would struggle to align industrial inputs, production capacity, manpower allocations, and consumer demand, or to decide wisely which crops were to be cultivated, when, where, and how. Burma's administration certainly struggled, partly because, in terms of broad experience, it had been left relatively threadbare in 1948 when the more senior British and Indian officials who had dominated the colonial civil service had left, but also because very few of the Burmese officials who now filled those ranks had commercial expertise or managerial experience.

There is a further point here. Independent Burma took the road to socialism in part because, emerging from colonial rule, there were too few Burmese with the business experience and resources to fill the commanding positions in the economy recently vacated by foreign interests. But this also suggested that few officials would be found in the ministries and departments, or indeed soldiers in the barracks, capable of running the state's new enterprises efficiently and profitably. And yet, as just indicated, during the decades of BSPP rule, it was common practice to appoint active and retired military officers – with no managerial abilities, experience, or knowledge – to executive positions in state economic enterprises and as managers of new industrial projects.[90] All were aware that military commanders knew little about running a business.[91] But they continued to be sent to manage, and almost invariably mismanage, the state's economic enterprises.

The unswerving road to socialism

With the economic strategy of Burma's civilian government in the first decade or more of independence focused on state-led industrialization, hostility towards foreign economic interests, and the curtailing of the market, by the early 1960s, GDP per capita, in real terms, remained substantially below the level that had been achieved under the British in the late 1930s. But despite that poor performance, the military, seizing power in 1962, not only maintained the strategy but, in important respects, drove it far harder. It was a strategy rejected by many of

[90] Tin Maung Maung Than, *State Dominance in Myanmar*, p. 281, fn. 49.
[91] Indeed it would appear that this was a constant theme of Ne Win himself. 'The men from our Defense Services know only how to wage war', he told a BSPP seminar in 1965: Mya Maung, *The Burma Road to Poverty*, p. 109.

Burma's economists outside government, most notably by Hla Myint who, in exile from 1960, argued for growth through the expansion of exports, first primary commodities but then manufactures. It was also on occasion re-examined within government itself, for example, in the early 1970s when the BSPP re-plotted Burma's route to socialism, and in August 1987, when Ne Win acknowledged Burma's economic failure and called for economic and political reform. Of course empty shelves and riots driven by economic hardship – in each decade of BSPP rule – were the most devastating and persistent criticism of the strategy, the most immediate evidence of economic failure. This raises a central question: why did Burma's military rulers persist with a demonstrably flawed and failing economic strategy for more than a quarter of a century until it finally bankrupted the country? The answer is surprisingly complex.[92]

It might first be noted that a number of the specific economic measures taken by government in these decades are difficult to fathom. For example, in 1965 the Revolutionary Council issued a directive that savings held in the Village Banks 'could not be used for lending purposes'. That prohibition on the re-employment of savings in lending was, in the view of one exasperated writer, 'Inexplicable... truly mystifying'.[93] Elsewhere were measures that *could* be explained, but the explanation often seemed to some to be bizarre. Thus shortly after the demonetization of K25, K35, and K75 currency notes in early September 1987, two new denominations, K45 and K90, were put into circulation. The separate numerals on each of the new notes add up to nine $(4+5 = 9$ and $9+0 = 9)$, which to Ne Win and indeed to most Burmese was a number with great mystical power.[94]

However there are dangers in focusing on specific unfathomable or perhaps unsettling economic measures. First, it draws an arguably exaggerated attention to the often unpredictable and suspicion-ridden

---

[92] The central question of Burma's economic failure under the BSPP has also been considered at length by Tin Maung Maung Than. His approach is to compare the BSPP-led state, which clearly sought development, with the successful developmental states of East and South East Asia: Tin Maung Maung Than, *State Dominance in Myanmar*, pp. 303–24.

[93] Turnell, *Fiery Dragons*, p. 243. It must be added that the author then offers an explanation for the inexplicable. The prohibition left the Village Banks 'dependent on disbursements from the government. Of course, this may well have been the intention of the measure.'

[94] Mya Maung, *The Burma Road to Poverty*, pp. 224–5.

character of General Ne Win. Ne Win was undeniably powerful. But it is unlikely that the failure of the Burmese way to socialism can be tied to his decisions alone, despite, in the words of Robert Taylor in a related context, 'The penchant of populist writers and politically constrained journalists... to blame one man'.[95] Second, it is easy to slip from a characterization of specific economic measures as unfathomable or bizarre to the dismissal of the economic strategy itself as unfathomable or bizarre. The Burmese way to socialism was seriously flawed and it eventually bankrupted Burma. But it was not incomprehensible.

The economic strategy pursued by Burma's independent government right from 1948 had three core elements – nationalization, Burmanization, and industrialization. Each was a reaction against the colonial experience. State ownership would overturn the brutal exercise of private interest that had marked the colonial economy; Burmanization would see the expulsion of the British and Indian commercial and financial concerns that had dominated the modern economy under British rule; and industrialization would end Burma's extreme dependence on the production and export of a narrow range of primary commodities. Those core strategic economic ambitions were, in the words of U Thet Tun in the mid-1960s quoted in the previous chapter, 'the very roots on which the state of Burma was founded'.[96]

That strategy had been set before Burma had become independent and, it is important to note, had been driven by Aung San himself. On 6 June 1947, he had called a meeting of Burmese politicians and senior officials, held at the Sorrento Villa in Rangoon. The ambition of those present was, in the words of a near contemporary observer, 'to bring to an end the "colonial economy", based on the export of raw materials, and to create a new Socialist system with the accent on

---

[95] Robert H. Taylor, *The State in Myanmar*. London: Hurst, 2009, p. 391. The same point has been made, slightly differently, by Mary Callahan: 'Among Burma scholars and journalists, there is a tendency... to hold up Ne Win as the residual explanation behind Burma's unusual policies and politics.' Callahan, *Making Enemies*, p. 204.

[96] U Thet Tun, 'A critique of Louis J. Walinsky's "Economic Development in Burma 1951–1960"', *Journal of the Burma Research Society*, 47, 1 (June 1964), p. 181. David Steinberg has made the closely parallel observation that the 'ardent' socialist tradition in Burmese economic and political thinking since before independence was 'treated [by government] with almost mystical reverence': David I. Steinberg, *Burma's Road toward Development: Growth and Ideology under Military Rule*. Boulder, CO: Westview Press, 1981, p. 76.

nationalization and industrialization'.[97] Just six weeks later, Aung San was assassinated, and it can be argued that the tragedy of his violent death – he had led Burma to an independence that he himself would never see – made it extremely difficult for the leaders who followed him to challenge the economic strategy that had been set at Sorrento Villa. The fact was that despite his death – indeed arguably reinforced by his death – Aung San remained a hugely powerful presence, his speeches and writings constantly quoted by politicians, military officers, and senior officials to promote or defend a position or policy.[98] His word had unchallengeable authority. In summary, the core elements in Burma's economic strategy from 1948 – nationalization, Burmanization, and industrialization – defined the independent state and bore the immense authority of the martyred national hero.

During the two decades and more of BSPP rule, there did not exist in Burma a core of economics expertise, that is an expertise respected by the political leadership, which might question the defining commitments to state ownership, the rejection of foreign interests, and the heavy emphasis on import substitution industrialization, or indeed which could challenge the unfathomable and the bizarre. It is interesting to note here that in Indonesia, when General Soeharto assumed power from President Sukarno in early 1966, and inherited an economy close to collapse, he appointed a group of five young economists from the Faculty of Economics at the University of Indonesia as his 'expert advisers'.[99] Soeharto had first come to know and respect the group in the late Sukarno years when he had taken courses in economics and other social sciences at the Army Staff and Command School in Bandung. The Indonesian New Order economic technocrats, commonly referred to as the 'Berkeley Mafia' as many of them had studied at Berkeley, stabilized the economy, principally by insisting on

[97] Hugh Tinker, *The Union of Burma: a Study of the First Years of Independence*, 4th edn. London: Oxford University Press, 1967, p. 93.

[98] Steinberg, *Burma's Road toward Development*, pp. 184–5. The irony is that had Aung San lived, it is almost certain that his views, tempered by further experience of government, would have evolved. Addressing an AFPFL convention in May 1947, just a few weeks before Sorrento Villa, he said: 'no political or economic system can be permanent. They change with circumstances.' Josef Silverstein (ed.), *The Political Legacy of Aung San*, revd edn. Ithaca, NY: Cornell University, Southeast Asia Program, 1993, p. 153.

[99] The following draws on Thee Kian Wie, 'Introduction', in Thee Kian Wie (ed.), *Recollections: the Indonesian Economy, 1950s–1990s*. Singapore: Institute of Southeast Asian Studies, 2003, pp. 21–5.

the importance of balanced budgets, and secured a fundamental redirection of Indonesia's economic strategy. The inward-looking policies and anti-capitalist anger of the Sukarno period were abandoned and replaced by an outward-looking strategy focused on the expansion of foreign trade, the attraction of private foreign direct investment, and the seeking of substantial foreign aid. In the three decades from 1967, Indonesia's per capita GDP grew at an average annual rate of 4.5 per cent. It is also interesting to note that in Thailand, the end of the 1950s saw the creation of a number of institutions in government, notably the National Economic Development Board, to plan and promote development. These institutions were led by a core of Western-trained technocrats, who then had a major influence in the determination and implementation of Thailand's development strategy.[100] In the 1960s, GDP in Thailand grew at an average annual rate of 8.2 per cent, and in the 1970s, at 7.2 per cent. Of course Burma too had fine economists, indeed a generation of remarkably fine economists, as was outlined in the previous chapter. But unlike the economic technocrats in Indonesia and in Thailand from the 1960s, Burma's economists had no influence in government or on economic strategy. Many, including the very best, had therefore left.

A number of circumstances might explain the exclusion of Burma's economists from influence during the years of BSPP rule. It should first be noted that when Soeharto turned to the Berkeley Mafia in the mid-1960s, the economy was close to collapse. Indonesia was in default on foreign debt of $2.4 billion, and the annual rate of inflation was approaching 600 per cent. In other words, a radical change in economic strategy was forced on government. Moreover the change was secured by a sharp break with Indonesia's political past, in the removal of Sukarno, president since independence in 1949 and on frequent occasion fiercely anti-West, and the succession of Soeharto. Although far less dramatic, the establishment of the Sarit Thanarat regime in Thailand in 1958 also marked a break with the past: and it produced a major redirection in economic strategy, as state capitalism was abandoned in favour of state promotion of private capital.[101] But when the military took power in Burma, although the economy had

[100] Chris Dixon, *The Thai Economy: Uneven Development and Internationalisation*. London: Routledge, 1999, pp. 79, 3.

[101] Pasuk Phongpaichit and Chris Baker, *Thailand: Economy and Politics*. Kuala Lumpur: Oxford University Press, 1997, pp. 277–8.

long performed poorly, it certainly did not face an imminent collapse, one that might force a radical change in economic strategy. Indeed, when the military took power for the second time, decisively, in March 1962, rather than reassess, it simply drove the established economic strategy harder still.

A second factor to explain the exclusion of Burma's economists from influence during the two decades or more of BSPP rule can be noted briefly. As established earlier, the core elements in Burma's economic strategy from 1948 – nationalization, Burmanization, and industrialization – were immensely powerful. They defined the independent state and bore the authority of Aung San. For the military-political leadership, Burma had no other path. It is interesting to note here that in the late 1960s, shortly after food shortages had led to serious unrest in parts of Burma, Ne Win invited former leading civilian politicians from the previous decade, including U Nu, to consider 'the nature and future of the state'.[102] A majority report, produced after six months, called on the Revolutionary Council to abandon the path that it had been taking since 1962. The report was ignored. It is also important to note that when the BSPP itself re-examined the Burmese way to socialism in the early 1970s, the reassessment created just one substantial change, a return to foreign borrowing and the acceptance of foreign aid and technical assistance on a substantial scale. State-led import-substituting industrialization remained, although it would now focus on processing and manufacturing from Burma's own natural resources. Elsewhere, adjustments were agreed – that material incentives would be built into Burma's economic structures; that local private capital had an important place in Burma's socialist economy – but they were not effectively implemented or indeed implemented at all in the remaining years of BSPP rule. And in one important respect, there was no revision in economic strategy. There was no return to foreign direct investment (except in offshore oil exploration by foreign oil companies), no return of foreign commercial interests. In other words, even the frank assessment of the failings of Burma's route to socialism undertaken by the BSPP in the early 1970s did not lead or drive the military-political leadership from the path on which it was set.

There is one further important consideration. In these same decades, a number of Burma's neighbours in South East Asia, including

---

[102] Taylor, *The State in Myanmar*, pp. 368–9.

Indonesia and Thailand, achieved sustained rapid growth in GDP, as noted above, and major structural change, away from agriculture and towards manufacturing. The transformation was created by economic strategies that were outward-looking – growth and structural change were in time driven principally by a major increase in the export of manufactures – and that abandoned state ownership in favour of private capital. That second principle required the presence from the very beginning of a substantial core of local capitalists with the capacity and abilities to exploit new business opportunities, not least as local partners in joint ventures with foreign capital. The local capitalists in Thailand and Indonesia, and elsewhere in South East Asia, were largely of immigrant origin, principally Chinese. In Thailand, during the decades of inward-focused state capitalism, they had often been stigmatized by Thai nationalist opinion as alien. But that hostility was now much diminished, although it would not disappear entirely, as the Sino-Thai capitalists were brought into the new, outward-looking and private capital driven, economic strategy.

The critical point is that in this period, Burma did not possess that substantial core of local capitalists. As was argued in the previous chapter, despite the expansion in domestic private manufacturing in the 1950s, in the early 1960s the sector remained fragile and modest. Certainly there were no powerful local capitalists to match, for example, the Chearavanont family in Thailand or William Soeryadjaya in Indonesia. And of course, the Indian financiers and businessmen, so prominent in British-ruled Burma and who might in time have become substantially integrated, had left in their tens of thousands at the beginning of the 1940s, had struggled to return after the war, and finally, had been effectively kicked out of the country in the early 1960s. In brief, even if Burma's military-political leadership had overcome its ideological commitment to state ownership, and its deep distrust of private capital, it did not have to hand the key instrument, a substantial, vigorous, experienced capitalist class, to implement that new economic strategy.

And finally, the fact that Burma's military rulers persisted with a demonstrably flawed and failing economic strategy for more than a quarter of a century until it finally bankrupted the country can be explained by the rigidly authoritarian nature of politics and administration under Ne Win. Within government, power was concentrated in that one man – known widely as *num-ber-one-gyi* (big number one) or *a-foe-gyi* (big old man) – who demanded above all loyalty and obedience from those below him.[103] Those individuals or groups he mistrusted, and there were many, Ne Win removed. Thus in its first years, the Revolutionary Council retired some 2,000 senior civil servants who had held responsible administrative positions in the first decade or so of independence, and indeed many had served in the British colonial administration before that; experienced officials, but now dismissed by the military 'as effete'.[104] Later the Revolutionary Council also removed the core of military officers who, in effect, had run the government during the earlier period of military rule from 1958. Those experienced senior civilian officials and military officers were replaced in high administrative positions by military men whose key qualification, it would appear, was loyalty to the Revolutionary Council and specifically to Ne Win.

In order to advance, or even simply to survive, senior BSPP party-state officials were forced to concentrate above all on meeting the expectations of their superiors, ultimately of Ne Win himself. On occasion this could be spectacularly difficult, as *num-ber-one-gyi* was frequently impulsive or contradictory in his behaviour, cryptic and impenetrable in his commands. As a result, senior officials 'came to practise the three *mas* – *ma-loke* [not doing any work], *ma-shote* [not getting involved in any complication] and *ma-pyoke* [not getting dismissed]'.[105] Initiative and responsibility were thereby drained from the government administration, crucial failings that were then covered up in distorted reporting to higher authority, hiding the bad news and often inventing the good. Government and administration in BSPP Burma thus became self-deceiving and sclerotic, simply incapable of coherent reform.

There is a particularly telling contrast to be noted from the final year of BSPP rule. In August 1987, Ne Win, acknowledging Burma's economic failure, called on the Central Committee of the Burmese Socialist

---

[103] Kyaw Yin Hlaing, 'Reconsidering the failure of the Burma Socialist Programme Party government to eradicate internal economic impediments', *South East Asia Research*, 11, 1 (2003), p. 25.

[104] Steinberg, *Burma's Road toward Development*, pp. 164–5.

[105] Kyaw Yin Hlaing, 'Reconsidering the failure of the Burma Socialist Programme Party government', p. 35. In this fine paper, Kyaw Yin Hlaing provides an extended description and analysis of the behaviour of BSPP party-state officials – for those officials, it was 'the politics of survival': pp. 24–42.

Programme Party and the various People's Councils to create plans for economic and political reform within one year. But within a few weeks of calling for reform, *num-ber-one-gyi*, ignoring all, sought to wipe out one of the regime's most serious economic failings, the ubiquitous presence of the black market, by ordering a third and extremely brutal demonetization. That action was not economic reform, considered and calculated. It was economic violence.

5 | Toward the market: the economy from 1988

Reform and its limitations

In March 1989, the State Law and Order Restoration Council (SLORC), the new military government that had taken power the previous September, revoked legislation of 1965 that had established the socialist economic system. The stated ambition of the new administration, in contrast, was to secure the evolution of a market-oriented economy. A key figure in this apparently major realignment was Brigadier General David Abel, at that time Minister of Trade and Minister of National Planning and Finance, and who, in the 1990s, would be 'the most articulate and internationally well-known spokesman for the SLORC'.[1] But in fact the dismantling of the socialist economy had begun in the final year of BSPP rule, for, as noted in the previous chapter, on 1 September 1987 the BSPP had removed the long-established controls on domestic trade in nine agricultural commodities, including, crucially, rice.

A year later, in October 1988, the SLORC lifted the ban on the private export of agricultural commodities – although not the export of rice.[2] The following month, the new government made it clear that, after almost three decades of near-total exclusion, Myanmar would again allow, indeed would encourage, investment by foreign private capital. The Foreign Investment Law of November 1988 made provision for full foreign ownership of concerns operating in Myanmar – it did not insist on joint ventures – with approval of investment applications from foreign interests being overseen by a Foreign Investments

---

[1] Mya Maung, *The Burma Road to Capitalism: Economic Growth versus Democracy*. Westport, CT: Praeger, 1998, pp. 53, 55.

[2] Ikuko Okamoto, 'Transformation of the rice marketing system after market liberalization in Myanmar', in Koichi Fujita, Fumiharu Mieno, and Ikuko Okamoto (eds), *The Economic Transition in Myanmar after 1988: Market Economy versus State Control*. Singapore: NUS Press, 2009, pp. 216–17.

Commission.[3] In the first decade, the fiscal years 1989 to 1998, over 300 FDI (foreign direct investment) applications, with a total value close to $7,200 million, were approved, principally in oil and gas exploration and extraction, hotels and tourism, manufacturing and light industry (notably garment manufacture), real estate, and construction.

From the early 1990s, the SLORC began to privatize a number of the state economic enterprises that had been taken over or created during the socialist period, at first through leasing and joint venture arrangements with foreign capital.[4] In January 1995, the Myanmar Privatization Commission was established not simply to facilitate the transfer of state-owned concerns to local entrepreneurs, but also to assist the latter in acquiring essential business skills, thus promoting 'the emergence of national economic enterprises in the hands of the national entrepreneurs'. This decade also saw the establishment in Myanmar of twenty-one domestic private commercial banks – private commercial banking had been banned from 1963 – permitted to offer virtually the full range of banking services except foreign exchange transactions.[5] Indeed this period saw reform in many further areas of the economy: for example, Myanmar's previously illegal border trade was regularized; fishing and forest rights were leased to foreign interests; industrial zones were established; public sector wages were substantially increased; laws governing commercial taxation, the insurance sector, mining, forestry, fisheries, and the hotel and tourism industries were introduced; and the Myanmar Chamber of Commerce and Industry was re-established. The legislative energy of the SLORC in these years was impressive.[6]

[3] Toshihiro Kudo and Fumiharu Mieno, 'Trade, foreign investment and Myanmar's economic development in the transition to an open economy', in Fujita et al. (eds), *The Economic Transition in Myanmar after 1988*, pp. 117, 119–22.
[4] Tin Maung Maung Than, *State Dominance in Myanmar: the Political Economy of Industrialization*. Singapore: Institute of Southeast Asian Studies, 2007, p. 360.
[5] Sean Turnell, *Fiery Dragons: Banks, Moneylenders and Microfinance in Burma*. Copenhagen: NIAS Press, 2009, pp. 258–60.
[6] The major economic reforms in this period are listed in tabular form in Tin Maung Maung Than, *State Dominance in Myanmar*, pp. 356–7; and Koichi Fujita, Fumiharu Mieno, and Ikuko Okamoto, 'Myanmar's economic transformation after 1988', in Fujita et al. (eds), *The Economic Transition in Myanmar after 1988*, p. 5.

That said, it is important to emphasize that for the new government, economic reform had a lower priority than the securing of
political control – or perhaps more accurately, the new government
saw economic reform primarily as a means to strengthen its political control.[7] Most importantly, by delivering more goods and services,
specifically to those loyal to the regime, economic growth would secure
the population's acquiescence to military rule, and perhaps more than
acquiescence. More broadly, economic progress would enhance the
regime's legitimacy.[8] In addition, as the new business opportunities
being created in a more market-oriented economy were to be commonly channelled towards the military's own commercial interests,
economic growth would directly enhance the wealth and power of the
regime itself. This last ambition implied that few business opportunities would be given to interests beyond the control of the military, or
to interests that might come to challenge the military's control.

The argument that economic reform was undertaken primarily to
strengthen political control partly explains why the evolution toward
a market-oriented economy under the SLORC frequently turned out
to be hesitant, partial, or easily reversed. Those characteristics were
clearly evident in the reforms introduced in the marketing of Myanmar's principal crop, rice.[9] Thus in brief detail, the compulsory procurement of rice by the state at a low, inflexible price was at first abolished – in 1987, at the same time, presumably, as the long-established
controls on the domestic trade in rice were removed. Burma's rice cultivators were now free to sell all their production to whomever they
wished at whatever price they could secure. But in 1989 compulsory
procurement was reinstated, although the state's demands were now
set substantially below the levels imposed during the socialist period.
The compulsory procurement of rice, accounting for just under 10
per cent of total production in the early 2000s, was then maintained
until 2003, when it was abolished for a second time. In addition, the

[7] David I. Steinberg, *Burma: the State of Myanmar*. Washington, DC:
Georgetown University Press, 2001, p. 292.
[8] For a valuable exploration of the complex concept of 'legitimacy by economic
performance' in rural Burma from the late 1970s, see Ardeth Maung
Thawnghmung, *Behind the Teak Curtain: Authoritarianism, Agricultural
Policies and Political Legitimacy in Rural Burma/Myanmar*. London: Kegan
Paul, 2004.
[9] The following draws principally on Okamoto, 'Transformation of the rice
marketing system after market liberalization in Myanmar'.

new military government retained from the socialist period the state monopoly on the export of rice, now conducted through Myanma Agricultural Produce Trading. However provision for the export of rice by private traders was included in proposals for reform announced in 2003 although it was later withdrawn. Then in late 2007, the government indicated that in the following year it would allow a number of private companies to export around 400,000 tons of rice: but after cyclone Nargis struck Myanmar in May 2008, the licences were suspended, as there were fears that domestic shortages could force prices to rise sharply. And finally, the SLORC retained from the socialist period, although with modifications, the rice ration system, a procedure that secured for designated households a stipulated quantity of rice at substantially below the market price. Under the BSPP, the rice ration had been allocated for all households. But now it was retained only for civil servants and the military, and for certain institutions such as hospitals, in an attempt, presumably, to secure support for the regime from those important constituencies. However the rice distributed under the ration system was often of poor quality, for it was acquired by the government through its compulsory procurement mechanism, and not surprisingly, cultivators were delivering their inferior production to the state depots and selling their better grain on the market. In the 1990s, the rice ration system therefore earned less gratitude from the select recipients than might have been hoped, and in early 2004 it was abolished.

By means of these three instruments – compulsory procurement, the ration system, and its monopoly of exports – the SLORC and its successor, the SPDC (State Peace and Development Council), retained a measure of control of the rice market, and thus were better able to secure for the domestic consumer a stable supply of rice at a low price. This was critically important for the stability of the regime. In 1967 and again in 1974, the BSPP rulers had faced major unrest across the country, caused on the first occasion principally by shortages of rice and on the second by a sharp increase in rice prices. The regime had good reason to fear that high prices for basic necessities could provoke serious political unrest.[10]

---

[10] Arguably the principal cause of protests that took place in September 2007, the so-called 'Saffron Revolution', was a sudden sharp rise in natural gas and petrol prices following the removal of government subsidies: Michael

The hesitant, partial, and easily reversed character of the new military government's reform ambitions was also evident in the privatization of state economic enterprises.[11] Despite the establishment of an apparently powerful Myanmar Privatization Commission (MPC) in January 1995, chaired by Secretary-1 of the SLORC with the Minister for National Planning and Economic Development as secretary, and including twelve further ministers, the attorney-general, the auditor-general, and four senior civil servants, progress was extremely slow. In the mid-1990s there were almost 1,800 state-owned enterprises. But in the first six years of the MPC, from the beginning of 1995 through to early 2001, just 138 state-owned assets were privatized: and of the 138, no less than 87 were cinema halls. The slow progress partly reflected government fears that new private owners of state enterprises would cut jobs and raise prices. It is interesting to note that in its first years at least, the MPC required private purchasers to continue in the same line of business (the cinema hall must remain a cinema hall) and with no retrenchment of staff. But slow progress also reflected a lack of management expertise and financial capacity in Myanmar's private sector. In other words, there were too few private interests with the skills and capital to take over state enterprises: and of those few, fewer still would think of taking on concerns that they could not then restructure and reform.

From the late 1990s, Myanmar's slow privatization went into reverse, as the Ministry of Industry 1 established a substantial number of new industrial enterprises. More than seventy were being implemented across the country in the early 2000s. One seasoned Burmese observer of the economy was driven to distraction. '[O]nly a handful of people, if any, will know why [the government] can expect state-led industrialization under military rule to succeed this time around after it had failed miserably in the past. This is incomprehensible.'[12] However, one possible explanation for the 'incomprehensible' was suggested immediately above: at that time there were too few local private

Aung-Thwin and Maitrii Aung-Thwin, *A History of Myanmar since Ancient Times: Traditions and Transformations*. London: Reaktion Books, 2012, p. 273; Michael W. Charney, *A History of Modern Burma*. Cambridge University Press, 2009, p. 196.

[11] The following draws principally on Tin Maung Maung Than, *State Dominance in Myanmar*, pp. 360–2.

[12] Myat Thein, *Economic Development of Myanmar*. Singapore: Institute of Southeast Asian Studies, 2004, p. 7.

interests in Myanmar with the skills and capital – and also perhaps too few foreign interests with the confidence – to take on new industrial projects.

Elsewhere, economic reform failed virtually from the outset. This was clearly the case with the Central Bank of Myanmar (CBM), established in July 1990.[13] The primary legal responsibility of the bank was 'to preserve the internal and external value of the Myanmar currency', and its founding legislation gave it the formal powers, for example to conduct open market operations in government securities and foreign exchange, to meet that responsibility. There is little need to emphasize that stable domestic prices and a stable value of the *kyat* against the world's major trading currencies were crucial elements for the macroeconomic stability that was essential if Myanmar, now in pursuit of an open-door market-oriented economy, was to achieve sustained growth. But neither was achieved. By 2002, the consumer price index, 1989 = 100, had soared to 1995, a twenty-fold rise, for the annual rate of inflation in the 1990s was between 20 and 30 per cent. Externally, the *kyat* was pegged to the IMF Special Drawing Rights to give a near-constant official rate against the United States dollar through the 1990s of roughly $1 = 6 *kyat*. But the rate at which the *kyat* was illegally traded, the black market rate, was far lower, deteriorating hugely in this period. In 1988, one dollar would exchange on the illegal market for approximately 30 *kyat*. In 2002 it secured approximately 960 *kyat*. With the value of the *kyat*, both internally and externally, falling, and perhaps too with the recent demonetizations in mind, as opportunities arose, the population turned to the United States dollar, and consequently financial transactions in important sectors of the Myanmar economy – prominently in hotels and tourism – came to be conducted almost exclusively in that currency. The 'dollarization' of Myanmar in the 1990s was not only a demonstration of the failure of macroeconomic management, but also a further obstacle to securing sustained stable economic growth.

The deterioration in the position of the *kyat* should not be seen simply in terms of the failure by the Central Bank of Myanmar to discharge its primary legal responsibility 'to preserve the internal and external value of the Myanmar currency'. Rather it should be seen primarily as a reflection of fundamental weaknesses in the economy over which

---

[13] The following draws principally on Turnell, *Fiery Dragons*, pp. 289–93.

the central bank had little or no control. Thus the deterioration in the internal value of the *kyat* – the inflation of the 1990s – was caused principally by the repeated failure of government to balance its budget and the consequent financing of the deficit by printing money. In other words, reform – here the creation of a central bank with considerable formal powers – broke on a fundamental economic reality. This was a common theme.

The performance of the economy

The Myanmar economy appears to have experienced substantial growth in the 1990s and subsequently. GDP is reported to have increased by 9.7 per cent in real terms in 1992/93 and by 10.5 per cent in 1999/2000, although growth was lower, occasionally much lower, in other years.[14] And then from 2000 to 2005, GDP reportedly grew at rates in excess of 10 per cent a year, on occasion considerably in excess.[15] Two reservations should be noted. As the economy had contracted very substantially in the second half of the 1980s – GDP fell some 11 per cent in the three years from 1985/86 – growth in the early 1990s was simply recovery. Myanmar GDP was not restored to its mid-1980s level, in real terms, until 1993/94, and per capita income not until 1996/97. Second, it would be unwise to put great faith in official statistics on the Myanmar economy, and in particular in the GDP figures. It need only be noted that while the government reported that GDP grew by 13.6 per cent in 2004, the Economist Intelligence Unit estimate was 0.2 per cent.[16]

Certainly the two decades and more of SLORC/SPDC rule saw marked physical change in important sectors of the economy. In anticipation of an increase in tourist and business arrivals, a number of new international-standard hotels were constructed – the Shangri-La group, based in Hong Kong, opened Traders Hotel on Sule Pagoda Road in Yangon in late 1996 – and the Strand, first opened in 1901 and one of the most famous colonial-era hotels in South East Asia but

[14] Myat Thein, *Economic Development of Myanmar*, Table 5.1, p. 127.
[15] Robert H. Taylor, *The State in Myanmar*. London: Hurst, 2009, Table 6.11, p. 456.
[16] For some valuable comments on the official statistics and their critics, see Sean Turnell, 'Burma's economy 2004: crisis masking stagnation', in Trevor Wilson (ed.), *Myanmar's Long Road to National Reconciliation*. Singapore: Institute of Southeast Asian Studies, 2006, pp. 78–80.

Figure 5.1 Naypyidaw, Myanmar's new capital
Source: Paula Bronstein/Getty Images News/Getty Images

poorly maintained from 1948, was renovated, and reopened, under private management, in 1995. At the same time, the government itself invested substantially in the country's infrastructure, in the construction of dams and reservoirs, electricity generation, postal, telegraph, and telecommunications services, highways, roads, and bridges, airfields, and in railways.[17] For example, over three and a half thousand miles of highways and main roads and over one hundred major bridges were constructed in the 1990s.

But by far the largest of the government's infrastructure projects in this period, indeed a huge commitment, was the construction of a new capital city, Naypyidaw, in central Myanmar, some 350 kilometres north of Yangon.[18] The main construction started in 2004 (preparatory work had been undertaken from the late 1990s) with the relocation of ministries and their officials from Yangon beginning in late 2005. The financial cost of the construction alone is said to be running – the work continues – at hundreds of millions of dollars. The reason given by the government to build the new capital was that, located in central Myanmar, it would more effectively secure the

[17] Myat Thein, *Economic Development of Myanmar*, pp. 207–11.
[18] The following draws on Dulyapak Preecharushh, *Naypyidaw: the New Capital of Burma*. Bangkok: White Lotus, 2009.

development of the country, notably economic development in that core hinterland between the dry zone and the frontier areas. But many observers have sought dark motives for the relocation. For example, a capital far inland would reduce the possibility of a seaborne invasion by United States forces sent to bring down the regime. Or relocation to Naypyidaw would place the regime safely beyond any future resurgence of serious protest in Yangon. There may have been another important consideration. David Steinberg has argued that the SLORC/SPDC 'used the construction of infrastructure of all varieties as demonstrations of [its] economic and political efficacy'.[19] In other words, new highways, bridges, dams and reservoirs, indeed a new capital city for Myanmar, rising in Burma's historic heartland, were to be seen as impressive physical evidence of the SLORC/SPDC's command of economic progress. And indeed the contrast with the drab decay of the socialist years was often striking.

But beneath that physical evidence of progress, beneath too the official reports of impressive GDP growth, the Myanmar economy under the SLORC/SPDC was marked by a considerable number of critical weaknesses. For example, the apparent growth, the recovery, of GDP in real terms in the 1990s is explained principally by the strong performance of agriculture, secured initially by the decontrol of prices in 1987 but then supported by further government initiatives, notably the introduction of summer paddy from 1992.[20] However it was a performance that could not be sustained. From the mid-1990s, the growth in agricultural production, and therefore the growth in GDP in real terms, slowed. A number of short-term factors appear to have undermined the continued expansion in agricultural output, notably adverse weather in those years and shortages of imported diesel fuel and fertilizer because of a restricted availability of foreign exchange. But it has also been argued that, long term, the potential for expansion was limited by Myanmar's agrarian structure.[21]

---

[19] David I. Steinberg, 'Myanmar: the roots of economic malaise', in Kyaw Yin Hlaing, Robert H. Taylor, and Tin Maung Maung Than (ed.), *Myanmar: Beyond Politics to Societal Imperatives*. Singapore: Institute of Southeast Asian Studies, 2005, p. 110.

[20] Myat Thein, *Economic Development of Myanmar*, pp. 129–33, 178–85.

[21] The following draws in part on Koichi Fujita, Fumiharu Mieno, and Ikuko Okamoto, 'Myanmar's economic transformation after 1988', in Fujita et al. (eds), *The Economic Transition in Myanmar after 1988*, pp. 6–10; and Koichi Fujita, 'Agricultural labourers in Myanmar during the economic transition: views from the study of selected villages', in Fujita et al. (eds), ibid., pp. 246–52.

As was noted in the previous chapter, although *The Burmese Way to Socialism* in 1962 had stated that all forms of production would be owned by the state or by cooperatives, the BSPP government had not brought agricultural land into state ownership. In other words, in contrast to the People's Republic of China and the Democratic Republic of Vietnam, for example, there was no collectivization of agriculture. Rather, Burma's cultivators worked the land as individuals, although they could not sell or mortgage their holding or purchase further holdings. For this last reason, but perhaps also because land redistribution had apparently tended to favour those cultivators with few resources, holdings remained small, too small to secure major economies of scale in cultivation or to produce for the household the surplus income needed to invest substantially in high-yield inputs and methods. In brief, the reform of Burma's agrarian structure – the redistribution of land – stressed equity rather than increased productivity.

One further feature of land redistribution must be noted. The stress on equity did not usually extend to the landless agricultural labourer, for priority in redistribution appears to have been given to (the poorer) tenants and owners. Consequently, a high proportion of the agricultural population remained without land: agricultural labour households are estimated to have accounted for perhaps a quarter of all households in rural Myanmar in the 2000s, nearly ten million people, largely dependent on labouring wages alone. That substantial rural presence, vulnerable to even small increases in the cost of living, provided a further important reason for the SLORC/SPDC to keep rice prices low, even though decontrol – the incentive of higher prices – would raise agricultural productivity and production. Maintaining social order was more important than raising productivity.

A strong agricultural sector was essential if Myanmar were to achieve sustained economic growth. Rising agricultural exports would secure the foreign exchange needed to import the capital goods, technology, and raw materials demanded by industrialization; a larger agricultural surplus, if captured by the state, would provide resources to invest in industry and infrastructure; larger rural incomes would create increased demand for local manufacturing. There was some progress in agriculture in this period. Restrictions on the trade in pulses and beans had been removed in 1987, and in the following decade, production soared, from 875,000 tons in 1992/93 to 1,882,000 in

1999/2000.[22] In that last year, 'pulses and beans' was Myanmar's second most valuable export. But, manacled by the continuing compulsory procurement of rice at fixed low prices and the state monopoly of rice exports; by an agrarian structure that emphasized equity and social order above increased productivity; and also by shortages of imported fuel, fertilizer, and high-yield seeds, and a provision of rural credit that remained substantially below cultivation costs, the agricultural sector was still far from providing a firm foundation for sustained economic growth in Myanmar.

There were critical weaknesses too in the industrial sector. Perhaps most striking, the sector remained small. After half a century, five decades in which the core economic ambition of Burma's governments, ceaselessly pursued, had been to build an industrial economy, in 2000, industry accounted for just 9.1 per cent of GDP, in fact down from 10.5 per cent in 1990.[23] There was some progress under the SLORC/SPDC, perhaps most notably a major expansion in the garment industry, producing for export.[24] In the early 1990s, a number of state-owned, military-related textile and garment factories established joint ventures with foreign companies, principally Korean or from Hong Kong, to produce to orders from overseas buyers. In addition, other foreign firms built their own, wholly foreign-owned, factories in Myanmar. And then, from the mid-1990s, local private firms began to enter the industry, and indeed soon took a leading role. The value of Myanmar's garment exports rose from almost nothing at the beginning of the decade to some $270 million in 1998, before soaring to $868 million in 2001, becoming Myanmar's single most valuable export at that time. Throughout the decade, about 90 per cent of garment exports went to the United States and the European Union. However in 2003, the United States imposed financial and trade sanctions – imports from Myanmar were banned – and inevitably garment exports fell sharply. It is reported that 160 garment factories were then closed, and over 80,000 workers, mainly female, dismissed.[25]

---

[22] Myat Thein, *Economic Development of Myanmar*, pp. 182–3.
[23] Ibid., p. 179.
[24] The following draws mainly on Toshihiro Kudo, 'Industrial policies and the development of Myanmar's industrial sector in the transition to a market economy', in Fujita et al. (eds), *The Economic Transition in Myanmar after 1988*, pp. 79–85.
[25] Tin Maung Maung Than, *State Dominance in Myanmar*, p. 410, fn. 129.

As indicated above, the remarkable growth in Myanmar's garment industry in the 1990s was led by private capital, foreign and local. Indeed in the first years of the following decade, local private capital alone accounted for no less than two-thirds of garment exports. But with that important exception, under the SLORC/SPDC, local capital struggled to establish new manufacturing concerns. There were many obstacles, not least severe difficulties in raising finance, a poor infrastructure, and the unpredictability and complexity of government regulations and procedures. In addition, private business was often caught between relentlessly rising costs, as factor markets were freed, and a restriction on earnings arising principally from an over-valued exchange rate.[26] Thus manacled, local private capital, even where there were the individuals with the necessary experience and expertise, would not take a leading position in the decisive industrial expansion that Myanmar was still seeking.

It was partly for this reason, surely, that, as noted earlier, a substantial number of new state-owned industrial enterprises were established from the late 1990s. Ministry of Industry 1, responsible for light industry, built thirty new factories in the period to 2001, manufacturing, for example, textiles and garments, noodles and soft drinks, soap, cement, tiles, bricks, newsprint, bicycles, shoes, and caustic soda, chlorine, and bleach. And it planned a further fifty-six thereafter.[27] In addition, Ministry of Industry 2, responsible for heavy industry, and the Ministry of Agriculture and Irrigation, as well as other economic ministries, also established a number of new state-owned industrial enterprises in this period. But as in earlier decades, the performance of the state economic enterprises was poor.[28] Capacity utilization was low: and each year in the 1990s, the state enterprises, as a sector, incurred substantial financial deficits, indeed huge deficits towards the end of the decade. The reasons for that poor performance are again familiar from earlier decades: a severe shortage of foreign exchange, which restricted essential imports of machinery, raw materials, and technology; an absence of financial discipline, for the deficits being incurred year-after-year by state-owned industrial enterprises were covered by government subsidy and were thus left uncorrected; and a near-total

---

[26] Ibid., pp. 392–3.
[27] Ibid., pp. 408–9, fn. 119; Myat Thein, *Economic Development of Myanmar*, pp. 260–1.
[28] Myat Thein, *Economic Development of Myanmar*, pp. 205–6.

absence of delegation and local responsibility in decision-making. The state-owned enterprises remained firmly shackled to their past.

Two final important weaknesses in the economy of Myanmar under the SLORC/SPDC must be noted. In each fiscal year from 1988 through to 2002, and beyond, the government ran a substantial budget deficit, commonly the equivalent of 3 per cent or more of GDP.[29] The deficits were caused in part by low government revenue (a serious structural problem that will be considered in some detail in the final section of this chapter) but also by high government expenditure on, notably, infrastructure projects, including the creation of the new capital, Naypyidaw, the armed forces, and on financing the losses of the state-owned economic enterprises. The budget deficits were financed principally through an expansion in central bank credit – a huge increase in the money supply – and the result, as noted earlier, was an annual rate of inflation in the 1990s of between 20 and 30 per cent.

The final critical weakness was a collapse in confidence from early 2003 in the private commercial banks that had been established during the previous decade.[30] The crisis was triggered by a series of failures in late 2002 among certain private finance companies, institutions that had been promising investors high rates of return but were in fact often little more than gambling syndicates and ponzi schemes, schemes paying out high returns to existing members from the new deposits of fresh members – for as long as fresh members can be found. Those failures rapidly unnerved the customers of Myanmar's private commercial banks, recently established and hitherto growing at an extraordinary rate. In early 2003, long queues formed outside the banks as depositors sought to withdraw their money.

The crisis was exacerbated by a number of further factors. First there were accusations by an OECD (Organization for Economic Cooperation and Development) task force and by the US State Department that private banks in Myanmar had long been involved in laundering the huge funds being generated by the drugs trade, Myanmar then being the world's second largest producer of illicit opium after Afghanistan. And second, in an attempt to stem the loss of deposits, the banks,

[29] Tin Maung Maung Than, *State Dominance in Myanmar*, Figure 9.7, p. 370.
[30] This paragraph draws on Turnell, *Fiery Dragons*, ch. 10; and Sean Turnell, 'Burma's economy 2004: crisis masking stagnation', in Trevor Wilson (ed.), *Myanmar's Long Road to National Reconciliation*. Singapore: Institute of Southeast Asian Studies, 2006.

apparently marshalled by the Central Bank of Myanmar, imposed increasingly tight limits on the amount that could be withdrawn by each customer in a given period. The banks also recalled loans, ignoring the capacity of borrowers to repay immediately, on demand. Inevitably those measures merely increased the sense of panic. By mid-2003, Myanmar's private banks had effectively closed their doors. A number reopened the following year but two of the largest, the Asia Wealth Bank and the Myanmar Mayflower Bank, directly accused by the United States Treasury of laundering drug money, remained closed. Their banking licences were revoked by the Myanmar authorities in March 2005. That the 2003 bank crisis had a serious impact not only immediately on production and trade, but also longer-term on the confidence of individuals in the security of property rights in Myanmar – depositors were denied access to their funds – requires no emphasis.

Manacled reform

Writing at the end of the 1980s, shortly after the SLORC took power, U Tun Wai, one of that remarkable generation of Burmese economists that had first emerged in the 1950s but who had spent almost all his career not in Burma but as a senior official with the International Monetary Fund in Washington, at first offered an encouraging assessment of the prospects for the Myanmar economy 'at the crossroads', as he put it.

Myanmar is well endowed with natural resources and if economic adjustment and stabilization programmes are well designed and implemented for a period of about four years, the country would be able to correct the mistakes of the past few decades and lay the foundations for solid economic growth and perhaps catch up with some of its more prosperous Asian neighbours.[31]

Three paragraphs later, U Tun Wai had become less sanguine. 'It will take many years, maybe even longer than the four years indicated here to put Myanmar on a sound economic footing because there are deep-seated problems in all sectors of the economy.'[32] But even that more

---

[31] U Tun Wai, 'The Myanmar economy at the crossroads: options and constraints', in Mya Than and Joseph L. H. Tan (eds), *Myanmar Dilemmas and Options: the Challenge of Economic Transition in the 1990s*. Singapore: Institute of Southeast Asian Studies, 1990, pp. 49–50.

[32] Ibid., pp. 50–1. In the mid-1990s, U Tun Wai had come to doubt the economic reform ambitions of the new military government: 'the initiatives of the

cautious assessment turned out to be far too confident. It was going to take many more than four years to put Myanmar on a sound economic footing: the economy's problems were very deep-seated.

It was clearly evident by the late 1980s, and arguably much earlier, that the Burmese way to socialism had failed. Burma had been bankrupted. And yet the subsequent transition to an open, market-oriented economy in the two decades and more of SLORC/SPDC rule was, as outlined in some detail above, hesitant, partial, and often abandoned. This final section of the chapter will seek to establish the reasons why that pursuit of the market was hesitant and far from complete. The reasons are undoubtedly complex. But they could also explain why, looking forward, Myanmar might well continue to struggle to find the path to sustained economic growth and development.

Although the stated ambition of the SLORC on taking power in the late 1980s was to secure a transition to an open, market-oriented economy, it is clear that through the two decades and more of SLORC/SPDC rule, the state's managers, senior military officers, failed to internalize the ethos of the market.[33] It is tempting to suggest that they failed to grasp fully what was required: but it is more likely that they understood full well but resisted the implications of that understanding. Thus few would dispute that an essential requirement for a market-oriented economy to perform with even modest efficiency is for government regularly to publish comprehensive and accurate economic data, including data on its own finances. But as indicated earlier, the official statistics on the Myanmar economy published in this period are, in the words of one observer, '[s]ubject to almost every conceivable obstruction to statistical best practice – from the low pay, scant resources and corruption of Burma's civil service . . . to plain wishful thinking'.[34] In addition, and in this context perhaps more telling, from the end of the 1990s, the Myanmar government simply stopped publishing a full set of national accounts. Finally it might be

---

SLORC government could be characterized as economic liberalization at the fringe, rather than a thoroughgoing restructuring of the economy': U Tun Wai, 'Myanmar', in Pradumna B. Rana and Naved Hamid (eds), *From Centrally Planned to Market Economies: the Asian Approach: Vol. III: Lao PDR, Myanmar and Vietnam*. Hong Kong: Oxford University Press, 1996, p. 281.

[33] This discussion draws partly on Myat Thein, *Economic Development of Myanmar*, pp. 167, 243; and Tin Maung Maung Than, *State Dominance in Myanmar*, pp. 353, 392.

[34] Turnell, 'Burma's economy 2004', pp. 78–9.

noted that in its management of the economy, the senior military of the SLORC/SPDC, like the BSPP ministers before them, chose not to bring in (or indeed bring back) experienced Myanmar economists from outside the ruling core, economists who would possess an understanding of and commitment to the market.

Despite the support given to the expansion of the private sector – seen perhaps most notably in the establishment of the private commercial banks in the 1990s, and in the dominant position taken by local private capital in the expansion in garment exports from the end of that decade – the implacable distrust of the self-interest of the capitalist that was so prominent during the BSPP years was clearly still present in the SLORC/SPDC. The founding principle of the market economy, that the individual pursuing self-interest in a free market secures benefit for the community as a whole, was an alien concept for the senior military. Theirs remained a mentality of command and control.

In some important respects, the SLORC/SPDC could not responsibly abandon control. This was the position, for example, with the rice market. As was noted earlier, although the compulsory procurement of rice by the state at a low, inflexible price was abolished in 1987, it was reinstated two years later and then maintained until 2003. In addition the SLORC retained from the socialist period, although with modifications, the rice ration system, until it too was abolished, early in 2004. And finally, throughout this period, the SLORC/SPDC retained the state monopoly on the export of rice, although provision for export by private traders was included in proposals for reform announced in 2003 but later withdrawn. Again as noted earlier, in retaining control of the rice market, the authorities were able to secure for the domestic consumer – a high proportion of Myanmar's population – a stable supply of rice at a low price. Full decontrol, particularly if implemented rapidly, would almost certainly have sent rice prices soaring, and thus caused serious economic hardship and social unrest. A similar argument might have applied to the privatization programme. The transfer of state industries to private interests and the rationalization that would inevitably follow to make them more efficient was almost certain to increase unemployment. However, as noted earlier, in its first years at least, the Myanmar Privatization Commission required private purchasers to avoid retrenchment of staff. But then if unemployment was the principal concern, perhaps the enterprises should have remained within the state sector in the first place.

The broad argument being made here is that after a quarter of a century in which the military had pursued a seriously flawed economic strategy that eventually brought Burma to bankruptcy, the economy of Myanmar in the 1990s was so severely dislocated – hugely bloated, loss-making state economic enterprises; a rice economy long drained of incentives – that deregulation on a major scale could well have led to chaos and collapse. In other words, if the economy was to continue to function, even at far below its potential, it was essential to retain a substantial measure of state control, and to implement the transition to the market gradually and subtly in order to minimize the disruptive consequences. Of course it is doubtful whether the senior military in the SLORC/SPDC had the understanding, or the government administration the experience, to achieve that essential subtlety.

At the same time it was clearly in the interest of the SLORC/SPDC itself to retain state command of the economy, beyond the obvious point that it had no wish to preside over an economic collapse, or face the severe social disorder and political challenge that a collapse would surely provoke. Thus, for the military there was concern that the emergence of powerful private interests in a market-oriented economy would undermine not only the economic but also in time the political authority of the state.[35] In other words, the transition to the market would threaten the military's position: ultimately, it would argue, its self-defined position as guardian of national sovereignty and unity. It is therefore interesting to note that prominent in Myanmar's modern private sector from the 1990s were two military-owned and military-operated conglomerates.[36] Burma's armed forces had long maintained substantial economic interests. Starting operations in 1951, with a loan from the Ministry of Defence and with military officers occupying the senior management positions, the Defence Services Institute (DSI) had initially been designed to supply goods and services to the troops, on the model of the British NAAFI. However, during the two years of military caretaker government at the end of the 1950s, the interests of the DSI had expanded enormously. Thus in 1960 it ran banks,

[35] Tin Maung Maung Than, *State Dominance in Myanmar*, p. 394.
[36] The following draws on Andrew Selth, *Burma's Armed Forces: Power without Glory*. Norwalk, CT: EastBridge, 2002, pp. 145–8; Maung Aung Myoe, *The Tatmadaw in Myanmar since 1988: an Interim Assessment*. Canberra: Australian National University, Strategic and Defence Studies Centre, 1999, pp. 11–13.

shipping lines, and Burma's largest import-export concern; and it controlled a hotel company, fisheries and poultry distribution businesses, a construction firm, a bookshop, a bus company, and the largest department store chain in Burma. The DSI was now 'the largest and most powerful business organization in the nation'. Shortly after the March 1962 coup, the DSI was nationalized. But as active and retired military officers were detailed to run the state economic enterprises established under the Burmese way to socialism, the position of the armed forces in the economy was maintained, indeed strengthened, as no business enterprise outside the state sector was permitted.

With the collapse of the BSPP at the end of the 1980s and the declared transition to a market-oriented economy, the military substantially reworked its economic interests. In 1990 the SLORC established the Union of Myanmar Economic Holdings (UMEH), with 40 per cent of the capital shares being held by the Ministry of Defence, the remainder by members of the armed forces, serving and retired, and veterans and regimental welfare organizations. By the end of the decade, the UMEH had created almost fifty joint ventures with foreign firms in a notably wide range of fields, including garment manufacturing, the food and beverage trade, supermarkets, a bank, galvanised iron sheet production, hotels and tourism, the gem trade, wood-based manufacturing, coach services and an airline, construction and real estate, cement production, and cosmetics. A second economic organization backed by the military, the Myanmar Economic Corporation (MEC), was formed in 1997. It came under the Ministry of Defence. Crucially, the MEC was exempted from earlier legislation that reserved certain key economic sectors for state-owned enterprise, and it was therefore able to establish interests in, notably, natural gas and petroleum exploration, production, and marketing, mineral and gem extraction, commodity trading, and telecommunications, as well as banking, finance, and insurance, construction, and hotels and tourism. But in addition to the dominant presence of the UMEH and the MEC, there was also 'considerable private participation in the economy by senior military officers'. Indeed, as one observer noted in 2002, 'It is now very difficult to establish any major business in Burma without the support of senior military officers.'[37] In other words, controlling access to the modern sector, the SLORC/SPDC was able to curb or prevent entirely the emergence of

[37] Selth, *Burma's Armed Forces*, p. 148.

independent private interests, local or foreign, that might undermine not only its economic position but also in time its political authority – although presumably this was achieved at the cost of excluding more experienced and innovative capital.

In summary, the fact that the transition to an open, market-oriented economy in the two decades and more of SLORC/SPDC rule was hesitant, partial, and often abandoned, reflected – the point is an obvious one – the understandings and perspectives of the military: its continuing distrust of the self-interest of the capitalist and its failure to internalize the ethos of the market; its fear that rapid deregulation on a major scale could lead to economic and social collapse; and its concern that the emergence of powerful private interests in a market-oriented economy would undermine not only the economic but also the political authority of the state. But there were other factors too.

The first was the refusal of the Western nations to engage economically with Myanmar. From 1962, Burma had sought to isolate itself from the world, banning foreign private investment and accepting only a small volume of official development assistance (ODA), although a far greater volume from the early 1970s. It is therefore ironic that when, from the late 1980s, Myanmar sought the return of foreign private capital and certainly needed substantial ODA to haul itself back from bankruptcy, it was isolated by the Western bloc. Reacting to the violent suppression of the anti-regime protests that had taken place throughout much of 1988 and then to the apparent failure of the military to honour the results of multi-party elections held in May 1990, in which the opposition National League for Democracy (NLD) had secured a clear majority, the United States terminated economic aid to Myanmar and blocked loans and grants to Myanmar from the World Bank and the International Monetary Fund.[38] The detention of Aung San Suu Kyi, the 1991 Nobel Peace Laureate, held under house arrest for a total of fifteen years in the period from 1989 to 2010, and near-constant reports that the SLORC regime was committing serious

---

[38] Ian Holliday, *Burma Redux: Global Justice and the Quest for Political Reform in Myanmar*. New York: Columbia University Press, 2011, pp. 22, 115, 117–18. The SLORC position on the 1990s election was that 'those elected could not form a new government until there was a new constitution'. In contrast, after its electoral success, the NLD claimed that it had the right to govern, and demanded that the military transfer power immediately: David I. Steinberg, *Burma/Myanmar: What Everyone Needs to Know*. New York: Oxford University Press, 2010, pp. 90–3.

human rights abuses, further hardened the hostility of Western administrations. In 2006, Myanmar received just $2.88 per capita in ODA, the lowest figure among the world's fifty poorest countries, far below the average of $58 per capita for that group. But in addition, Western private capital, just recently welcomed to return, now also retreated. In the early 1990s, Levi Strauss, Apple Computers, Kodak, Motorola, Disney, and PepsiCola pulled out of Myanmar, and in 1996 the European brewers Carlsberg and Heineken withdrew from major projects. Important in each withdrawal was the campaigning work of activist communities, particularly strong in the United States and the United Kingdom, in organizing consumer boycotts in Western markets of companies that would trade with or invest in a SLORC-ruled Myanmar. The activists also put pressure on their governments, no doubt encouraged by the fact that, partly because of Burma's earlier isolation, Western policy-makers were clearly listening to the activist communities. In 1997, an Executive Order signed by President Clinton banned US citizens from making new investments in Myanmar. In 2003, the Burmese Freedom and Democracy Act, together with an Executive Order signed by President Bush, banned imports into the United States from Myanmar.

Western trade sanctions had a significant impact on the Myanmar economy. As noted earlier, the 2003 ban on imports into the United States is reported to have led to the closure of 160 garment factories in Myanmar, with the loss of 80,000 jobs. In addition, it is clear that activist campaigns seriously affected a hoped-for growth in tourism. A 'Visit Myanmar' promotion in 1996 is said to have failed, and for year after year, hotels built in anticipation of a tourist boom struggled to find much business, even at rock-bottom room rates. In 2010, Myanmar had just over 300,000 international arrivals, against 16 million for neighbouring Thailand.[39]

The withdrawal of Western investment after a brief, modest return had perhaps a less significant impact on the Myanmar economy, in part because private capital was simultaneously being attracted from outside the Western economies. The commitment of Korean and Hong Kong interests to joint ventures in garment manufacturing from the early 1990s was noted earlier. There was also significant investment in Myanmar by interests in Malaysia, Singapore, Thailand,

---

[39] Holliday, *Burma Redux*, p. 68.

Indonesia, and Japan, although inward investment from those countries fell sharply with the onset of the Asian financial crisis in 1997.[40]
Official figures indicate that inward investment from China in the
1990s was modest – the cumulative value at March 2000, just under
$32 million, was below the figure for investment from Canada – but
it increased greatly in the following decade, dramatically so in the late
2000s. In July 2010, the value of investment in Myanmar from interests in China, including interests in Hong Kong, was officially given as
$12.3 billion, pushing China ahead of Thailand as Myanmar's princi-
pal source of foreign direct investment.[41]

There is a further reason to suggest that the forced disengagement of
Western investment from Myanmar from the early 1990s had only a
limited impact. For reasons to be noted below, Myanmar in this period
was not a particularly attractive prospect for foreign investment, and
therefore, even in the absence of sanctions and the threat of consumer
boycotts, it is unlikely that Western companies would have invested
on a substantial scale. In this context it is interesting to note that,
despite significant investment by, notably, Thailand and Singapore, in
the 1990s Myanmar was attracting far less foreign direct investment
than Vietnam, which at that time was also seeking to re-engage with
the world economy.[42]

It is also important to note that a major part of approved foreign
direct investment in Myanmar – one-third, as of January 2005 – was
in the extraction of oil and natural gas.[43] Thus a principal objective
of China, Myanmar's major source of foreign investment by the end
of this period, for investing in the country was to meet its own vastly
increasing energy needs. China sought access to the huge natural gas
reserves in the Gulf of Martaban and in the Bay of Bengal; it undertook major hydro-power projects in Kachin State; and it proposed

[40] Myat Thein, *Economic Development of Myanmar*. Singapore: Institute of
Southeast Asian Studies, 2004, pp. 163, 165.
[41] For detail on China's investments in Myanmar from 1988, see David I.
Steinberg and Hongwei Fan, *Modern China-Myanmar Relations: Dilemmas of
Mutual Dependence*. Copenhagen: NIAS Press, 2012, pp. 228–33.
[42] Myat Thein, *Economic Development of Myanmar*, p. 162.
[43] Tin Maung Maung Than, *State Dominance in Myanmar*, p. 373. For details
on the investments in the sector, see Sean Turnell, 'Finding dollars and sense:
Burma's economy in 2010', in Susan L. Levenstein (ed.), *Finding Dollars,
Sense, and Legitimacy in Burma*. Washington, DC: Woodrow Wilson
International Center for Scholars, 2010, pp. 29–30.

construction of an oil pipeline from Rakhine State into Yunnan to deliver much of China's oil imports from the Middle East. But – and this is the central point here – the oil and natural gas sector is an enclave, with few direct linkages to other parts of the Myanmar economy. The foreign investments in oil and natural gas clearly boosted Myanmar's export earnings, its foreign exchange reserves, and the government's revenues. But it created very little local employment, and did little or nothing directly to secure a significant restructuring of the economy. The latter would require substantial investment in manufacturing, perhaps too in hotels and tourism: but foreign investors had less interest in those sectors.

This returns the argument to its central focus – the further factors that might explain the partial, incomplete character of the transition to an open, market-oriented economy in the two decades and more of SLORC/SPDC rule. A principal consideration in attracting foreign investment into manufacturing in Myanmar was undoubtedly the presence of a large, low-wage, disciplined but low-skilled labour force. However Myanmar also presented a number of deep-seated obstacles to the potential foreign investor – to the local capitalist as well – and in a competitive world in which many economies could offer a cheap industrial labour force, these appear to have been highly damaging. Perhaps the most serious obstacle was poor infrastructure, and in particular the frequent dips and cuts in electricity supplies (somewhat ironic in a country which was now beginning to export energy on a substantial scale) and unreliable but expensive telecommunications services.[44] Investment in manufacturing was also discouraged by unpredictable and often inexplicable changes in government regulations; the belief, noted earlier, that it was 'very difficult to establish any major business in Burma without the support of senior military officers'; and by routine reports that Myanmar was among the most corrupt countries in the world.[45] The huge gap between the official rate for the *kyat* (approximately $1 = 6 *kyat*) and the market rate (in the region of $1 = 1,000 *kyat* at the end of this period), in creating an

---

[44] Myat Thein, *Economic Development of Myanmar*, p. 163; Tin Maung Maung Than, *State Dominance in Myanmar*, p. 372.

[45] On occasion, official regulations were simply bizarre. In the early 2000s, hotels were apparently required to provide for the authorities a photograph of every item they wished to import. Personal communication from Robert Taylor, 27 September 2012.

image of economic malfunction and by providing obvious opportunities for corruption, further discouraged foreign direct investment.[46]

It is interesting in this context to note one explanation for the success of garment manufacturing in this period, the great exception in
Myanmar's industrial stagnation in the two decades of SLORC/SPDC
rule.[47] The structure of the garment industry in Myanmar, as in other
low-wage emerging economies, was such that the foreign partner or
overseas buyer was responsible for all operations except the production itself, the cutting, sewing, and packing for export. Crucially, the
foreign interests supplied to the local factories all the basic materials,
procured from outside Myanmar, the cloth, buttons, zips. In this way
local garment production avoided Myanmar's tight import restrictions
and, to some degree, its treacherous business regulations and administrative procedures. In brief, the garment industry was in crucial respects
an enclave, distanced from the hostile reality of conducting business in
Myanmar.

There is one final argument. The factors noted above that hindered the transition to an open, market-oriented economy under the
SLORC/SPDC – the unreliable infrastructure; administrative regulations and procedures that were complex, unpredictable, and often inexplicable – persisted largely undiminished through these two decades
principally because the regime did not possess the leverage to tackle
them. The state was weak. That weakness had many aspects, and there
is space here to focus on just three of the most important.

As was explained in some detail in the previous chapter, from the
time of independence in 1948, Burma's governments had only a limited
and often fragile capacity to raise revenue. The revenue take was low
partly as a consequence of poor administration and widespread evasion, but there were also major weaknesses in the tax structure itself,
as described earlier. Despite reform under the SLORC/SPDC, including broadening the tax base, adjusting tax rates, and strengthening tax
administration, collection, and enforcement, and despite too attempts
to clean up a corrupt tax machinery – the entire central customs administration was prosecuted in 2006 – revenue remained desperately low,

---

[46] Turnell, 'Finding dollars and sense', p. 22.
[47] The following draws on Toshihiro Kudo, 'Industrial policies and the
    development of Myanmar's industrial sector in the transition to a market
    economy', in Fujita et al. (eds), *The Economic Transition in Myanmar after
    1988*, pp. 79, 82.

the equivalent of just 5 per cent or so of GDP in the first half of the 2000s.[48] Indeed in this period the state actually lost sources of income which had been important in the socialist decades, notably when the compulsory procurement of rice was finally abolished in 2003.

The weakness of the state in raising revenue was highly damaging. It was the fundamental reason for the persistent large budget deficits that scarred the government's finances through these decades, deficits that were covered by borrowing from the Central Bank of Myanmar – printing notes – and thus led to entrenched inflation and large falls in the market value of the *kyat*. In addition, the regime's weakness in raising revenue left it with too few resources once its priorities for expenditure – the armed forces, the building of a new capital city, covering the losses of the state-owned industries – had been met. Health and education, but also repairing a long-neglected infrastructure to encourage private investment, were starved. However it should be added that from the end of this period, Myanmar's natural gas exports provided the state with a new major source of income. It is said that new fields in the Bay of Bengal could yield an annual revenue in excess of one billion US dollars for thirty years, perhaps sufficient to restore the budget to surplus, although interestingly, the government's dollar earnings from the export of natural gas were apparently hugely undervalued in its published accounts.[49]

Turning to the second aspect, as was noted earlier, in this period there were accusations that private banks in Myanmar were involved in laundering the huge funds being generated by the drugs trade. According to the United States Treasury in 2003, the Asia Wealth Bank and the Myanmar Mayflower Bank were 'controlled by and used to facilitate money lending for such groups as the United Wa State Army – among the most notorious drug trafficking organizations in Southeast Asia'.[50] The alleged activities of these two banks point to a larger phenomenon,

---

[48] Mya Than and Myat Thein, 'Mobilization of financial resources for development in Myanmar: an introductory overview', in Mya Than and Myat Thein (eds), *Financial Resources for Development in Myanmar: Lessons from Asia*. Singapore: Institute of Southeast Asian Studies, 2000, p. 17; Robert H. Taylor, *The State in Myanmar*. London: Hurst, 2009, pp. 457–8, 460.

[49] Turnell, 'Finding dollars and sense', pp. 30–1. Those earnings are recorded in the government's published accounts at the official dollar: *kyat* rate, rather than the market rate. This understates the *kyat* value of Myanmar's natural gas earnings by over 150 times.

[50] Quoted in Turnell, *Fiery Dragons*, p. 307.

the channelling through various mechanisms of the earnings from the narcotics trade into Myanmar's legal economy. It has been argued that those earnings were so substantial that, laundered into legitimate investment – real estate, the retail trade, hotels, tourism – and into covering Myanmar's huge balance of trade deficit and adding to its reserves of hard currency, they saved the economy from collapse.[51]

In the preceding socialist period, the black market, supplying even basic necessities, had made it possible for the people to survive. But at the same time, the BSPP regime was severely weakened by this vast illegal trade, for it deprived the state of revenue and constituted a surrender of the state's control over the economy. This could not be tolerated. Therefore in the demonetizations of November 1985 and September 1987, the BSPP government finally set out to break the *hmaung-kho* (illegal) traders and reassert control – but with devastating consequences. If the economy of Myanmar under the SLORC/SPDC was indeed saved by the laundering of drug money, as has been argued, then there is a potent parallel with that earlier situation.[52] The SLORC/SPDC was clearly under great pressure, not least from international opinion, to break the trade in heroin and methamphetamines. But to have attempted to do so, seriously, would have been to invite economic collapse.[53]

The final aspect of the weak state to be noted here was the inadequacy of the government machinery itself. In the words of two observers in the 1990s, 'While the bureaucracy in Myanmar is both more complex and more competent than is often supposed, it remains

---

[51] This is the argument advanced by Bertil Lintner, 'Drugs and economic growth in Burma today', in Morten B. Pedersen, Emily Rudland, and Ronald J. May (eds), *Burma-Myanmar: Strong Regime, Weak State?* Adelaide: Crawford House Publishing, 2000.

[52] 'Burma has become Asia's first and only state that survives on the export of narcotics': Lintner, 'Drugs and economic growth in Burma today', p. 189.

[53] See Patrick Meehan, 'Drugs, insurgency and state-building in Burma: why the drugs trade is central to Burma's changing political order', *Journal of Southeast Asian Studies*, 42, 3 (October 2011). Meehan argues that by offering legal impunity, money-laundering services, and business opportunities to the drugs trade, which thereby directs a far higher proportion of its earnings into the legal economy, the Myanmar state has greatly strengthened its economic position. Thus Janus-like, it portrays 'itself to the West as committed to tackling drugs whilst at the same time continuing to use the drugs trade as an arena through which to construct and consolidate state power': Meehan, p. 404.

ill-equipped as a mechanism for economic reform.'[54] Poor performance was partly a reflection of woefully inadequate civil service salaries, for, paid little, at every opportunity, officials extracted extra payments from the public even for tasks that were little more than routine duties. In addition, low standards in schools – not least because teachers were poorly paid and lacked motivation – and the frequent closure of schools, colleges, and universities for lengthy periods because of political and social unrest, considerably weakened the quality of recruits into the government service. But even more damaging to the competence of the government machinery was the fact that throughout the half century since independence, it had been drained of initiative and resilience.[55] The civilian politicians of the 1950s had treated the civil service 'with contempt and disdain', seeing it as a legacy of British rule. And from 1962, the military, viewing the government administration with deep suspicion, had purged the senior grades, installed its own officers, and demanded unquestioning loyalty from those who remained.[56] In brief, in Burma-Myanmar, the resourceful official, or even the merely competent, was too often discarded, constrained, or simply left.

It was the severe inadequacy of the government machinery, perhaps more than any other factor, which manacled the evolution towards a market-oriented economy under the SLORC/SPDC. And looking to the future, it may well be the creation of a competent, resilient, and trusted government administration – to implement policies effectively and to engage constructively with the political leadership in the making

---

[54] Paul Cook and Martin Minogue, 'Economic reform and political change in Myanmar (Burma)', *World Development*, 21, 7 (1993), p. 1157. See also Paul Cook and Martin Minogue, 'Economic reform and political conditionality in Myanmar', in Peter Carey (ed.), *Burma: the Challenge of Change in a Divided Society*. London: Macmillan, 1997, p. 196.

[55] In the mid-2000s, one observer suggested that the Myanmar bureaucracy was virtually 'a synonym for inflexibility, lethargy, anachronism, unresponsiveness, and interference': Alex M. Mutebi, '"Muddling through" past legacies: Myanmar's civil bureaucracy and the need for reform', in Kyaw Yin Hlaing, Robert H. Taylor, and Tin Maung Maung Than (eds), *Myanmar: Beyond Politics to Societal Imperatives*. Singapore: Institute of Southeast Asian Studies, 2005, p. 154. This essay includes a brief history of Burma-Myanmar's civil bureaucracy from the final years of British rule.

[56] Tin Maung Maung Than, *State Dominance in Myanmar: the Political Economy of Industrialization*. Singapore: Institute of Southeast Asian Studies, 2007, pp. 312–13.

of policy – that will prove to be the most intractable obstacle to major economic reform. In 2000, a group of prominent Burmese economists, from both inside and outside the country, published a vision and strategy for the economic development of Burma.[57] Their approach was founded on belief in the market and the private sector. But crucially, they repeatedly stressed the importance for the market of an effective institutional framework.

The open market economy can operate effectively only within a transparent, publicly accountable and consistent administrative system. It is essential for the government to set up the appropriate legal framework and establish an efficient, impartial and result oriented administrative system. The development of a cadre of efficient and dedicated public servants, appropriately compensated and motivated, will be one of the main requirements in the reform process ... We should ... make institutional effectiveness a cardinal imperative in our strategy.[58]

The huge gulf between the condition of the government machinery – drained of initiative and resilience – and what it would need to be for a market-oriented economy to function effectively – efficient, impartial, result-oriented, dedicated, appropriately compensated, motivated – is a striking measure of the challenge of economic reform in Myanmar at the beginning of the twenty-first century. It may also be seen as a measure of the damning legacy of the past for Myanmar's development prospects. Burma's weak administrative provision on independence, the contemptuous disregard of senior officials as colonial remnants in the 1950s, and then, from 1962, the purging of the higher administrative grades and the insistence on military loyalty and obedience, has left Myanmar with a debilitating inheritance.

---

[57] Khin Maung Kyi, Ronald Findlay, R. M. Sundrum, Mya Maung, Myo Nyunt, Zaw Oo, et al., *Economic Development of Burma: a Vision and a Strategy*. Stockholm: Olof Palme International Center, 2000. Although seen as 'an opposition tract', it was translated into Burmese for government ministers to read: personal communication from Robert Taylor, 27 September 2012.

[58] Khin Maung Kyi et al., *Economic Development of Burma*, p. 35.

Conclusion: themes and threads

'The tragedy of Burma', asserted an editorial in *The Times* in April 2012, 'is that, on most measures, it held the brightest prospects of any country in South-East Asia when it won independence in 1948.'[1] As an earlier chapter in this book made clear, this is far from the truth. On independence, Burma was a barely functioning state. Its transport infrastructure and industrial plant – the oilfields and the refinery at Syriam, the rice mills and timber mills at the ports – had suffered huge damage during the war, and only limited reconstruction had been completed in the two years since the British had reoccupied Burma at the end of the war. With the departure of British and Indian officials at the close of colonial rule, there were too few trained and experienced Burmese to run a modern economy, society, and administration. And finally, the stability – the very survival – of the new state was seriously threatened by communist and ethnic insurrections. Burma's prospects in 1948 were poor.[2]

Much of Burma's damaged inheritance on independence was not beyond repair. Railway lines could be relaid and the oil refinery rebuilt; with education and training, an effective Burmese administration could be created, although this would certainly be a greater challenge than rebuilding the railway network; and, a still greater challenge, the communist and ethnic insurgents might in time be defeated or reconciled.

---

[1] *The Times*, 2 April 2012, p. 2.
[2] And yet the untruth is continually repeated, as in the later *Times* editorial quoted at length in the opening pages of this book: 'On gaining independence from Britain in 1948, its [Burma's] economic prospects appeared as bright as any nation's in South East Asia.' Of course the 'bright prospects' myth underpins the argument that the military have brought ruin to a potentially prosperous country. Thant Myint-U has also drawn attention to this 'enduring myth', when arguing that it is important not simply to point to the disastrous policies of the military but to understand Burma's 'deeper history of misfortune': Thant Myint-U, 'What to do about Burma', *London Review of Books*, 29, 3 (8 February 2007).

But there was one, arguably damaging, inheritance that was hugely resilient. This was the Burmese rejection of the colonial economic structure, manifest in the three core ambitions of independent Burma's economic strategy – the nationalization of foreign interests, the Burmanization of the modern labour force, and state-led industrialization.

It was of course common, although far from inevitable, for the newly independent nations of Asia and Africa in the 1940s, 1950s, and 1960s to reject the colonial economic structures that, they felt, had long oppressed them.[3] The foreign trading companies, banks, mills and refineries, shipping lines, the mines and plantations that had so dominated the economy under colonial rule were nationalized, expropriated, excluded, or regulated and restricted. The entrepreneurial minorities – Indians, Arabs, and Chinese – who had dominated trade and moneylending in colonial times were expelled, squeezed out, or sharply curtailed. Local industry meeting the needs of the domestic market would break the colonial stranglehold of commodity production and trade. The state would replace, or at least temper, the market. Burma pursued that orthodoxy in the first decade or more of independence. But then, for the quarter of a century after the military seized power in 1962, Burma stood out among the new independent nations of Asia and Africa for the sheer ferocity with which it rejected its colonial economic structure.

One explanation for this extreme reaction would be that the economic structures of colonial Burma were exceptionally disadvantageous to the Burmese, or were seen by them as such. If this was the case, the exceptionality did not lie in Burma's extreme specialization in primary production and trade or in the powerful position occupied by British commercial interests, for this was commonplace in the colonial world. Rather it lay in the exclusion of the Burmese from the modern economy, except of course as cultivators of rice. Among the large-scale enterprises of colonial Burma's modern economy, the rice millers-merchants, the shipping lines, the teak companies, the banks, the oil companies, none were Burmese. Perhaps more importantly, relatively few Burmese found employment in the modern enterprises and institutions brought to Burma by colonial rule. The positions there

---

[3] Much of my thinking here was initially stated in an article, Ian Brown, 'Tracing Burma's economic failure to its colonial inheritance', *Business History Review*, 85, 4 (Winter 2011). Substantial passages in this conclusion are taken, with modifications, from that article.

were dominated by Indians. And of course, where the Burmese *had* engaged directly with the modern world, in the cultivation of rice for export, by the final complete decade of British rule, they were left debt-ridden, impoverished, and landless.

As was noted in an earlier chapter, writing at the end of the 1940s, J. S. Furnivall had observed that the Indian domination of colonial Burma's modern economy and administration 'erected a barrier between Burmans and the modern world that has never been broken down'.[4] Reflecting on Furnivall's intellectual legacy almost half a century later, Robert Taylor argued that the barrier identified by Furnivall 'is crucial for understanding the extremely strong character of Burmese nationalism', including of course its ferocious rejection of the colonial economic structure.[5] To be specific, as a result of the existence of the barrier, or rather of their position on the wrong side of it, 'most Burmese saw modernity [controlled by foreign interests] as the key to the means of their exploitation [at the hands of those interests]'. Thus in their increasingly determined pursuit of socialism, Burma's political leaders, the civilians in the 1950s but, with extreme intent, the military after 1962, sought to destroy the barrier by removing those who occupied the other side of it. Foreign interests were nationalized, squeezed out, or expelled. Foreign capital was excluded. It is possible to see in this the origins of Burma's development failure. But, Taylor argues, to an earlier generation of Burmese emerging from the colonial experience, the destruction was not an economic disaster but an act of release from the colonial structures that had long exploited them.[6]

At this point, it would be as well to pause: after all, during the colonial period, all the major territories in South East Asia experienced substantial immigration of Indians or Chinese, or both, who then came to dominate the modern economy, relegating, as in colonial Burma, the local population to cultivation. But at the end of colonial rule, the independent state did not invariably reject the colonial economic structure. And nowhere in South East Asia was it rejected with the sustained ferocity seen in Burma. For example, from the final decades of the nineteenth century, British Malaya experienced exceptionally

---

[4] J. S. Furnivall, *Colonial Policy and Practice: a Comparative Study of Burma and Netherlands India*. New York University Press, 1956, p. 46.

[5] R. H. Taylor, 'Disaster or release? J. S. Furnivall and the bankruptcy of Burma', *Modern Asian Studies*, 29, 1 (1995), p. 53.

[6] Ibid., pp. 56–7.

high levels of both Chinese and Indian immigration, such that, at the beginning of the 1930s, Chinese accounted for 41 per cent and Indians 22 per cent of the population of the Federated Malay States (the FMS), the states in which British Malaya's modern economy was principally located.[7] The indigenous Malay population accounted for only 35 per cent of the FMS total. Chinese and Indian labourers worked, respectively, in the tin mines and on the rubber plantations; Chinese and Indians dominated the internal trade of British Malaya and the local provision of credit; and Indians were prominent in the government services.

And the British colonial administration in Malaya really did erect a barrier between the indigenous Malays and the modern world. Most prominently, its Malay vernacular schools focused on creating 'a vigorous and self-respecting agricultural peasantry', while through a combination of legislation and administrative action, the authorities sought to discourage, indeed prevent, the Malays from cultivating rubber, British Malaya's principal agricultural export from the first decades of the twentieth century. In other words, the colonial government sought to restrict the rural Malays not simply to cultivation, but to subsistence cultivation: it erected a barrier between the Malays and the external market.[8] And yet when Malaya became independent in 1957, with a constitutionally secured Malay political dominance, there was no rejection of the colonial economic structure. Rather, that structure's most serious failing, the economic retardation of the Malays, was in time addressed by a redistribution of ownership and opportunity in favour of the Malays. At the same time, the colonial integration into the international economy, in trade and investment, was retained.[9] The colonial inheritance was not rejected: it was reworked.

Undoubtedly, many factors shaped the economic strategies pursued by Malaya-Malaysia after independence. I will focus on just two that provide, I suggest, an interesting perspective on Burma. The first is that the domination of colonial Malaya's modern economy by Chinese and Indian interests was not complemented by the political presence of

---

[7] Calculated from Lim Teck Ghee, *Peasants and their Agricultural Economy in Colonial Malaya 1874–1941*. Kuala Lumpur: Oxford University Press, 1977, p. 245.

[8] For colonial policy and practice toward the Malay agricultural economy, see Lim, *Peasants and their Agricultural Economy in Colonial Malaya*.

[9] For the modern economic history of Malaya (Malaysia from 1963), see John H. Drabble, *An Economic History of Malaysia, c.1800–1990*. London: Macmillan, 2000.

either China or India. In contrast, India had a huge political presence in Burma from the beginning of British rule in the 1820s, and indeed earlier, to independence in 1948. As noted in earlier chapters, it was the British need to secure the eastern border of India and its approaches against, first, the Burmese themselves and later against feared French intervention that was arguably the principal factor in Britain's annexation of Burma in the nineteenth century. On the completion of the British advance – the conclusion of the final Anglo-Burmese war in 1885 – Burma became not a colonial territory under the direct authority of London, but a province of British India. And it remained an Indian province, an integral part of the structures of British India, until 1937. One important consequence of this position was that from around 1920, constitutional advance in Burma was in crucial respects tied to constitutional advance in India proper. Indeed, in the 1920s and 1930s, Burmese nationalists were concerned that separation from India, desirable on so many other grounds, might slow Burma's advance to self-government. And finally, it could well be argued that British India pulled Burma into Britain's war against Japan in 1941, condemning the land and its people to more than three years of destruction and devastation. In essence, Burma was caught in the conflict not because of what it was or what it offered, but simply because it was located on the eastern border of British India.

These observations are intended to establish not simply that under British rule the Burmese had good reason to be anti-India and anti-Indian.[10] The argument here is far broader. By the end of British rule, the Burmese had good reason to fear the outside world and to sense their vulnerability to external intervention.[11] This did not end with the departure of the British. In 1949, Chinese Nationalist forces, in retreat following the communist victory in China's civil war, entered

[10] They did, and not only for the reasons given here but also, for example, because of the dispossession of the Burmese cultivator by the Chettiars during the Depression. Anti-Indian riots in 1930 and 1938 were an important measure of Burmese feeling.

[11] The influence of Burma's wartime experience has been particularly powerful. 'Today [2007], the perception strongly held by the [Myanmar] government is that all of its political opponents, foreign and domestic, are set upon subverting the country's independence and breaking its territorial coherence. This perception has its origins in the lessons of the [Second World] war': Robert H. Taylor, 'The legacies of World War II for Myanmar', in David Koh Wee Hock (ed.), *Legacies of World War II in South and East Asia*. Singapore: Institute of Southeast Asian Studies, 2007, p. 62.

Burma over the border with Yunnan.[12] Covertly supported by the US Central Intelligence Agency, the Nationalists established control over a large part of the eastern Shan states, reinforced by air from their stronghold in Taiwan. They remained for decades. The Chinese Nationalist presence, maintained with American support, was not simply a serious violation of Burmese sovereignty. From the late 1960s, those who stayed – some moved to Taiwan – were key figures in the opium and heroin trade, which in turn further fuelled a number of Burma's ethnic insurgencies. At the same time, China's communists were supplying arms, ammunition, and volunteer fighters on a substantial scale to the Burma Communist Party. This is the broad political-historical context in which to understand why, in its economic strategy in the 1960s and 1970s, Burma sought self-reliance and isolation.[13] With the world excluded, Burma would at last control its economic destiny. The ambition to exclude the world may well have been futile: and it led Burma to disaster. But in historical context, it is possible to understand the ambition.

The second circumstance that shaped the economic strategies pursued by Malaya-Malaysia after independence, providing an interesting perspective on Burma, is that at the end of British rule, the Indians and Chinese were still present and still dominated the modern economy. Consequently, the Malays, rather than contemplating the destruction of the structures that had led to their economic retardation under British rule, sought a substantial redistribution of ownership and opportunity away from the Indians and Chinese. For their part, the Indians and Chinese had little choice, given the constitutionally secured Malay political dominance, but to accept accommodation with Malay economic aspirations.

In contrast, at the end of British rule in Burma, the Indian presence was hugely weakened. The economic position of the Indians had deteriorated considerably in the 1930s, when the collapse in rice prices during the depression and the consequent default by vast numbers of indebted cultivators had frozen much of the Chettiars' business, and

---

[12] Thant Myint-U, *Where China Meets India: Burma and the New Crossroads of Asia*. London: Faber and Faber, 2011, pp. 88–90. See also Robert H. Taylor, *Foreign and Domestic Consequences of the KMT Intervention in Burma*. Ithaca, NY: Cornell University, Southeast Asia Program, Data Paper no. 93, 1973.

[13] It is interesting to recall here the comment by Ne Win in the mid-1960s that an export-oriented economic strategy 'would put the country into the hands of the CIA'.

when the eruption of racial violence – the anti-Indian riots of 1930 and 1938 – had dampened Indian immigration. But the critical break came in late 1941 and early 1942, when close to two-thirds of the Indian population fled Burma for India, ahead of the advancing Japanese. In the 1931 census, the Indian population had been recorded at fractionally above one million.[14] The Burma census of 1953 reported the number of persons of Indian origin in urban areas (there was no figure for rural areas) at a little over a quarter of a million, roughly half in Rangoon. They were largely the stateless and poor. Many of the most substantial Indians, the traders, millers, and moneylenders, had abandoned Burma a decade earlier.

The Indian departure, I would argue, was to have highly important consequences for the economic strategies pursued by independent Burma. This argument is most effectively presented by posing a counterfactual: in which respects and to what extent would the strategic options for Burma's economy, specifically in the 1950s and 1960s, have been different had the Indian business community, so important before the war, still been present in strength, instead of having abandoned Burma when the Japanese attacked in the early 1940s? It is certain that, after 1948, Burma's government would have imposed tight restrictions on Indian economic activity, reflecting its determination to break the colonial domination of the economy by foreign interests. But given the scale and location of the Indian population being assumed here – around one million, perhaps the majority in Rangoon – and assuming too that the substantial numbers of Indian traders, merchants, lenders, and rice mill-owners had firm possession of their concerns when Burma regained its independence in 1948, then the new government's restriction of Indian interests is less likely to have extended to the most extreme measures, that is, expropriation and expulsion.[15] In other words, some form of accommodation would

---

[14] Nalini Ranjan Chakravarti, *The Indian Minority in Burma: the Rise and Decline of an Immigrant Community*. London: Oxford University Press, 1971, pp. 15, 186.

[15] Citing the expulsion of the Indians from Uganda by Idi Amin in 1972, it might be argued that a substantial presence would not provide secure protection for a minority against being expelled en masse. However, the Indian population of Uganda – just 76,000 at the end of the 1960s – was far smaller than the number of Indians in Burma being assumed here. Hugh Tinker, 'Indians abroad: emigration, restriction, and rejection', in Michael Twaddle (ed.), *Expulsion of a Minority: Essays on Ugandan Asians*. London: The Athlone Press, 1975, p. 15.

have been reached between Burmese and Indian interests. It would not have been a balanced accommodation, as perhaps was to be achieved in Malaysia: the Chinese and Indian populations there were far more substantial – relative to the local population – than the assumed Indian population in Burma. But the central point is that an accommodation between Burmese economic ambitions and Indian interests after 1948, no matter how unequal, implied a continued Indian presence.

That in turn would have broadened the strategic options for Burma's economy in the 1950s and 1960s. An Indian business community, even one severely constrained, would have provided experienced partners for Burmese enterprise determined to advance into sectors of the economy previously dominated by foreign interests. Indeed that process could have been forcibly created by making it a requirement that Indians acquire Burmese partners if they wished to remain in business in Burma. It would be part of the accommodation. An Indian business community would also have provided experienced partners for foreign capital seeking joint ventures, should Burma have pursued an open economy strategy. In fact, a continued – immovable though constrained – outward-looking Indian presence, tempering the isolationist ambitions of Burma's political leaders, might have encouraged the adoption of such a strategy. But in reality, these paths were not open, for the Indian presence, so powerful before the war, was, by independence in 1948, broken. The Indian business community had largely abandoned Burma at the beginning of the decade.

The argument being built on the counterfactual posed above might finally be put in two different, but closely related, ways. When the military took power in 1962, it was able to drive towards socialist isolation – and bankruptcy – as no substantial economic interests stood in its path. Alternatively, when the military took power in 1962, it was forced to pursue socialist isolation because, in the absence of a substantial outward-looking Indian (or indeed Burmese) business community, it had no alternative.

The argument is now perilously close to being a demonstration of the historical determinism of which the introductory chapter warned. In brief summary: it is being argued that the domination of colonial Burma's modern economy and administration by foreign interests erected a barrier between the Burmese and the modern world. Once Burma regained its independence, the earlier exclusion of the Burmese provoked a ferocious rejection of the colonial economic structure and a determined pursuit of Burmanization, nationalization, and state industrialization – in an extreme form, a pursuit of socialist isolation. Indeed, so ferocious was the rejection of the colonial economic structure that to the generation of Burmese emerging from the colonial experience, its destruction, even when this eventually led to the bankruptcy of Burma, was an act of release. At the same time, the departure of the foreign interests which had so dominated colonial Burma's modern economy, and in particular the departure of the Indian business community, either cleared the way for Burma's military rulers to drive the economy towards socialist isolation or forced them to do so. In this last case, the military were imprisoned by Burma's colonial past.

The influence of the colonial inheritance on the economic strategy pursued by independent Burma – the inheritance of the exclusion of Burmese from the modern economy; the domination by and then departure of the Indians; the war damage; the stripping out of the senior levels of administration as the British left; and even Burma's political fragility on independence – was clearly extremely powerful. It was most starkly evident in the final expulsion of foreign interests and disengagement from the international economy in the 1960s, in the pursuit of socialist isolation. But at the same time, it is clear that the colonial influence, no matter how powerful, did not absolutely have to be obeyed. In other words, Burma's colonial inheritance was, in the final analysis, open to rejection. Thus, to be specific, it was open to the Burmese military in the 1960s to choose a different economic strategy. Indeed when, in 1965, General Ne Win asked Chan Aye and his associates – U Thet Tun, Professor Aye Hlaing, and Dr Ronald Findlay – to propose their economic strategy for the government, as described in Chapter 4, an opportunity to reject the powerful influence of the colonial economic legacy, to reject the rejection, was laid before the government.

In seeking to understand why that opportunity was not taken, it is important to emphasize that Burma's governments from 1948 – and not simply Ne Win in 1965 – have had one concern that overrides all others: the need to secure Burma from disorder and disintegration. Those threats have indeed been severe and immediate: from communist and ethnic insurgencies, intense and unresolved for decades on end; from foreign invasion – the CIA-backed Chinese Nationalist occupation of the eastern Shan states; and from periodic eruptions of social-political protest, in 1967, 1974, and of course in 1988.[16]

The response of Burma's military governments from 1962 was to build the coercive power of the state and to attempt to impose the tightest control over all aspects of economic, social, and political life. The implications for government economic strategy were very considerable. Building the coercive power of the state involved heavy investment in the military, which left far fewer resources for social and economic development. Moreover, tight state control implied, for the economy, rejection of the market and of any economic strategy that might create powerful independent interests that could challenge the state's domination. Thus for three decades and more, the state procured Burma's agricultural production at low and inflexible prices, severely limiting the exploitation of Burma's agricultural potential but, by holding down food prices, maintaining some measure of social order. In addition, for almost three decades, the regime excluded foreign private capital, severely limiting the growth of the manufacturing sector but leaving the state's economic and indeed political authority beyond potential challenge from that quarter. In such ways, the one overriding concern of Burma's governments since 1948, to secure Burma from disorder and disintegration, has been met. Of course, the cost has been very great, and not only in terms of development failure and the poverty of the people.

But then, perhaps the choice as it is being posed here – between, on the one hand, securing Burma from disintegration and, on the other, sustained development – is a false one. Thus it would surely have been possible to allocate the state's resources to achieve both ambitions: or to introduce the market and engage with the international economy sufficiently to produce a sustained economic growth that did not

---

[16] Focusing on the external threat, writing in 2001, David Steinberg commented that the 'Burmese regime believes that the country is surrounded by enemies – real and potential', before adding that its 'fears are based on a reality once extant but now completely outmoded': David I. Steinberg, *Burma: the State of Myanmar*. Washington, DC: Georgetown University Press, 2001, pp. 292–3. However, writing a decade later, Mary Callahan argued that the regime's heightened concerns about foreign interference or intervention 'are real and current . . . the regime has reason to distrust foreign influence': Mary Callahan, 'The endurance of military rule in Burma: not why, but why not?', in Susan L. Levenstein (ed.), *Finding Dollars, Sense, and Legitimacy in Burma*. Washington, DC: Woodrow Wilson International Center for Scholars, 2010, pp. 65–6.

inevitably create economic and political challenges for the established order. Moreover, sustained economic growth could surely secure the integration and stability of the state and society rather than undermine them. But if this is the case, then it would appear that Burma's governments, certainly the military from 1962, did not see these subtle strategic economic options. Rather they sought, with a near-exclusive determination but at great economic cost, to secure Burma from political disintegration and disorder.

Bibliography

Official publications

Binns, B. O., *Agricultural Economy in Burma*. Rangoon: Government Printing and Stationery, 1946

Couper, T., *Report of Inquiry into the Condition of Agricultural Tenants and Labourers*. Rangoon: Government Printing and Stationery, 1924 (reprint: Rangoon: Central Press, 1966)

Economic Survey of Burma 1962. Rangoon: Government Printing and Stationery, 1962

Economic Survey of Burma 1963. Rangoon: Central Press, 1964

Is Trust Vindicated? A Chronicle of the Various Accomplishments of the Government Headed by General Ne Win during the Period of Tenure from November, 1958 to February 6, 1960. Rangoon: Director of Information, Government of the Union of Burma, 1960

Kyaw Min, *Preliminary Report on New Industries for Burma*. Rangoon: Government Printing and Stationery, 1947

Report of the Burma Provincial Banking Enquiry Committee, 1929–30. Rangoon: Government Printing and Stationery, 3 vols, 1930

Other published primary sources

Burma Chamber of Commerce, *Annual Reports for 1959–1960*

Published secondary sources

Adas, Michael, *Prophets of Rebellion: Millenarian Protest Movements against the European Colonial Order*. Cambridge University Press, 1987

The Burma Delta: Economic Development and Social Change on an Asian Rice Frontier, 1852–1941. Madison, WI: University of Wisconsin Press, 1974

Allen, Louis, *Burma: the Longest War 1941–45*. London: J. M. Dent, 1984

Andrus, J. Russell, *Burmese Economic Life*. Stanford University Press, 1948

Ardeth Maung Thawnghmung, *Behind the Teak Curtain: Authoritarianism, Agricultural Policies and Political Legitimacy in Rural Burma/Myanmar*. London: Kegan Paul, 2004

Aung Tun Thet, *Burmese Entrepreneurship: Creative Response in the Colonial Economy*. Stuttgart: Steiner Verlag Wiesbaden GmbH, 1989

Aung-Thwin, Maitrii, 'Genealogy of a rebellion narrative: law, ethnology and culture in colonial Burma', *Journal of Southeast Asian Studies*, 34, 3 (October 2003), 393–419

The Return of the Galon King: History, Law, and Rebellion in Colonial Burma. Athens, OH: Ohio University Press, 2011

Aung-Thwin, Michael, and Maitrii Aung-Thwin, *A History of Myanmar since Ancient Times: Traditions and Transformations*. London: Reaktion Books, 2012

Aye Hlaing, 'Trends of economic growth and income distribution in Burma, 1870–1940', *Journal of the Burma Research Society*, 47, 1 (June 1964), 89–148

Ba Maw, *Breakthrough in Burma: Memoirs of a Revolution, 1939–1946*. New Haven, CT: Yale University Press, 1968

Badgley, John H., 'Burma's zealot wungyis: Maoists or St. Simonists', *Asian Survey*, 5, 1 (January 1965), 55–62

Bayly, Christopher, and Tim Harper, *Forgotten Armies: the Fall of British Asia, 1941–1945*. London: Allen Lane, 2004

Forgotten Wars: the End of Britain's Asian Empire. London: Allen Lane, 2007

Bayne, Nicholas, *Burma and Tudor History: the Life and Work of Charles Bayne 1860–1947*. Bideford: Edward Gaskell, 2008

Booth, Anne, 'The Burma development disaster in comparative historical perspective', *South East Asia Research*, 11, 2 (2003), 141–71

Colonial Legacies: Economic and Social Development in East and Southeast Asia. Honolulu: University of Hawai'i Press, 2007

Brown, Ian, *A Colonial Economy in Crisis: Burma's Rice Cultivators and the World Depression of the 1930s*. London: RoutledgeCurzon, 2005

'British firms and the end of empire in Burma', *Asian Affairs*, 40, 1 (March 2009), 15–33

Economic Change in South-East Asia, c.1830–1980. Kuala Lumpur: Oxford University Press, 1997

'South East Asia: reform and the colonial prison', in Frank Dikötter and Ian Brown (eds), *Cultures of Confinement: a History of the Prison in Africa, Asia and Latin America*. London: Hurst, 2007, 221–68

'The economics of decolonization in Burma', in Toyin Falola and Emily Brownell (eds), *Africa, Empire and Globalization: Essays in Honor of A.G. Hopkins*. Durham, NC: Carolina Academic Press, 2011, 433–44

'Tracing Burma's economic failure to its colonial inheritance', *Business History Review*, 85, 4 (Winter 2011), 725–47

Brown, Rajeswary Ampalavanar, *Chinese Big Business and the Wealth of Asian Nations*. Basingstoke: Palgrave, 2000

Bryant, Raymond L., *The Political Ecology of Forestry in Burma 1824–1994*. London: Hurst, 1997

Cady, John F., *A History of Modern Burma*. Ithaca, NY: Cornell University Press, 1958

Callahan, Mary P., *Making Enemies: War and State Building in Burma*. Ithaca, NY: Cornell University Press, 2003

'The endurance of military rule in Burma: not why, but why not?', in Susan L. Levenstein (ed.), *Finding Dollars, Sense, and Legitimacy in Burma*. Washington, DC: Woodrow Wilson International Center for Scholars, 2010, 54–76

Chakravarti, Nalini Ranjan, *The Indian Minority in Burma: the Rise and Decline of an Immigrant Community*. London: Oxford University Press, 1971

Charlesworth, Neil, *Peasants and Imperial Rule: Agriculture and Agrarian Society in the Bombay Presidency, 1850–1935*. Cambridge University Press, 1985

Charney, Michael W., *A History of Modern Burma*. Cambridge University Press, 2009

Cheng Siok-Hwa, *The Rice Industry of Burma 1852–1940*. Kuala Lumpur: University of Malaya Press, 1968 (reprinted Singapore: Institute of Southeast Asian Studies, 2012)

Christian, John Leroy, *Modern Burma: a Survey of Political and Economic Development*. Berkeley, CA: University of California Press, 1942

Collis, Maurice, *Into Hidden Burma: an Autobiography*. London: Faber and Faber, 1953

Last and First in Burma (1941–1948). London: Faber and Faber, 1956

Trials in Burma. London: Faber and Faber, new edn, 1945

Cook, Paul, and Martin Minogue, 'Economic reform and political change in Myanmar (Burma)', *World Development*, 21, 7 (1993), 1151–61

'Economic reform and political conditionality in Myanmar', in Peter Carey (ed.), *Burma: the Challenge of Change in a Divided Society*. London: Macmillan, 1997, 183–208

Corley, T. A. B., *A History of the Burmah Oil Company 1886–1924*. London: Heinemann, 1983

A History of the Burmah Oil Company, Vol. II: 1924–1966. London: Heinemann, 1988

Dixon, Chris, *The Thai Economy: Uneven Development and Internationalisation*. London: Routledge, 1999

Donnison, F. S. V., *Public Administration in Burma: a Study of Development During the British Connexion*. London: Royal Institute of International Affairs, 1953

Drabble, John H., *An Economic History of Malaysia, c.1800–1990*. London: Macmillan, 2000

Rubber in Malaya 1876–1922: the Genesis of the Industry. Kuala Lumpur: Oxford University Press, 1973

Dulyapak Preecharushh, *Naypyidaw: the New Capital of Burma*. Bangkok: White Lotus, 2009

Dutt, Amitava K., 'International trade in early development economics', in Jomo K. S. and Erik S. Reinert (eds), *The Origins of Development Economics: How Schools of Economic Thought have Addressed Development*. London: Zed Books, 2005, 99–127

Englehart, Neil A., 'Liberal Leviathan or imperial outpost? J. S. Furnivall on colonial rule in Burma', *Modern Asian Studies*, 45, 4 (2011), 759–90

Fenichel, Allen, and Gregg Huff, 'Colonialism and the economic system of an independent Burma', *Modern Asian Studies*, 9, 3 (1975), 321–35

The Impact of Colonialism on Burmese Economic Development. Montreal: McGill University, Centre for Developing-Area Studies, 1971

Fisher, Charles A., *South-East Asia: a Social, Economic and Political Geography*, 2nd edn. London: Methuen, 1966

Foley, Matthew, *The Cold War and National Assertion in Southeast Asia: Britain, the United States and Burma, 1948–1962*. London: Routledge, 2010

Fujita Koichi, 'Agricultural labourers in Myanmar during the economic transition: views from the study of selected villages', in Koichi Fujita, Fumiharu Mieno, and Ikuko Okamoto (eds), *The Economic Transition in Myanmar after 1988: Market Economy versus State Control*. Singapore: NUS Press, in association with Kyoto University Press, 2009, 246–80

Fujita Koichi, Fumiharu Mieno, and Ikuko Okamoto, 'Myanmar's economic transformation after 1988', in Koichi Fujita, Fumiharu Mieno, and Ikuko Okamoto (eds), *The Economic Transition in Myanmar after 1988: Market Economy versus State Control*. Singapore: NUS Press, in association with Kyoto University Press, 2009, 1–19

Furnivall, J. S., *An Introduction to the Political Economy of Burma*. Rangoon: Burma Book Club, 1931; 3rd edn, Rangoon: Peoples' Literature Committee and House, 1957

Colonial Policy and Practice: a Comparative Study of Burma and Netherlands India. New York University Press, 1956

Netherlands India: a Study of Plural Economy. Cambridge University Press, 1944

Ghosh, Parimal, *Brave Men of the Hills: Resistance and Rebellion in Burma, 1825–1932*. London: C. Hurst, 2000

Harvey, G. E., *British Rule in Burma 1824–1942*. London: Faber and Faber, 1946

Herbert, Patricia, *The Hsaya San Rebellion (1930–1932) Reappraised*. Clayton, Victoria: Monash University, Centre of Southeast Asian Studies, Working Paper 27, 1982

Hill, Hal, and Sisira Jayasuriya, *An Inward-Looking Economy in Transition: Economic Development in Burma since the 1960s*. Singapore: Institute of Southeast Asian Studies, 1986

Hla Myint, *Southeast Asia's Economy: Development Policies in the 1970's: a Study Sponsored by the Asian Development Bank*. New York: Praeger, 1972

　'The "Classical Theory" of international trade and the underdeveloped countries', *Economic Journal*, 68, 270 (June 1958), 317–37

　'The gains from international trade and the backward countries', *Review of Economic Studies*, 22, 2 (1954–1955), 129–42

　'The inward and outward looking countries of Southeast Asia', *Malayan Economic Review*, 12, 1 (1967), 1–13

Holliday, Ian, *Burma Redux: Global Justice and the Quest for Political Reform in Myanmar*. New York: Columbia University Press, 2011

Ireland, Alleyne, *The Province of Burma: a Report Prepared on Behalf of the University of Chicago*. Boston, MA: Houghton, Mifflin, 2 vols, 1907

Khin Maung Nyunt, *Foreign Loans and Aid in the Economic Development of Burma 1974/75 to 1985/86*. Bangkok: Institute of Asian Studies, Chulalongkorn University, 1990

Khin Maung Kyi, Ronald Findlay, R. M. Sundrum, Mya Maung, Myo Nyunt, Zaw Oo, et al., *Economic Development of Burma: a Vision and a Strategy*. Stockholm: Olof Palme International Center, 2000

Khin Win, *A Century of Rice Improvement in Burma*. Manila: International Rice Research Institute, 1991

Kin Oung, *Who Killed Aung San?* Bangkok: White Lotus, 1993

Kratoska, Paul H., 'The impact of the Second World War on commercial rice production in mainland South-East Asia', in Paul H. Kratoska (ed.), *Food Supplies and the Japanese Occupation in South-East Asia*. Basingstoke: Macmillan, 1998, 9–31

Kudo Toshihiro, 'Industrial policies and the development of Myanmar's industrial sector in the transition to a market economy', in Koichi Fujita, Fumiharu Mieno, and Ikuko Okamoto (eds), *The Economic Transition in Myanmar after 1988: Market Economy versus State Control*. Singapore: NUS Press, in association with Kyoto University Press, 2009, 66–102

Kudo Toshihiro, and Fumiharu Mieno, 'Trade, foreign investment and Myanmar's economic development in the transition to an open economy', in Koichi Fujita, Fumiharu Mieno, and Ikuko Okamoto (eds), *The Economic Transition in Myanmar after 1988: Market Economy versus State Control*. Singapore: NUS Press, in association with Kyoto University Press, 2009, 103–27

Kurasawa Aiko, 'Transportation and rice distribution in South-East Asia during the Second World War', in Paul H. Kratoska (ed.), *Food Supplies and the Japanese Occupation in South-East Asia*. Basingstoke: Macmillan, 1998, 32–66

Kyaw Yin Hlaing, 'Reconsidering the failure of the Burma Socialist Programme Party government to eradicate internal economic impediments', *South East Asia Research*, 11, 1 (2003), 5–58

Lim Teck Ghee, *Peasants and their Agricultural Economy in Colonial Malaya 1874–1941*. Kuala Lumpur: Oxford University Press, 1977

Lintner, Bertil, *Burma in Revolt: Opium and Insurgency since 1948*, 2nd edn. Chiang Mai: Silkworm Books, 1999

'Drugs and economic growth in Burma today', in Morten B. Pedersen, Emily Rudland, and Ronald J. May (eds), *Burma-Myanmar: Strong Regime, Weak State?* Adelaide: Crawford House Publishing, 2000, 164–94

Outrage: Burma's Struggle for Democracy, 2nd edn. London and Bangkok: White Lotus, 1990

McCrae, Alister, and Alan Prentice, *Irrawaddy Flotilla*. Paisley: James Paton, 1978

McEnery, John H., *Epilogue in Burma 1945–1948: The Military Dimensions of British Withdrawal*. Bangkok: White Lotus, 2000

Mali, K. S., *Fiscal Aspects of Development Planning in Burma 1950–1960*. Rangoon: Department of Economics, University of Rangoon, 1962

Maung Aung Myoe, *The Tatmadaw in Myanmar since 1988: an Interim Assessment*. Canberra: Australian National University, Strategic and Defence Studies Centre, 1999

Maung Maung, *The 1988 Uprising in Burma*. New Haven, CT: Yale University Southeast Asia Studies, 1999

Maung Shein, *Burma's Transport and Foreign Trade (1885–1914) in Relation to the Economic Development of the Country*. Rangoon: Department of Economics, University of Rangoon, 1964

Maung Shein, Myint Myint Thant, and Tin Tin Sein, '"Provincial Contract System" of British Indian Empire, in relation to Burma – a case of fiscal exploitation', *Journal of the Burma Research Society*, 52, 2 (December 1969), 1–27

Meehan, Patrick, 'Drugs, insurgency and state-building in Burma: why the drugs trade is central to Burma's changing political order', *Journal of Southeast Asian Studies*, 42, 3 (October 2011), 376–404

Mizuno Asuka, 'Identifying the "agriculturists" in the Burma Delta in the colonial period: a new perspective on agriculturists based on a village tract's registers of holdings from the 1890s to the 1920s', *Journal of Southeast Asian Studies*, 42, 3 (October 2011), 405–34

Mole, Robert, *The Temple Bells are Calling: a Personal Record of the Last Years of British Rule in Burma*. Bishop Auckland: Pentland Books, 2001

Morehead, F. T., *The Forests of Burma*. London: Longmans, Green, 1944

Mutebi, Alex M., '"Muddling through" past legacies: Myanmar's civil bureaucracy and the need for reform', in Kyaw Yin Hlaing, Robert H. Taylor, and Tin Maung Maung Than (eds), *Myanmar: Beyond Politics to Societal Imperatives*. Singapore: Institute of Southeast Asian Studies, 2005, 140–60

Mya Maung, *The Burma Road to Capitalism: Economic Growth versus Democracy*. Westport, CT: Praeger, 1998

The Burma Road to Poverty. New York: Praeger, 1991

Mya Sein, *The Administration of Burma*. Kuala Lumpur: Oxford University Press, 1973 (first published, in Burma, in 1938)

Mya Than, *Growth Pattern of Burmese Agriculture: a Productivity Approach*. Singapore: Institute of Southeast Asian Studies, 1988

Myanmar's External Trade: an Overview in the Southeast Asian Context. Singapore: Institute of Southeast Asian Studies, 1992

Mya Than and Myat Thein, 'Mobilization of financial resources for development in Myanmar: an introductory overview', in Mya Than, and Myat Thein (eds), *Financial Resources for Development in Myanmar: Lessons from Asia*. Singapore: Institute of Southeast Asian Studies, 2000, 1–22

Mya Than and Nobuyoshi Nishizawa, 'Agricultural policy reforms and agricultural development in Myanmar', in Mya Than, and Joseph L. H. Tan (eds), *Myanmar Dilemmas and Options: the Challenge of Economic Transition in the 1990s*. Singapore: Institute of Southeast Asian Studies, 1990, 89–116

Myat Thein, *Economic Development of Myanmar*. Singapore: Institute of Southeast Asian Studies, 2004

'Monetary and fiscal policies for development', in Mya Than, and Joseph L. H. Tan (eds), *Myanmar Dilemmas and Options: the Challenge of Economic Transition in the 1990s*. Singapore: Institute of Southeast Asian Studies, 1990, 53–88

Nisbet, John, *Burma under British Rule–and Before*. Westminster: Archibald Constable, 2 vols, 1901

Okamoto Ikuko, 'Transformation of the rice marketing system after market liberalization in Myanmar', in Koichi Fujita, Fumiharu Mieno, and Ikuko Okamoto (eds), *The Economic Transition in Myanmar after 1988: Market Economy versus State Control*. Singapore: NUS Press, in association with Kyoto University Press, 2009, 216–45

Orwell, George, *Burmese Days*. London: Penguin Books, 1989 (first published in New York, 1934)

Pasuk Phongpaichit, and Chris Baker, *Thailand: Economy and Politics*. Kuala Lumpur: Oxford University Press, 1997

Perry, Peter John, *Myanmar (Burma) since 1962: the Failure of Development*. Aldershot: Ashgate, 2007

Pham, Julie, 'Ghost hunting in colonial Burma: nostalgia, paternalism and the thoughts of J. S. Furnivall', *South East Asia Research*, 12, 2 (2004), 237–68

    'J. S. Furnivall and Fabianism: reinterpreting the "Plural Society" in Burma', *Modern Asian Studies*, 39, 2 (2005), 321–48

Piness, Edith L., 'The British administrator in Burma: a new view', *Journal of Southeast Asian Studies*, 14, 2 (September 1983), 372–8

Pointon, A. C., *The Bombay Burmah Trading Corporation Limited 1863–1963*. Southampton: Millbrook Press, 1964

Rothermund, Dietmar, *An Economic History of India from Pre-Colonial Times to 1986*. London: Croom Helm, 1988

Saito Teruko, and Lee Kin Kiong (comp.), *Statistics on the Burmese Economy: the 19th and 20th Centuries*. Singapore: Institute of Southeast Asian Studies, 1999

Sarkisyanz, E., *Buddhist Backgrounds of the Burmese Revolution*. The Hague: Martinus Nijhoff, 1965

Scott, James C., *The Moral Economy of the Peasant: Rebellion and Subsistence in Southeast Asia*. New Haven, CT: Yale University Press, 1976

Scott, Sir J. G., *Burma: a Handbook of Practical Information*. London: Daniel O'Connor, 1921

Seekins, Donald M., *State and Society in Modern Rangoon*. London: Routledge, 2011

Selth, Andrew, *Burma's Armed Forces: Power without Glory*. Norwalk, CT: EastBridge, 2002

Silverstein, Josef (ed.), *The Political Legacy of Aung San*, revised edn. Ithaca, NY: Cornell University, Southeast Asia Program, 1993

Slim, Field Marshal the Viscount, *Defeat into Victory*, abridged edn. London: Cassell, 1962

Steinberg, David I., *Burma: a Socialist Nation of Southeast Asia*. Boulder, CO: Westview Press, 1982

Burma: the State of Myanmar. Washington, DC: Georgetown University Press, 2001

Burma/Myanmar: What Everyone Needs to Know. New York: Oxford University Press, 2010

Burma's Road toward Development: Growth and Ideology under Military Rule. Boulder, CO: Westview Press, 1981

'Myanmar: the roots of economic malaise', in Kyaw Yin Hlaing, Robert H. Taylor, and Tin Maung Maung Than (ed.), *Myanmar: Beyond Politics to Societal Imperatives*. Singapore: Institute of Southeast Asian Studies, 2005, 86–116

Steinberg, David I., and Hongwei Fan, *Modern China-Myanmar Relations: Dilemmas of Mutual Dependence*. Copenhagen: NIAS Press, 2012

Stifel, Lawrence D., 'Economics of the Burmese Way to Socialism', *Asian Survey*, 11, 8 (August 1971), 803–17

Taylor, Robert H., 'Burma in the Anti-Fascist War', in Alfred W. McCoy (ed.), *Southeast Asia under Japanese Occupation*. New Haven, CT: Yale University Southeast Asia Studies, 1980, 132–57

'Disaster or release? J. S. Furnivall and the bankruptcy of Burma', *Modern Asian Studies*, 29, 1 (1995), 45–63

Foreign and Domestic Consequences of the KMT Intervention in Burma. Ithaca, NY: Cornell University, Southeast Asia Program, Data Paper no. 93, 1973

'The legacies of World War II for Myanmar', in David Koh Wee Hock (ed.), *Legacies of World War II in South and East Asia*. Singapore: Institute of Southeast Asian Studies, 2007, 60–73

The State in Myanmar. London: Hurst, 2009

Thant Myint-U, *The Making of Modern Burma*. Cambridge University Press, 2001

The River of Lost Footsteps: Histories of Burma. London: Faber and Faber, 2007

'What to do about Burma', *London Review of Books*, 29, 3 (8 February 2007), 31–3

Where China Meets India: Burma and the New Crossroads of Asia. London: Faber and Faber, 2011

Thee Kian Wie, 'Introduction', in Thee Kian Wie (ed.), *Recollections: the Indonesian Economy, 1950s-1990s*. Singapore: Institute of Southeast Asian Studies, 2003, 3–43

Thet Tun, 'A critique of Louis J. Walinsky's "Economic Development in Burma 1951–1960"', *Journal of the Burma Research Society*, 47, 1 (June 1964), 173–81

Burma's Experience in Economic Planning. Rangoon: Government Printing and Stationery, 1960

'The writings of John Sydenham Furnivall (on Myanmar)', in *Selected Writings of Retired Ambassador U Thet Tun*. Yangon: Myanmar Historical Commission, 2004, 119–50

Waves of Influence. Yangon: Thin Sapay, 2011

Tin Maung Maung Than, *State Dominance in Myanmar: the Political Economy of Industrialization*. Singapore: Institute of Southeast Asian Studies, 2007

Tinker, Hugh (ed.), *Burma: the Struggle for Independence 1944–1948*. London: HMSO, 2 vols, 1983, 1984

'Burma's struggle for independence: the transfer of power thesis re-examined', *Modern Asian Studies*, 20, 3 (1986), 461–81

'Indians abroad: emigration, restriction, and rejection', in Michael Twaddle (ed.), *Expulsion of a Minority: Essays on Ugandan Asians*. London: The Athlone Press, 1975, 15–29

'The contraction of empire in Asia, 1945–48: the military dimension', *Journal of Imperial and Commonwealth History*, 16, 2 (January 1988), 218–33

The Union of Burma: a Study of the First Years of Independence, 4th edn. London: Oxford University Press, 1967

Trager, Frank N., *Building a Welfare State in Burma 1948–1956*. New York: Institute of Pacific Relations, 1958

Tun Wai, *Burma's Currency and Credit*, revd edn. Calcutta: Orient Longmans, 1962

'Myanmar', in Pradumna B. Rana and Naved Hamid (eds.), *From Centrally Planned to Market Economies: the Asian Approach: Vol. III: Lao PDR, Myanmar and Vietnam*. Hong Kong: Oxford University Press, 1996, 149–331

'The Myanmar economy at the crossroads: options and constraints', in Mya Than and Joseph L. H. Tan (eds), *Myanmar Dilemmas and Options: the Challenge of Economic Transition in the 1990s*. Singapore: Institute of Southeast Asian Studies, 1990, 18–52

Turnell, Sean, 'Burma's economy 2004: crisis masking stagnation', in Trevor Wilson (ed.), *Myanmar's Long Road to National Reconciliation*. Singapore: Institute of Southeast Asian Studies, 2006, 77–97

Fiery Dragons: Banks, Moneylenders and Microfinance in Burma. Copenhagen: NIAS Press, 2009

'Finding dollars and sense: Burma's economy in 2010', in Susan L. Levenstein (ed.), *Finding Dollars, Sense, and Legitimacy in Burma*. Washington, DC: Woodrow Wilson International Center for Scholars, 2010, 20–39

Walinsky, Louis J., *Economic Development in Burma 1951–1960*. New York: The Twentieth Century Fund, 1962

Warren, James, 'The Rangoon jail riot of 1930 and the prison administration of British Burma', *South East Asia Research*, 10, 1 (2002), 5–29

White, Herbert Thirkell, *A Civil Servant in Burma*. London: Edward Arnold, 1913

Wright, Arnold, H. A. Cartwright and O. Breakspear (eds.), *Twentieth Century Impressions of Burma: its History, People, Commerce, Industries, and Resources*. London: Lloyd's Greater Britain Publishing Company, 1910

Unpublished dissertations

Diokno, Maria Serena I., 'British firms and the economy of Burma, with special reference to the rice and teak industries, 1917–1937'. PhD, University of London, 1983

Maung Myint, 'Agriculture in Burmese economic development'. PhD, University of California, Berkeley, 1966

Nelson, Joan Marie, 'Central planning for national development and the role of foreign advisors: the case of Burma'. PhD, Radcliffe College, 1960

Private papers

Louis Walinsky Papers: Division of Rare and Manuscript Collections, Cornell University Library

Interviews

Professor Hla Myint, Bangkok, 29 January 2012

U Thet Tun, Yangon, 25 January 2012

Index